Technology Offsets in International Defence Procurement

Technology offsets, a nonconventional international trade-financing tool, is used by governments (buyers) to obtain industrial and technological benefits from companies (sellers) as part of international procurement. Offsets deals involve billions of dollars and this practice exists in around 80 countries around the world. Though offsets is a popular practice in defence, it is increasingly gaining popularity in civil sectors. Offsets is often tainted by controversy and receives bad press. What then makes offsets popular? Governments claim that offsets delivers technology and knowledge transfer, skills in high technology sectors and employment, and offsets expands export opportunities through participation in OEM supply chains. For companies, offsets is mainly employed as a tool to obtain a competitive edge and win sales in international business. In the past, there have been mixed results of case studies on the impact of offsets successes and failures.

Considering the mismanagement of globalisation, unfair trade agreements and current political and economic discontent, there is a stronger need for governments and companies to use vehicles such as offsets to create a relationship of trust and commitment for sustainable development. This book fills the gap in offsets and focuses on how to manage offsets more effectively by addressing issues of strategy, policy and implementation, technology management, governance and risk.

Technology Offsets in International Defence Procurement is designed for those studying international procurement, international trade, international business, technology management, defence policy and industrial policy. This book will also be of interest to practitioners and policy makers in both government and industry.

Kogila Balakrishnan is currently the Director for Client and Business Development (East Asia) at WMG, University of Warwick. She began her career in the Malaysian civil service where she was instrumental in the development of national offsets policy and subsequently retired as the Under Secretary for Defence Industry in 2016. Kogila holds an BA (Hons) from University of Malaya, LLB (Hons) degree from the University of London and an MA in Strategy and Diplomacy from the Malaysian National University. She won a Fulbright Scholarship in 2003 and held a Chevening Scholarship during 2004–2007, when she obtained her PhD in offsets and technology policy from the Defence College of Management and Technology, Cranfield University, UK Defence Academy. She presently holds an Adjunct Professorship at the Malaysian National Defence University and continues to advise governments and organisations on offsets policy. Kogila is married and has three wonderful children.

RIOT! Routledge Studies in Innovation, Organization and Technology

For more information about the series, please visit www.routledge.com/Routledge-Studies-in-Innovation-Organizations-and-Technology/book-series/RIOT

Technology Offsets in International Defence Procurement

Kogila Balakrishnan

Routledge
Taylor & Francis Group

LONDON AND NEW YORK

First published 2019
by Routledge
2 Park Square, Milton Park, Abingdon, Oxon OX14 4RN

and by Routledge
52 Vanderbilt Avenue, New York, NY 10017, USA

First issued in paperback 2020

Routledge is an imprint of the Taylor & Francis Group, an informa business

British Library Cataloguing-in-Publication Data
A catalogue record for this book is available from the British Library

Library of Congress Cataloging-in-Publication Data
Names: Balakrishnan, Kogila, author.
Title: Technology offsets in international defence procurement / Kogila Balakrishnan.
Description: Abingdon, Oxon ; New York, NY : Routledge, 2018. | Series: Routledge studies in innovation, organizations and technology | Includes bibliographical references and index.
Identifiers: LCCN 2018019996 | ISBN 9780815367192 (hardback) | ISBN 9781351258005 (ebook)
Subjects: LCSH: Arms transfers. | Technology transfer. | Defense industries—Government policy. | Government purchasing. | Commercial policy. | International trade.
Classification: LCC HD9743.A2 B35 2018 | DDC 382/.456234—dc23
LC record available at https://lccn.loc.gov/2018019996

ISBN 13: 978-0-367-58695-9 (pbk)
ISBN 13: 978-0-8153-6719-2 (hbk)

Typeset in Times New Roman
by Apex CoVantage, LLC

Contents

Figures

Tables

Foreword

Offsets are a policy tool used by governments globally to address critical economic, industrial and technological development priorities. In the UK, Europe and the United States, offsets have largely been used to develop the defence sector. In recent years, the tool has become increasingly popular in the civil sector, notably in the aerospace and automotive industries of emerging economies.

For governments, offsets deals with foreign suppliers of goods and services not available in local markets and provides a mechanism for local manufacturing and service sectors to improve capability.

For firms, the transfer of technology through offsets can stimulate innovation in local product and process development. Offsets can also support broader education, training, research and development projects. This impact on human capital development can lead to stronger labour markets and improved productivity.

Naturally, the implementation of offsets programmes creates debate, even controversy, over the extent desired policy outcomes are achieved in practise.

The results of offsets projects, as with any other economic policy, should be evaluated on objective economic measures and measurable policy impacts. For policy goals to be met, governments must provide the leadership to set standards and ambitions, provide careful assessment of proposed programmes and rigorous evaluation of implementation to ensure that offsets policy delivers on the stated objectives.

Such an evaluation and improvement process requires strong support from foreign partners in genuinely developing a long-term agenda of sustainable development.

This book on offsets comes at a time when governments are keen to find a middle ground between policies of protectionism and globalism. I congratulate Dr Kogila Balakrishnan, a leading expert in the field of technology offsets, for putting this book together.

Guided by her years of work in academia, policy and industry, this book is based on her robust understanding of the theory and practice of offsets. Further, she provides a crucial insight into the field from her personal experience in advising governments, the corporate sector and SMEs.

I wish her all the best.

Professor Lord K Bhattacharyya
Chairman and Founder
WMG, University of Warwick

Acknowledgements

To write a book for academics and practitioners of offsets requires in-depth knowledge and experience in this field. Only with the help, guidance and advice from so many offsets experts from government, industry and academia over the many years have I been able to pin down my thoughts into this book. The content and ideas of this book have translated mainly from high-level discussions with many offsets practitioners; government offsets officials, academics and fellow students. The opportunity to gain insights into offsets availed to me mainly in the course of my teaching, training and supervision through the challenging questions posed by my students during lectures and syndicate exercises; through feedback from offsets managers and government authorities; from my offsets training teammates at team GOCA and from various government- and company-led workshops worldwide.

I have so many individuals and organisations to thank in actualising this book. WMG, University of Warwick provided all the support and created the environment for me to complete this book. I obtained my motivation to write this book through witnessing the successful collaboration and relationships that exist within academia, industry and government at WMG and the resultant thriving economic development in the Midlands. Lord K Bhattacharya and my fellow colleagues and friends at the university have been continuously supportive of my decision to write this book.

A special thanks to my husband Robert for inspiring me and for giving me the utmost confidence to write this book. I would also like to thank my son Jai for his immense contribution in editing, proofreading and putting the whole book together for me on time. I take this opportunity to thank so many others who were involved directly or indirectly in providing me with knowledge, encouragement and in teaching me the 'nooks and corners' of offsets management. I wish to thank Professor Ron Matthews at Cranfield University for introducing me to the academic world of offsets. His writings and thoughts on offsets had been inspirational for my own work later. I also thank Dr Kevin Burgess of Cranfield University for his constant motivation, in encouraging me to write this book and in ensuring that I completed the project. I cannot forget to thank Dr Jesbil Singh who worked with me in various offsets projects at the Ministry of Defence Malaysia and then the National Defence University for his valuable insights into offsets. I would also like to thank to Dr Alan Colegrove, Offset Collaboration,

Incorporated, for introducing me to the world of offsets when he was the country manager for Boeing Malaysia.

I would also like to thank my offsets training team at GOCA who have always been supportive and continue to provide me with the platform to appreciate and learn how companies manage offsets. Special thanks to my dear friends Dov Hyman, Greg Clugston, Roger Bulgin and Mitch Butta for their constant support. I would also like to thank Christian Sylvian of AREVA who always invited me to ECCO meetings and provided me the platform to share my thoughts on offsets.

I must also make a special mention of Dr Dhafir and Paul Williams from the Partnership for Development programme (PfD), Oman; Matar Romaithi at Tawazun Economic Council (TEC), UAE; Wan Ashraf at the Defence Industry Division (DID) at the Ministry of Defence Malaysia; the Bulgarian Ministry of Economy and Ministry of Defence; Adrian Dalton (retired) of Defence and Security, UKTI; officials at Department of Defence Technology Institute (DTI) and National Science and Technology Development Agency (NSTDA), Thailand; Indonesian Defence University; Institute of Strategic Studies, Brunei; the Brazilian Armed Forces and Nanyang Technology University Singapore for their engagement with me in offsets policy formulation and implementation. I would also like to thank THALES, BAES, DCNI, MBDA, L3, QINETIC, SAVIS and Embraer for valuing my input on offsets policy. Special thanks also to colleagues at Cranfield University, colleagues at the National Defence University Malaysia, friends at RSIS, Nanyang Technology University and to friends at the Indonesian Defence University for their support.

I would also like to thank all my students who have chosen to undertake research in this field and also for their intellectual contributions to the discussions. Finally, I thank the publisher Routledge, especially to Kristina Abbott, Laura Hussey, Georgia Priestly and Kate Fornadel for assisting me with all the editing work and for the trust in me to commit to publishing this book.

Abbreviations

BD	business development
BIS	Bureau of Industry and Security
BOT	build, operate, transfer
CTO	Countertrade and Offset
EC	European Commission
ECCO	European Club for Countertrade and Offset
FDI	foreign direct investment
GOCA	Global Offset and Countertrade Association
GPA	Government Procurement Agreement
IC	international collaboration
IJV	international joint venture
IPR	intellectual property rights
LDCs	less developed countries
MNC	multinational corporations
MOU	Memorandum of Understanding
MRO	maintenance, repair and overhaul
NDA	non-disclosure agreement
NICs	newly developed countries
NITF	Nonconventional International Trade Financing
OEM	original equipment manufacturers
OMO	offset management office
PMO	project management office
R&D	research and development
SME	small and medium enterprise
SP	strategic partnership
TAC	technological absorption capability
TC	technology collaboration
TCB	technological capability building
TI	Transparency International
TNC	transnational corporations
TOT	transfer of technology
WTO	World Trade Organization

Phase I

1   An introduction to offsets

1.1   Setting the scene

'Rules of the game' set by Bretton Wood institution, WTO and major organisations are set against forms of government intervention to promote industry. In the near future, government will have almost none of the instruments of policy used through history to promote industrial development. Yet, targeted intervention in trade, industry and supporting institutions have played a critical role in industrialisation through history.

Working papers no 48, Selective Industrial and Trade Policies in Developing Countries, Theoretical and Empirical Issues, Sanjaya Lall, OEH Writing Paper series, OEHWPS. 2000, August

This quote by Professor Sanjaya Lall[1] describes the crucial role which targeted government intervention will come to play as traditional economic tools become less utilised. This shift from sweeping intervention to specialised policy has provided the space and justification for the emergence of offsets in international business. In principle, government intervention can be harmful and a dose of liberalisation is a precondition for industrialisation. However, there is still considerable scope for legitimate industrial policy. Targeted interventions in trade, industry and supporting institutions have played a critical role in industrialisation throughout history. For example, all major industrialised countries utilised extended protectionism and other selective measures to promote industry, while simultaneously developing the institutions needed to support industrial and technological activity. Offsets has very much been used for similar purposes around the world.

Offsets, or offset,[2] is not a widely used term. Due to its relative unfamiliarity, it is often misinterpreted as an economic tool similar to carbon trading, sometimes courting controversy in the face of accusations of being illusive and non-transparent. Offsets is a policy tool used by buyers[3] to seek additional economic, industrial and technological benefits from sellers[4] as part of international procurement.

The aim of introducing offsets is to ensure that buyers do not participate in face value transactional activities by simply being net importers of products and services. Instead, deeper engagement with sellers is encouraged by including developmental activities such as employment creation, technology transfer and joint ventures as part of the terms of transaction. In the long-term this would promote global cooperation and provide another source of economic benefit to buyer nations, further reducing inequality between nations (Stiglitz, 2017, pp. xii–xli).[5]

This book arrives after my 20 years of experience both in the theory and practice of offsets.[6] Stephen Martin published a volume of papers on arms trade offsets, part of a series of studies in defence economics which was then published by Harwood (Martin, 1996). The book was comprehensively cited and used as a primary reference by those who had limited knowledge of offsets at a time when there was little in the way of published material on offsets. Eight years later Jurgen Brauer and John Paul Dunne (Brauer and Dunne, 2004) published another volume of papers which examined the theory and policy applications of arms trade offsets and looked at a dozen case studies drawn from across Europe, Africa, Asia and the Americas. These two works share some similarity in style, both composed of a compilation of case studies, written from an academic perspective, predominantly by defence economists. Most critically, both sets of authors conclude that offsets does not bring net benefits to a country's economic development, and, indeed, offsets deals make arms trades more expensive.

Its intrinsically pervasive nature makes it difficult to pigeonhole offsets into a specific field. Previous authors have primarily approached the topic as part of economic theory, but when considering real world implementation, offsets can also be studied as a field within technology management, public policy and international business. The content of this book reflects this more holistic view, with a focus on technology offsets within an international business focus combining theories of economic development, aspects of technology management, and public policy as well as incorporating various aspects of practicality of offsets.

Thus, this book is aimed at a broader section of the offsets community than previous publications, including government decision makers, corporate leaders, politicians, academics, policy makers and business students, as well as everyday practitioners of offsets in government and industry.

I have written this book based on my deep understanding of the theory and practice of offsets. My initial years were focused on the development and implementation of an offsets programme at the Ministry of Defence in Malaysia. I gained first-hand experience in negotiating, finalising contracts and working with sellers in implementing offsets contracts and programme closure. Curiosity as to the effectiveness of offsets in Malaysia's industrial and technological development led me to undertake a PhD at the Defence College of Management and Technology (DCMT) at Cranfield University, UK Defence Academy, for four years (2004–2007). During this time, I researched the impact of offsets on Malaysia's defence industry, whilst also sharpening my theoretical knowledge in offsets and technology policy. I was appointed as the Under Secretary for Defence Industry at the Ministry of Defence Malaysia in 2007. This was when I took a direct involvement in drafting and formulating offsets policy for the government of Malaysia. In this time my involvement in the formulation and implementation of Malaysian offsets policy was challenging but also fascinating, as I was able to work closely with both international suppliers and local subcontractors to understand offsets policy fundamentals and to see where issues arose during implementation. From 2011 to 2014, during my secondment to the Warwick Manufacturing Group (WMG) at the University of Warwick, my involvement in offsets was mainly focused on advisory work for foreign governments, large transnational corporations and SMEs, as well as running offsets academic and training courses. These multifaceted interactions with offsets practitioners were beneficial to reflect, compare and contrast the various offsets practices around the world. From 2015, as Director for Client and Business Development (East Asia) at WMG, besides undertaking knowledge transfer programmes for the university, I spent most of my time assisting sellers in putting together offsets proposals as part of a bid process, consulting for foreign governments and teaching offsets.[7] This book draws upon my first-hand experience but also is vitally composed of facts and discussions based on my PhD thesis, lecture notes, presentations from various conferences and some of my published papers.

I believe this book will be a valuable reference for those who wish to have a comprehensive understanding of offsets strategy and policy formulation. In addition, I hope to provide further rationale for offsets, as well as a perspective from government and industry. Nonetheless, I discuss the challenges and criticism that offsets faces, and conclude with a look at the future for offsets as it stands today. It is extremely difficult to obtain much information in the public domain about offsets and how it works, as this subject is closely associated to defence. All the more reason why I believe this book is important for offsets practitioners, policy makers and academics in the field of international business and management.

1.2 Why the need for this book?

- This book sets the foundation and shares best practices on offsets policy and implementation in the defence sector. While in itself a useful study, it can be looked at as a type of policy transfer by other sectors such as aerospace, healthcare, transport, energy and telecommunication.
- Offsets as an integral component of defence procurement is estimated to form at least 30–40% of overall defence procurement (Holtom, Bromley, Wezeman and Wezeman, 2012; Avascent, 2012; Sobolev and Alden, 2014). This is both a significant sum of money and an important aspect of defence that should be more openly discussed.
- Evidence suggests that the number of countries embracing some form of offsets, whether written or unwritten, is increasing (Spear, 2013). It is claimed today that around 80 countries around the world have some form of offsets policy in place (Behera, 2009). This development certainly requires nations to have some form of policy guidance and advice on offsets and how it works.
- This book also provides guidance to organisations on how offsets policies are formulated, issues in implementation and an awareness of national aspirations and requirements for offsets.

- At the same time, buyers as smart customers should be perceptive of corporate offsets strategy and implementation (Ajaxon., 2006). This book discusses company offsets strategy as well as the offsets management cycle, including cost and associated risk.
- There are several books and articles written on the effectiveness and impact of offsets, but none focus on offsets practice from a technology transfer and management perspective.
- Governance in defence and often in offsets practice has led to much public scrutiny in the past decade (Pyman, 2013). It is important to discuss issues of governance and ethical practice in an offsets environment.
- This book also aims to establish some form of standardisation and uniformity in the terminology and concepts used when discussing offsets, in order to create a foundation for greater competency and professionalism for offsets specialists and the wider industry community.
- This book also aims to dispel misinformation and prevent the misinterpretation of offsets by increasing awareness and providing a focal point of reference on offsets education.

1.3   Global offsets obligation and trends

One of the major challenges within offsets is obtaining consolidated data on the total offsets obligation globally. This difficulty arises as there is no unified published report on offsets transactions by international organisations such as the World Trade Organization (WTO) or the World Bank. The Bureau for Industry and Security (BIS) Offsets Report produced by the United States Department of Trade is the only published document on offsets obligation and transactions.[8] However, this report only covers American contractors' offsets obligations worldwide. It is often impossible to agree on total offsets obligations as most governments and companies are reluctant to publish or reveal this data on the pretext of political, commercial and security interests.

From the existing available reports in the public domain, it is can be seen that the value of offsets transactions worldwide is certainly increasing (Jane's Defence Industry, 2013; Ungaro, 2013). It is predicted that the total offsets obligation will increased from $214 billion in 2012 to $500 billion in 2016 (Avascent, 2012). However, there is no clarity as to whether this figure includes offsets obligations by countries such as China and Russia, who have a much different attitude both towards offsets practice and in how they operate in export markets (Andolenko, 2010; Anderson, 2012; Dodds, 1995, pp. 1119–1145; Felton, 2012).[9]

In terms of regional distribution, the Middle East (ME), followed by East and South Asia, shows a significant increase in offsets obligation (Avascent, 2012), whilst this figure has declined drastically within the European Union (EU) since the banning of offsets following Directive 2009.EC/81 except with the exclusion under Article 346 of the EU Treaty which allows offsets to be requested by EU member nations on the pretext of national security[10] (Welt and Wilson, 1998, pp. 36–53; Furter, 2014).

In terms of sectors, BIS reports that offsets obligations are highest in aircraft manufacturing, other parts and auxiliary equipment manufacturing, aircraft engine and engine parts manufacturing, guided missile sectors and spare vehicle manufacturing (BIS, 2016a).[11] The initial offsets work focused on the aerospace sector for it was seen as the area with the greatest potential for propelling buyer nations into high technology areas. This aimed to move national industrial and technological capability up the value chain, creating highly skilled, high-income jobs such as in aerospace and aeronautical engineering, advanced material such as composites and nano-composites, systems integration, advanced manufacturing, as well as enhancing the local supply chain to be part of the international supply chain, and creating new export opportunities in high tech sectors (Khan, 2010; United States Department of Commerce Bureau of Industry and Security, 2016).

The cycle of using offsets can be traced back to when the US entered the international market in the 1960s, when Boeing offered work packages to Western European countries. This then broke the aircraft industry monopoly with the birth of a consortium of European aerospace companies, Airbus. The formation and development of Airbus is an excellent case to demonstrate how the US used aerospace offsets to transfer technology and assist the European aviation industry (Niosi and Zhegu, 2005). This model was then copied by others such as Brazil, Japan, Taiwan, then later by Malaysia, Indonesia,[12] South Korea, India and recently by China, UAE and Saudi Arabia[13] (Zhang, 2009; Savitri, 2016). I discuss the historical development of offsets in the second chapter of this book. The trend of using offsets for development of the aerospace sector is slowly changing. I discuss the future trend in offsets usage in the final chapter.

Why has offsets obligation continuously increased? First, since the end of the Cold War, the defence market has shifted from a sellers' to a buyers' market. The oversupply of arms and weapons by defence industries worldwide has made the defence market extremely competitive (Bitzinger, 1999; Dunne and Freeman-Sam, 2003, pp. 23–41; Holtom, Bromley, Wezeman and Wezeman, 2012; Stockholm International Peace Research Institute, 2016). Buyers have had a wide choice as to where they could buy from and have become intelligent and savvy customers not only shopping for the best products and services but also for additional benefits such as offsets. Sellers, on the other hand, have had little choice but to offer additional carrots such as offsets as part of their competitive advantage in bids to win international business and capture export sales. Second, the proliferation of offsets practice and its subsequent impact on industrial and technological development mainly in Europe and the United States has created global awareness of the benefits of offsets. Countries in the process of industrialising are beginning to view it as a tool that can help them quickly and efficiently make up for lags in technological capability when compared to industrialised nations (Buckley, 2003) I discuss in detail the rationale for offsets in the third chapter of this book. Third, over the years, the wide network of offsets lobbyists such as offsets authorities, governments, politicians, defence and related companies, third party agents and academics have also directly or indirectly been involved in promoting and translating the impact of offsets for economic development through transfer policy mechanisms.

1.4   Offsets in international procurement

In studying offsets, it is important to appreciate that it can feature in international procurement activities. Though offsets is present in defence and civil procurement, offsets is only institutionalised and structured in defence procurement. Other sectors such as transport, healthcare, telecommunication, energy and construction widely practise offsets, but in more subtle ways due to strict international trade rules that forbid any form of protection in favour of local industrial and technological development. It is only in defence procurement where offsets is openly practised and discussed. This does not mean that offsets does not exist in civil procurement. In fact, some of the largest offsets deals are in civil automotive, aerospace, construction as well as energy and gas sectors (Hayward, 2013; Florio, Parikh and Hussain, 2017; Skynews, 2017; Bombardier, 2017).

Why introduce offsets in international procurement? Procurement takes many forms. Buyers have to make a choice as to the type of procurement they choose to enter into. Buyers can choose to source for products and services locally if available in-country, or to procure off-the-shelf products and services from abroad. If a buyer country wants to ensure that it does not continue to be a net purchaser of certain products and equipment, especially in strategic industries (Amara. and Pargac, 2009),[14] then offsets could be imposed as part of an international procurement transaction to ensure that some level of capability is retained in-country. In defence procurement, for example, imposing offsets with a view to total self-sufficiency and indigenous development theoretically means a nation will have independent capability, total control of equipment and benefits in terms of jobs and technology acquisition, though this may result in higher costs to the nation's economy (Kelly and Rishi, 2003, pp. 1–17; Kennedy, 1974, 1975). The opposite extreme is to procure off-the-shelf, which could be a cheaper option. This may result in a nation having to compromise or lose control over systems capability or miss out on industrial and technological benefits, and it increases the risk of discontinuation of support for the equipment purchased in the case of an embargo or refusal to continue supply (Brzoaka and Ohlson, 1986, p. 279; United States Bereau of Industry and Security (BIS, 2016b)). Therefore, the third option is to use offsets as part of a defence globalisation[15] agenda to venture into collaborative production and maintenance of equipment. Even in this middle way, collaboration has also proven to have its own share of difficulties (Chuter, 2010; Bitzinger, 1999, p. 306).

Despite the voices of Adam Smith, David Ricardo and neoliberals alike who hail the free market, condemn government intervention, argue for trade liberalisation and propose that globalisation is beneficial for all nations, the new discontent of the 21st century lies in the growing economic disparity both within and between nations. The Keynesian model of calculative state intervention to ensure balanced economic development requires policies such as offsets to continue to feature as part of international procurement.

1.5 Key research on offsets

Offsets is a new field in international business studies. Offsets has never gained prominence as it is seen as incompatible to free trade. If at all, the subject of countertrade as an alternative trade financing mechanism is discussed only briefly in international business textbooks. As earlier mentioned in this chapter, there remain only two major books solely on offsets. First, the book by Stephen Martin on *The Economics of Offsets: Defence Procurement and Countertrade*, published in 1996 by Harwood. The book was funded by the Economic and Social Research Council (ESRC). The book has 11 chapters of case studies on offsets practice in various countries around the world mainly written by academics with a background in defence economics, providing an overview of offsets and countertrade in Chapter 1. Eight years later, in 2004, Jurgen Brauer and John Paul Dunne edited another book on offsets called *Arms Trade and Economic Development: Theory, Policy and Cases in Arms Trade Offsets*. The first part of the book provides theoretical discussions to offsets whilst the second part consists of 14 case studies on offsets practice around the world. Most of these articles were contributed by economists with a few by offsets practitioners.

Trade journals that take an interest in offsets include *Countertrade and Offsets (CTO)*,[16] *Jane's Defence Weekly*, the *Economist*, *Aviation Week*, *Space Magazine* and *Defence News*. Several journals have published papers on offsets, including *Defence and Peace Economics*, *Security Challenges*, *Financial Management* and the *Royal United Services Institute (RUSI)*. The US Department of Defense (DOD) with the assistance of the Defense Institute of Security Management sponsors a quarterly journal called *DISAM* used to frequently publish on defence offsets. Several PhD and MSc dissertations have focused on the impact of offsets. Most of these studies were focused on the impact of offsets on a specific nation's industrial and technological development, suggesting a way forward through the effective utilisation of offsets[17] (Taylor, 2003b; Matthews, 2014; Eriksson et al., 2007; Matthews, 1996; Kirchwehm, 2014b).

Overall, there is still a dearth in offsets research as it is hard to undertake research in defence and security transactions shrouded in secrecy and confidentiality due to national security concerns, thereby limiting the number of people involved (Kirchwehm, 2013). Further, there is no coherent effort to undertake such research in non-defence sectors except in some studies that look at the impact of international collaboration, strategic alliances and localisation. Research focus on offsets should expand beyond impact analysis and economic development to analysing the role of offsets in strategy and strategic management, risk management, marketing and finance in international business.

1.6 Costs and benefits of offsets

In Chapter 3 I discuss the rationale for offsets backed by a theoretical underpinning. It is an ongoing debate as to whether offsets should be continued or disbanded. There is no definitive answer, but later in this book I argue that the effectiveness of offsets relies not on offsets strategy and policy but on its imple-mentation. In this section, I discuss the costs and benefits of offsets from supplier and buyer perspectives.

1.6.1   Benefit to suppliers

Some of the expected benefits to suppliers include the potential of securing sales in difficult markets by using offsets as part of company marketing strategy; tapping into a cheaper and broader supplier base in the buyer country (Hammond, 1990); corporate partnerships such as through international joint ventures (IJV) and stra-tegic alliances with a view to long-term in-country presence and continued sales. Other benefits include boosting the image of defence and security companies that are seen to be involved in socio-economic development in export markets. For supplier governments, offsets can serve as an important foreign policy and national security tool, where nation states can boost the industrial capability of allied nations, standardise military equipment and modernise allied forces (Chinworth, 1992; Peterson, 2011; Behera, 2015). At the same time, offsets arrangements can raise the value of technology transfers, as well as boosting the overall industrial and technological capability of allied nations (Chinworth, 2011, pp. 233–245).

1.6.2   Cost to suppliers

The expected costs to suppliers includes the possibility for distortion of existing supply chains and national security concerns as companies are pressured to transfer work elsewhere to comply with offsets regulations. In seller countries, this could also lead to a loss of jobs in critical sectors thus leading to a loss of specific skills in the long-term. Offsets can also increase competition, as firms that benefit from the tech-nology transfer could become new entrants in the market (Herrnstadt, 2008). Offsets could also increase administrative and transactional costs for suppliers. Offsets cost is often associated with supply documents, management and transport of sub-assemblies, auditing and building capability to close the technology gap in buyer countries as well as cost incurred due to international differences in language and culture (Chuter, 2013). In some cases, especially if it involves barter or counter-purchase deals, offsets can distort the existing market and lead to dumping products in third country markets (Mann, 2000, p. 49; Dehoff, Dowdy and Kwon, 2014).

1.6.3   Benefit to buyers

Buyers argue that offsets has many benefits. The strongest argument is that offsets in defence transfers technology for the development of indigenous defence indus-tries, helping buyer nations retain some level of self-sufficiency[18] in respect to its armed forces. Countries such as Brazil, South Korea and South Africa claim to have developed their defence industrial base through offsets. Others, for example India, have also attempted to follow suit but have struggled. For example, India decided to produce the R-MIG21 fighter aircraft from Russia under licence with the expectation that offsets through the procurement would provide India with the expected development of advanced aeronautics (Singh, 1990, p. 275; Ragunathan, 1990, pp. 29–31; Suman, 2005, pp. 1–2; Mitra, 2009, pp. 34–36). India is taking a similar approach now with the purchase of the Rafael aircraft from Dassault insisting on co-production, but the negotiation had been most difficult where the Indian government and the Indian defence industries claim that they were not offered the technology and expertise they had expected (Behera, 2016). Offsets are also credited with the creation of jobs in critical high technology sectors such as in defence, security and aerospace (Grey and Buchan, 1992). In Malaysia, for example, offsets was instrumental for the growth of advanced aerospace manufacturing, creating demand for aeronautics engineers and other related skilled jobs in-country (Balakrishnan, 2007). The British government claimed that more than 3,000 jobs were secured through the purchase of the Longbow Apache in 1995 for $4 billion (Financial Times, 1995). China has been extremely successful in using offsets to enhance its automobile and aerospace industry. A typical example is how the technology partnership between AVIC and China Aerospace with Boeing and Airbus resulted in the development of locally made C919 Chinese COMAC aircraft (Palia and Shenkar, 1991; Moretz, 2010). Some countries also claim that offsets reduces the cost of weapon purchases through co-production, licencing and subcontracting. Offsets help to develop new skills through education and training provided by original equipment manufacturers (OEMs) and associated subcontractors (Matthews, 1996). Offsets is also often used by politicians to justify military procurement, arguing the case for regional development programmes, employment creation and export opportunities.

1.6.4   Costs to buyers

In most countries the building of defence industry capability is the responsibility of the state, as public funds are used to support defence research and development (R&D) and domestic manufacturing. Most often, returns on investment (ROIs) in defence are negligible and often take a long time to materialise. Not all countries that aim to use offsets for defence industrialisation can achieve full potential. Some of these governments aspire to become major producers of defence goods and services, but fail to realise that there is an opportunity cost at the expense of forgoing other sectors of development. The volume of defence exports captured through offsets deals may be used to spread high fixed costs over small outputs, resulting in spiralling unit costs. Also, if export sales for defence or non-defence items can only be secured through offsets, this can make companies in buyer countries extremely vulnerable, as they have to be continuously dependent on their overseas partner for future export orders (Markowski and Hall, 2014).

1.7   Offsets stakeholders and their views

"One man's meat is another man's poison". Offsets is seen as distorting, corrupt and ineffective by some whilst others see offsets as an economic development tool that can be a catalyst towards national industrial and technological development. In this section, I briefly discuss the varying perspectives that exist within the offsets fraternity.

1.7.1   Economists

The majority of economists have a negative view towards offsets (Martin, 1996; Jurgen and Paul, 2004; Martin and Hartley, 1995). Offsets is labelled as 'free lunch' but someone still has to pay for the cost of offsets. Both theoretical and empirical discussions, mainly in the form of case studies, by the majority of the economists conclude that offsets overall has had very little positive impact on economic development. This conclusion necessitates severe analysis amongst offsets practitioners as to why, despite billions of dollars in global offsets obligations, evidence suggests that in most instances, offsets has not been successfully implemented. Does this suggest that data on offsets obligations and outcomes are not being effectively captured and measured, that there is a major issue with the implementation of offsets, resulting in a high number of offsets project failures that go unreported? Or is it the case that accurate indicators are not being used to measure offsets impact?

1.7.2   International organisations

The European Commission (EC) issued a directive in 2009 claiming that offsets is a distortion of European trade and should be constrained (Eliassen and Shriver, 2002). EC reasoned that banning offsets and other forms of trade protectionism would prevent duplication and waste, leading to an effective and cost-efficient European industrial defence base that would be much more competitive (Organization for Joint Armament Cooperation (OCCAR), 1996; Eriksson et al., 2007; Edwards, 2011; Briani, Marrone, Molling and Valasek, 2013). Directive 2009/81/EC (Directive 81) clearly calls for elimination of offsets practice in all EU member states except under Article 346 of TFEU for reasons of national security. Theoretically, the directive imposed by the European Defence Agency (EDA)[19] on EU nations seems like a robust policy but in practise the directive is not working, as nations find other options to still impose offsets but disguise it under some other name (Matthews and Ansari, 2015; Furter, 2014; Eisenhut, 2013, pp. 393–403; European Defence Industry Group [EDIG], 2011).

The World Trade Organization (WTO) agreement on government procurement generally forbids the use of offsets in government procurement except under Article 23 of the WTO on account of national security and public health (www.wto.org). The Government Procurement Agreement (GPA)[20] however does not explicitly ban offsets. The GPA provides flexibility and differential treatment depending on a nation's level of development. The agreement is subjective and negotiable by developing countries as long as GPA members adhere to core principles regarding transparency, competition and good governance in procurement of goods and services.

There is still flexibility over how offsets can be used for capacity and capability building especially in the developing market. The question however is whether such flexibility should also be applicable to many developed countries that are finding it equally hard to retain jobs, secure employment and create export opportunities in an environment where the difference between developed and emerging economies becomes less transparent. These nations are asking themselves why they should be subject to strict WTO rules leading to disadvantages for their in-country economic development.

US trade law clearly does not permit offsets. The US government views offsets for military export as economically inefficient and market distorting. No government agencies of the US government will directly enter into an offsets arrangement in relation to the sale of defence goods or services to foreign governments, with a strict policy that government funding should not be used to finance offsets activities. The decision whether to engage in offsets and the responsibility for negotiating and implementing offsets arrangement resides solely with the companies involved (Bush's Press Secretary, 1990). This official stance on offsets has been questioned and debated for the past two decades by the rest of the world, as the US government continues to strictly impose the 'Buy American Act' (BAA)[21] on foreign contractors importing into the US, stipulating rules on local content, employment creation and other restrictions. It is likely that under an 'America First' Trump administration, the US will continue to impose stronger rules for offsets flow into America through the BAA, whilst strongly discouraging the outflow of offsets from US companies to overseas markets.

1.7.3   Offsets industry community

The industry community is divided in their views of offsets. Some view offsets as a '*necessary evil*' that has to be offered as part of a winning bid in international sales. Offsets is seen as adding competitive advantage to business. The Chartered Institute of Purchasing and Supply Chain (CIPS), for example, has included offsets as part of global sourcing strategy (CIPS, n.d.).

Pro-offsets companies (POCs) develop a more positive attitude by including offsets as part of company corporate strategy. POCs develop dedicated offsets departments and train staff to work closely with foreign governments in comprehending offsets policy and delivering them effectively. I discuss OEM offsets strategy and implementation in detail in Chapter 6. POCs also put in place governance structure and compliance mechanisms as part of their company marketing and export strategy. This is discussed in further detail in Chapter 8 of this book. On the other hand, some companies view offsets as a burden to their core business, costly to develop and deliver, and have an anti-offsets attitude (AOA). AOAs often plead ignorance to the existence of offsets policy in buyer countries and would prefer not to take part in offsets transactions if they had an option. The AOAs understand that they face the danger of losing a bid if they refuse but sometimes choose not to as they are unable to deliver offsets programmes due to the additional cost and occasional non-existence of in-house offsets specialists that are able to handle offsets.

1.7.4   Government and offsets agencies

There is generally a widespread pro-offsets sentiment within governments and off-sets agencies. There is a strong endorsement from this community that offsets can be used as a leveraging policy tool to gain additional economic, industrial and technological benefits to balance the large outflow of currency following procurement activities. Many nations have developed offsets policies and created dedicated offsets agencies mandated to implement offsets. This is discussed in detail in Chapter 4 of this book. However, within government itself, there is an ongoing tension from different stakeholders such as end-users (armed forces for example), finance and procurement as to the allocation of resources for offsets in relation to long-term ROIs and whether offsets really benefits a nation (Petty, 1999; Trybus, 2014).

1.7.5   Offsets consultants and third party providers

Consultants and third party offsets providers are generally appointed for the following reasons:

- the original equipment manufacturer (OEM) or subcontractor does not want to have an offsets department or invest in offsets internally as it is too costly and strategically not feasible to maintain such operations in-company;
- obtaining specific external programmes or projects from individuals in areas not within the core business of the OEM, and where OEMs do not have such expertise in-house whilst customers have requested for such projects;
- out-of-house consultants are usually expert advisors on offsets with vast experience and knowledge on the subject, and a good track record with personal credentials. Such a consultant is able to provide impartial advice to governments and companies on how to develop and deliver offsets effectively and institute policy transfer.

1.7.6   Offsets-related trade associations

There are a few trade associations solely dedicated to offsets. These organisations are mainly industry-led and most are based in the US and Europe. The most well-known of these organisations are the Global Countertrade and Offsets Association based in New York (GOCA), the European Club for Countertrade and Offsets based in Paris (ECCO) and DKF in Germany. The aim of these associations is to assist their members in disseminating guidance and the latest developments in offsets policy around the world, creating platforms such as conferences for the sharing of best practice and networking opportunities. These organisations also run offsets training for their members.

1.7.7   Publishers

Countertrade and Offsets (CTO) is a well-known offsets magazine which is published monthly. CTO covers major development in offsets globally, and highlights issues and challenges in the offsets world. CTO also produces a quarterly bulletin on offsets policies. Many large companies and governments subscribe to CTO as a means of keeping abreast with industry activity and offsets policy development worldwide. Other magazines and journals that often cover offsets news include the *Economist, Financial Times, Journal of Defence and Peace and Economics* and *RUSI*.

1.8   The need for an offsets framework

As I discussed earlier in this chapter, offsets management is a new field and is still in its infancy. Though there are a few books, journal articles and papers that discuss the impact, benefit and effectiveness of offsets, a clear methodology or approach to offsets management has not emerged. Similar challenges were faced by many other management disciplines such as project mangement, quality management, innovation and strategic management when they too were in their infancy, but many of these disciplines have now flourished and become important components of business and management study being offered at universities. Offsets is new and there is so far a lack of an integrated methodology for offsets managers to think through and appreciate overall offsets framework.

Due to the pervasive nature of offsets, offsets managers require unique skill sets that combine knowledge of technology management, project management, supply chain, strategy and strategic management, contracts management, finance as well as soft skills such as communication, relationship management and negotiation skills, among others. This makes offsets management a complex challenge for aspirational managers.

Considering the need for an integrated methodology in offsets supported by a combination of hard and soft skills, an offsets management framework is necessary. Having had first-hand experience in offsets management coupled by many years of research on offsets, I realise that there is a need for consistency in offsets management.

Figure 1.1 illustrates a 3-P Framework for an effective offsets management life cycle. The figure is divided into three phases. The primary phase illustrates the foundation required by offsets managers before they embark on offsets management. This includes understanding and appreciating offsets typology, drivers, terminology and rationale for offsets both from sellers and buyers perspectives.

Phase two is the process phase and this phase focuses on two distinct phases for buyers and suppliers in offsets management, the development stage and the implementation phase, respectively. Both of these phases compliment each other and actvities within the two phases are interlinked as opposed to being linear.

Finally, phase three is the pillar to offsets management and reflects the essential ingredients to successful offsets management. This depends on mastering issues of technology, risk, governance and delivery in offsets management.

Figure 1.1 has been derived from a combination of my years of active research while engaging with govenments and companies worldwide over the past 20 years, the Offsets Business Framework (OBF) that I use when presenting to GOCA

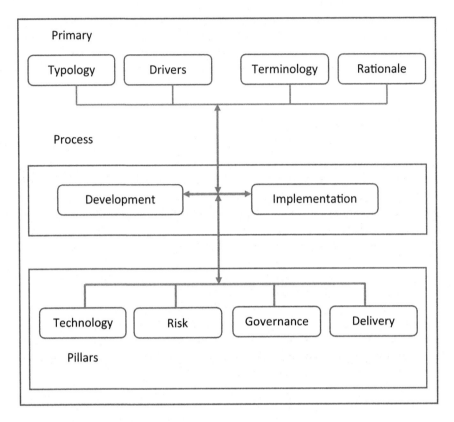

Figure 1.1 Offsets 3-P Framework

training participants and some elements of my PhD research framework (Bal-akrishnan, 2007). The 3-P Framework forms the foundation to the structure of this book and subsequent chapters.

1.9   Structure of the book

The structure of this book is based on the 3-P Framework with chapters as follows.

The second and third chapters discuss phase one. Chapter 2 explores keys aspects of offsets management, defines offsets, explains offsets typology and ter-minologies and discusses the drivers to offsets. Chapter 3 on offsets and economic development puts forward a justification for the use of offsets based on theoretical arguments from the perspective of buyers and suppliers. Phase two consists of Chapter 4, Chapter 5 and Chapter 6. Chapter 4 explains the role of government in offsets strategy and policy formulation, and explains how governments and offsets agencies develop offsets policy and manage different stakeholders. Chapter 5 discusses the role of government in implementing offsets, and explains the bid processes, evaluation, tender, contract negotiation, finalisation and finally the monitoring and reporting of an offsets programme. Chapter 6 on seller offsets strategy and implementation discusses the overall company offsets management life cycle consisting of before, during and after the offsets contract. This chapter also discusses functions of offsets in a corporate organisation, the successful ingredients to managing offsets and issues for sellers in delivering offsets. Phase three consists of Chapter 7, Chapter 8, Chapter 9 and Chapter 10. Chapter 7 on competitiveness, technology and offsets discusses the various roles and the relevancy of technology in offsets management. Chapter 8 on ethics and governance in offsets is focused on issues of transparency and corruption in offsets management, whilst Chapter 9 talks about how to identify and mitigate risks in offsets. This chapter also discusses the offsets risk matrix. Finally, Chapter 10 on the future of offsets concludes with direction for the future. In a globally challeging and dynamic international environment where businesses are becoming more competitive and governments are increasingly protective, how can offsets be leveraged more effectively for a win-win solution for buyers and sellers alike?

Notes

1 Professor Sanjaya Lall was one of the world's preeminent developmental economists with a 40-year career at Oxford University. Lall's pioneering research was mostly focused on the impact of foreign investment, the economics of multinational corporations and the emergence of technological capability and industrial competitiveness in a developing world. Lall passed away two weeks before I tried to contact him (July 2005) for a meeting regarding my PhD work whilst at Cranfield University. Most of my theoretical work on offsets is based on Lall's discussions and arguments.
2 There is a constant debate of whether it should be offset or offsets. One will notice these two being used interchangeably by many authors. In this book, I shall stick to offsets.
3 'Buyers' in the context of this book is defined as the government, public sector enterprises, government-linked companies, large private corporations and other entities that are all involved in the major overseas procurement of goods and services.
4 Sellers in the context of this book are defined as original equipment manufacturers (OEM), prime contractors or multinational companies that are involved in export sales.
5 Joseph Stiglitz's book *Discontent of Globalisation* (Stiglitz, 2017) is an excellent way to describe the need for targeted government intervention tools such as offsets to ensure balanced industrial and technological growth for both importing and exporting countries.
    Stigltitz argues that globalisation has failed but succeeded in the creation of global discontent due to the unequal distribution of wealth and reckless attitudes of corporate giants towards ensuring a balance between profit, shareholder satisfaction and ensuring that they are creating an impact through economic development activities in host countries.
6 My experience in offsets spans across formulating offsets policy for the government of Malaysia; being involved in offsets implementation; undertaking PhD research on the impact of offsets; working alongside OEMs and SMEs in preparing and executing offsets in my role as Director of Business Development for WMG, University of Warwick; running offsets training courses at GOCA, ECCO, universities and bespoke industry programmes as well as advising foreign governments on offsets policy and practice.

7 An offsets module was initially offered at Cranfield University in Shrivenham as part of the MSc in International Defence Marketing. This was later delivered as a standalone module by WMG in collaboration with Offsets 2000 a SME based in the UK. I also delivered offsets training to members of GOCA. ECCO invited me to deliver a one-day offsets module on 'customer perspective' in Paris, France, as part of their MBA programme with ESSEC Business School. I have run offsets training and worked in advisory roles for various governments and OEMs but am unable to go further in this book due to commercial sensitivity and customer confidentiality.

8 There are very few published documents on offsets data showing offsets obligations and transactions worldwide. Only the BIS produces a yearly report which highlights major US defence contractors' obligations overseas, types of obligations and amount of transaction by category, sector and region. Refer to 'Offsets in Defence Trade, 21st Study', *U.S. Department of Commerce, Bureau of Industry and Security* (2016), December, www.bis.doc.gov/index.php/documents/pdfs/1620-twenty-first-report-to-congress-12-16/file.

9 The increasing number of countries requesting the inclusion of offsets packages however cannot be used as a benchmark to claim that the total offsets obligation is increasing, though this is an indication that offsets is now becoming widely practised by more countries than ever. Countertrade and Offsets publishes a quarterly bulletin with a complete list of countries and their offsets policies. Refer to *Offsets Guideline Quarterly Bulletin*, January 2017, at http://cto-offsets.com/the-offsets-guidelines-quarterly-bulletin.

10 However, most OEMs operating in the EU claim that offsets practice within the EU has not gone away but is continuously being practised and disguised under other names such as the British 'Industrial Engagement Policy'. Several offsets managers doing business in the EU even go as far as to suggest that "offsets has become an underground activity", whereby offsets obligations are still being imposed by buyer nations but the transactions are not declared, making offsets even less transparent. See Furter, Denise, 2014 for discussion on 'Banning of offsets in the EU'.

11 The offsets obligation by sector published by BIS is limited to only defence and this does not include civil offsets, noticeably lacking in the civil aerospace sector which involves a large amount of work-sharing, co-production, licencing, technology transfer and subcontracting that are not covered in any report.

12 Dr Mahathir Mohammad, the fourth prime minister of Malaysia was instrumental for the development and growth of the Malaysian aerospace sector, as was Dr B.J. Habibie, an aeronautical engineer who became the CEO of Institute Pesawat Terbang Nusantara (IPTN) and was later appointed as the president of Indonesia between 1998 and 1999 in the post-Suharto era.

13 Refer to the unpublished PhD thesis by Zhang, N.Y 'China's Search for Indigenous Industrial Development: A Case Study of the Aviation Industry', 2009, Cranfield University unpublished thesis), for the development of aerospace industry and use of offsets in China, and Savitri (2016), 'Contribution of Offsets to Defence Industry in Indonesia, Cranfield Defence and Security' (PhD thesis) for development of defence and aerospace industry in Indonesia.

14 A strategic industry is defined as an industry that a government considers to be very important for the country's economy and security. However, this could vary for each country based on its geopolitical, economic and social considerations. In general, most nations would classify defence, security, energy and telecommunication as strategic industries. Others have also designated certain raw materials such as steel, oil and gas as strategic. There are continuous debates as to what constitutes a 'strategic industry'.

15 Defence globalisation is defined as "the shift away from the traditional single-country pattern of weapons manufacturing in favour of 'internationalising' the development, production, and marketing of arms".

16 *Countertrade and Offsets*, or CTO, is a bulletin on offsets published in London. It is by far the only bulletin that provides up-to-date news and information on offsets around the world. Although the information provided may not be unconditionally accurate, CTO is nonetheless relied upon as a major source for updates on offsets policy and practice by companies and governments worldwide. CTO can be accessed at http:// cto-offsets.com/ and anyone wanting to access the bulletin must pay a subscription fee.

17 For reference, several academic works include unpublished PhD theses by Balakrishnan (2007) for Malaysia, Gonzales (2012) for Spain, Furter (2014) for the European Union and Savitri, C. M. (2016) for Indonesia. For MSc theses, refer to William (1998) for United Kingdom, Villalon (1998) for Philippines, Gibson (1998) for United States ; Rapaz (2004) for Switzerland, O'Donnell (2004) for Saudi Arabia, Lim (2005) for South Korea, Learmont (2005) for South Korea, Chakraborty, S (2017) for India, Yunusa (2014) for Nigeria, Butt (2015) for the UAE and Kirchwehm (2014) for Switzerland.

18 Self-sufficiency or self-reliance is a subjective word and it is difficult to gauge when a country is fully self-sufficient. Most countries will aim to attain maximum level of self-sufficiency but this is only possible if countries have adequate capital resources to embark on this development strategy, or nations risk diverting all their resources from competing social demands such as health, education and welfare into defence.

19 The European Defence Agency (EDA) commissioned a study in 2007 to evaluate the effect of offsets on the development of a European Defence Industry and market. The outcome of the study was then used to call for a ban on all forms of protectionism in defence procurement. Although offsets was not directly mentioned in the EC directive, the spirit of the directive itself implicitly imposes a ban on offsets.

20 Offsets is defined in the Government Procurement Agreement as "any condition or undertaking that encourages local development and improves a party's balance of payment account such as use of domestic content, licencing of technology investment, countertrade and similar activities or requirements".

21 The BAA of 1933 acts to protect US businesses and labour by restricting the acquisition and use of end products and construction materials that are not 'domestic'. See Kate M. Manuel, 'The Buy America Act – Preference for "Domestic Supplies": In Brief'. Congressional Research Services.

2 Key aspects to offsets management[1]

2.1 Background

The aim of this chapter is to introduce the basic concepts, typology and terminology used in offsets practice. Buyers and sellers often define offsets terminologies differently. Trade associations linked to offsets like GOCA and ECCO have attempted to create some form of uniformity in offsets terminology, though each offsets policy document may vary in its definition, typology and terminology of offsets. Though the rationale and analysis may vary, the thrusts of these concepts are similar in application. This chapter does not aim to create harmonisation or standardisation in offsets concepts or terminologies. The intention of this chapter is to critically discuss key aspects of offsets management that could be used as guidance by offsets practitioners and academics. This chapter also investigates the evolution, historical development and analysis as to what drives offsets.

2.2 Nonconventional International Trade Financing (NITF)

Nonconventional financing practices such as countertrade were much more popular from the 1960s through to the mid-1990s.[2] There was much literature published on countertrade from the 1980s right up to the mid-1990s prior to the formation of the WTO (Hammond, 1987, p. 16; Korth, 1987, p. 23; Banks, 1983, pp. 14–16; Parsons, 1985, pp. 11–15; Verzariu, 1985). Often, offsets and countertrade are described as two distinctly separate activities where countertrade refers strictly to a reciprocal exchange of goods and services, while offsets consists in a framework agreement for a range of commercial and industrial practices required as a condition of purchase (Verzariu, 2000, pp. 36–37). However, when the WTO labelled countertrade and its associated activities as illegal and a distortion of the free market, there was a drastic decline in the publication of countertrade and offsets activities, though they were still widely practised. NITF suddenly became 'taboo' and was seen as some sort of underground activity that should not be discussed. It is only in the past decade that the topic of offsets has gained increasing attention due to pressure from offsets practising countries, the international business community and interest groups to make offsets activities and their impact more transparent. This chapter focuses on offsets but discusses various forms of NITF practice. There are several models available on countertrade and offsets typology (Ajaxon, 2006, p. 30, Martin, 1996, pp. 16–35; Balakrishnan, 2017b, p. 265). Considering the dynamic nature of NITF, I have created a model that explains offsets within alternative trade financing. Figure 2.1 details the range of NITF mechanisms available in international trade. The chart consists of three main categories: countertrade, offsets and industrial collaboration.

2.2.1   Defining countertrade in international trade

Countertrade is an umbrella term used for reciprocal trade arrangements when there is an exchange of goods or services between two parties. Countertrade takes many forms, involving cash and non-cash transactions. I have included barter, clearing arrangements, switch, swap and counter purchase under countertrade arrangements.

Arguments for and against the use of countertrading and its associated activities have long been put forward by the international trade community. What are the benefits of countertrade? (Martin, 1996, pp. 15–31). First, in the past countertrade was used largely to increase foreign currency reserves for nations in newly industrialised countries (NICs) and less developed countries (LDCs) with an inability to borrow. Reducing access to foreign exchange makes domestic currency more expensive or overvalued and tends to discourage exports and encourage imports (Elderkin and Norquist, 1987, p. 28; Biederman, 1999, pp. 171–222). In such instances, introducing countertrade led to the easing of foreign exchange shortages (all forms of countertrade) and the increased protection of foreign exchange reserves especially in the NICs and LDCs. Second, countertrade offers a good substitute to trade finance and other financial instruments used to manage the risks of international commercial transactions, in response to their increasing costs and declining availability (Kostecki, 1987, p. 11). Third, countertrade is said to be useful in spreading risk. This occurs when a buyer country commits to purchase a quantity of products and services from the vendor at some future date. These commitments ensure today's outlays of foreign exchange will be balanced by future inflows[3] (Hennart, 1986, pp. 9–10; Parsons, 1985, p. 7; Kogut, 1986, p. 18). Fourth, countertrade is also said to be useful to bypass price controls, exchange controls, and creditor monitoring of imports (Hennart, 1989, pp. 38–42). Through countertrade, producers have the ability to dispose of their products by undercutting the agreed price on the international market. This could provide an opportunity to dispose of export surplus, especially primary commodities.

However, the anti-countertrade school argues that countertrade is a distortion to the present multilateral trading system. The negative perception on countertrade has been challenged as to why some countries may find it in their interest to impose countertrade obligations to solve economic problems (Kogut, 1988, p. 14; de Miramont, 1985, p. 53; Parsons, 1985, p. 37; Mirus and Yeung, 1993, pp. 54–56; Hennart, 1989, pp. 24–29; Lecraw, 1988, p. 62). Countertrade faces criticism that it

Typology

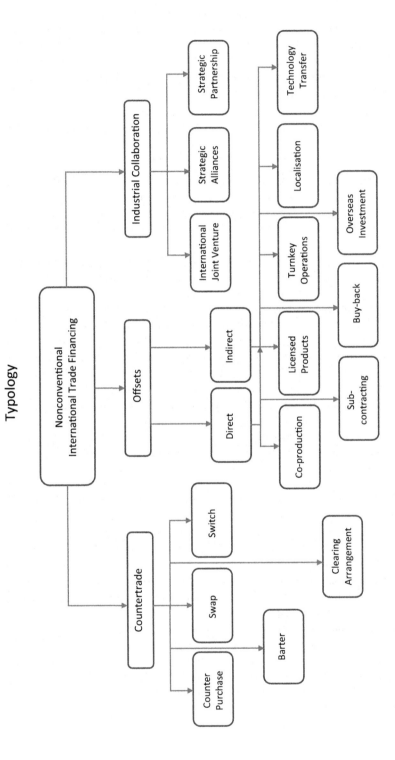

Figure 2.1 Nonconventional international trade financing model

Source: Author

arbitrarily fosters domestic corruption and abuse, especially when goods are not exchanged at market prices or when deals are not made public. It is also questionable whether countries truly resort to countertrade due to shortages of foreign currencies (Mirus and Yeung, 1986, p. 35). Countertrade is also seen as leading to activities such as dumping, price cutting and price discrimination.

However, in recent years a new style of thinking has developed on the use of countertrade and barter, demanding that they be seriously reconsidered as an alternative international trade practice. It is argued that the extremely negative views towards countertrade practices developed by the General Agreement on Tariffs and Trade (GATT) in the mid-1980s should be revisited in the WTO era[4] (Howse, 2010, pp. 2–18). Overarching the entire countertrade debate is the argument that the free market is simply not functioning at an acceptable level. On top of this banks are also charging more for letters of credit, and valuable trade financing is becoming harder to obtain (Stiglitz & Pleskovic, 1997, p. 12).

Simple barter

Countertrade in its traditional form is seen as a form of *simple barter*, defined as the exchange of goods and services without cash transactions or foreign exchange (Korth, 1987, p. 2). Barter refers to a single transaction, limited under a single compensation agreement, specifying the exchange of selected products or services by others. The earliest countertrade activities can be traced to forms of simple barter. This practice existed for a long time and flourished during periods of major economic turmoil in the 1930s, an era when governments and industry faced difficulties in paying for their imports and financing their exports due to exchange restrictions, large debts and low foreign currency reserves. Simple barter was popular until the end of the Second World War when a 'truly monetarised world economy' was established. Barter amongst all forms of countertrade was the most popular mode of transaction until the end of the Second World War (Korth, 1987, p. 3).

Clearing arrangement

When a number of barter transactions are grouped together under a single contract, whereby each party agrees to purchase a specified (usually equal value) amount of goods and services, this arrangement is known as a 'clearing arrangement'. Most of such transactions are accomplished on a government-to-government basis, in which each country sets up an account that is debited whenever one country imports from the other. This form of transaction used to be very popular amongst developing countries which lack foreign currency reserves or face difficulties with cash transactions. The account is cleared on an annual basis through hard currency payments or a transfer of goods to remove imbalances (Korth, 1987, p. 2). Clearing arrangements means one does not have to make instantaneous exchanges (Rubin, 1986, p. 15) and, for instance, if the debtor has a shortage of hard currency and the creditor does not want goods, the creditor can sells his credits to a third party or switch trader who will use these credits to buy the goods which will then be pure barter-exchange of one product for another (Korth, 1987, p. 2).

Switch trade

The third type of countertrade is *switch trade*. Switch trade is more flexible as it allows a country to exchange credits accrued under a clearing arrangement with a third party (hard currency or another product) (Weigand, 1977, p. 30).

Counter purchase

Another form of countertrade is counter purchase. Counter purchase is an agreement whereby the initial exporter buys or undertakes to find a buyer for a specified amount or value of unrelated goods from a set list determined by the buyer, during a specified time period and to the value of the initial export. The value of the counter purchased goods represents an agreed percentage of the price of the goods originally exported. This type of transaction is the most widely practised of all countertrade options. Counter purchase agreements are also said to also reduce transaction costs (Murrell, 1982, pp. 589–593; Kogut, 1983, pp. 15–16; Parsons, 1985, p. 6; Mirus and Yeung, 1986, pp. 30–32; Hennart, 1986, p. 15; Lecraw, 1988, pp. 17–19). Counter purchase agreements are seen particularly in key industrial sectors. The products traded under counter purchase could extend to manufactured products such as electronic goods, textiles and automobiles. There are two parallel hard currency contracts where the goods taken by the seller are not related to the equipment sold. The seller agrees to buy unrelated goods from a list set up by the importer. The list could vary from time to time but sellers are encouraged to stick to the latest list and price. Defence companies tend to avoid counter purchase agreements because they inevitably incur extra transaction costs.[5] In addition, many counter purchase agreements impose rigid specifications relating to the time for completion of the counter purchase and penalties for non-performance (Willett and Anthony, 2005, pp. 1–31).

The next component of NITF is offsets.

2.2.2   *What is offsets?*

It is challenging to define offsets in the clearest way possible without compromising on its intrinsically comprehensive nature. There is no simple way to define offsets. A very basic explanation is that offsets is a reciprocal trade arrangement over and above international procurement. Offsets relate to any normal 'reciprocity transactions' and are not limited to defence or government imports (Hall, 2011). The term 'offsets' is more recognised in the defence sector, but exists under different names in the civil sectors. Some such terms for offsets include industrial participation, industrial engagement, economic compensation or engagement and industrial collaboration.

I have attempted to define offsets in a way that considers the perspectives of both offsets obligors and offsets obligees.[6] In the past, most definitions of offsets were delivered from an offsets obligor's perspective. This was the case as most academics, trade associations and others that attempted to define offsets were from countries of sellers with offsets obligations. Thus the perception was that offsets in defence trade was considered as encompassing a range of industrial *compensation arrangements* required by foreign governments as a condition of the purchase of defence articles and services from nondomestic suppliers. Offsets was highlighted as a 'compensatory practice' agreed between the parties as a condition for the importation of goods, services and technology, with the intention of generating benefits of industrial, technological and commercial nature. Offsets was seen as a *trade obligation* in international defence business and one that was *contractual* when corporations enter into dealings with foreign governments. Offsets is even seen as a form of coercion (Brauer and Dunne, 2004, p. 4). Most of these definitions focus on words such as compensation, obligation and contractual which depict offsets as punitive or something that has to be done. In short, this implies that offsets are side agreements or sweeteners, ancillary to a government contract, that provide additional benefits to buyers (U.S. Department of Commerce, Bureau of Industry and Security, 2015; European Club for Countertrade and Offset (ECCO), 2011). Implicitly, there is a cynical view of offsets as intending to force relocation of activity from the supplier country to the purchasing nation (Martin, 1996, pp. 15–48; Harrigan, 1986).

However, in the past two decades, there has been increasing clamour to view offsets in a different light. As offsets business transcends across borders from developed to developing countries, receiving greater visibility and maturity, the definition of offsets has also evolved and taken on a more balanced perspective. A different school of thoughts view offsets as an economic development tool used to create industrial and technological activities at the back of government procurement and where benefits from the contract are directed back into the purchasing country (Matthews, 1996, p. 25; Balakrishnan, 2016a, p. 46; Savitri, 2016, pp. 46–70). Many national offsets policies recognise the importance of offsets for building up their economic, industrial and technological capabilities. For nations, offsets obligations represent the value added to the primary procurement investment and contractors have to fulfil them in the form of stipulated benefits. Today, it is seen as almost impossible to proceed with international defence procurement without offsets (Jang and Joung, 2007; Georgescu, Caraiani and Tutor, 2013).

Table 2.1 presents a variety of definitions of offsets by trade associations.

Direct and indirect offsets

Offsets is further divided into direct and indirect offsets (European Union, 1997, pp. 14–18; Figure 2.2).

Direct offsets in contractual agreements is often referred to as activity that is directly related to the products and services referenced in the sales agreement. For example, in military exports direct offsets would relate to transactions that are directly related to defence items or services exported by defence firms and are usually in the form of co-production, subcontracting, technology transfers,

Table 2.1 Definitions of offsets

Source	Definition
ECCO, or European Club for Countertrade and Offset	Offset refers to a specific kind of contractual obligation applying to major international public procurement markets, such as markets in the fields of defence, energy, transport, telecommunications or other kinds of infrastructure. Refer to 'Principles', ECCO, in www.ecco-offset.eu/what-is-offset/principles/, accessed online on 4 February 2018.
Brauer and Dunne (2004)	Offset agreements were defined as tools for international trade agreements, which requires the seller to **compensate** the buyer, through a reinvestment arrangement in favour of the latter in proportion to the amounts received from the sale of military equipment.
Department of Commerce (2015)	For US Bureau of Industry and Security (BIS), "offsets in defense trade encompass a range of industrial and commercial benefits provided to foreign governments as an **inducement or condition** to purchase military goods or services, including **benefits** such as co-production, licensed production, subcontracting, technology transfer, purchasing, and credit assistance" of Commerce (2015, p. 1). The agreement can be related to the purchased defence article or service or it can involve activities or goods unrelated to the defence sale. More colloquially, offsets are commonly defined as nonstandard contracts that require, as a **condition for the sale of goods or services**, that the vendor transfer a form of economic activity to the buyer's government.
European Defence Agency, (2008)	UN definition for Offset agreements by the European Commission, offset is used to reference the acquisitions involving defence equipment or services and involving more than one nation, or a country and foreign companies, and the counterparts may be of civilian nature.
B. Udis and K.E. Markus, 1991. 'Offsets as Industrial Policy: Lessons From Aerospace', *Defence Economics*, 2, 151–164 (Udis and Maskus, 1991, pp. 151–164)	"[A]n Offset is a contract imposing performance conditions on the seller of a good or service so that the purchasing government can recoup, or offset, some of its investment. In some way, reciprocity beyond that associated with market exchange of goods and services is involved".
P. Hall and S. Markowski, 1994. 'On the Normality and Abnormality of Offsets Obligations', *Defence and Peace Economics*, 5(3), 173–188 (Hall and Markowski, 1994, pp. 173–188)	"Offset is simply goods and services which form elements of complex voluntary transactions negotiated between governments as purchasers and foreign suppliers. . . . They are those goods and services on which a government chooses to place the label *offsets*".
S.G. Neuman, 1985. 'Co-Production, Barter and Countertrade: Offsets in the International Arms Market', *Orbis*, 29, Spring, 183–213 (Neuman, 1985, pp. 183–213)	"Of Offset, co-production, barter and countertrade are compensatory trade agreements that incorporate some method of reducing the amount of foreign exchange needed to buy a military item/some means of creating revenue to help pay for it".

Source	Definition
S. Martin and K. Hartley, 1995. 'UK Firms: Experience and Perceptions of Defence Offsets: Survey Results', *Defence and Peace Economics*, 6, 125 (Martin and Hartley, 1995, p. 125)	"Offset occurs when the supplier places work of an agreed value with firms in the buying country, over and above what it would have bought in the absence of the offsets".
Markowski and Hall, 2014, pp. 148–162	Offsets is "compensatory procurement arrangements designed to offset the cost of purchasing defence equipment from overseas by means of a reciprocal (countertrade) commitment by suppliers in support of a purchaser's domestic economy".
T.K. Taylor, 2002. *Using Offsets in Procurement as an Economic Development Strategy*, (College of Business, Alfred University, New York, September), 2 (Taylor, 2002, p. 2)	Offset often appears under the guise of compensation packages, industrial benefits programmes, cooperative arrangements and countertrade policy.
Agreement on Government Procurement, April 15, 2011, updated December 2011, entered into force April 6, 2014, *Marrakesh Agreement Establishing the World Trade Organization*, 1867 U.N.T.S. 154, annex 4(b), art. 1-1	World Trade Organization (WTO) Agreement on Government Procurement (GPA), which limits, and outside the defence sector prohibits, the use of offsets by its members, defines an offset as "any condition or undertaking that encourages local development or improves a Party's balance-of-payments accounts, such as the use of domestic content, the licensing of technology, investment, countertrade and similar action or requirement". Related terms include compensatory trade agreements, co-production, barter and buy-backs. The term 'offset' is most often used in the aerospace and defence industry, whereas other terms, such as countertrade, may be used in other sectors.
UNCITRAL, 1993 With the wide range of terms and definitions, the United Nations (UN) created the International Business Law Commission (UNCITRAL) through Resolution 2205 in 1966, of the General Assembly, which is responsible for the reduction or removal of barriers on the free flow of international trade. This commission created by the United Nations was to burden the creation of legal guides that consist of manuals standardising the terms used in foreign trade (UNCITRAL, 1993).	The Legal Guide defined the offset term and outlined lines use. According to the Legal Guide, offset agreements are business practices of large and varied goals, described to be the compensation that would normally involve the provision of high-value or high technological sophistication products including the transfer of technology and know-how as well as promotion of investments and facilitation of access to a particular market.

Source: Author

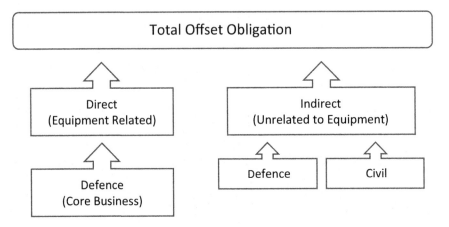

Figure 2.2 Direct and indirect offsets
Source: GOCA, 2015

buy-back schemes, joint ventures, marketing assistance, training, production, licenced production or financial assistance. Countries such as the UK, US, Singapore, India and South Korea adopt this interpretation. Others, such as Malaysia, Oman and South Africa, refer to all defence-related activities as direct offsets.

Indirect offsets relates to offsets activity in contractual agreements that involve goods and services unrelated to exports referenced in the sales agreement. In defence for example, indirect offsets may relate to defence-related activities but that which is not related to the product or service being purchased. In other cases, indirect offsets could refer to non-defence or commercial activities.

Offsets typology

There are various types of offsets activities both direct and indirect. These include licenced production, co-production, subcontracting, buy-backs, overseas investment, technology transfers, education and training, turnkey operations, research and development as well as localisation. I briefly explain these terms below.

SUBCONTRACTING

Subcontracting is one of the most popular offsets activities. Subcontracting is a straightforward activity that involves overseas production of parts or subsystems of a wider equipment or system. It refers to the production of a component originating from a foreign supplier. The subcontract does not necessarily involve a technical information licence and usually is a direct trade agreement between the OEM and a foreign producer. Subcontracting can involve a contract with one or a more firms to assemble or manufacture parts. Subcontracting depends on an interrelationship between enterprises to provide not only an outlet for production by suppliers but also the establishment of a relationship between linked enterprises. This promotes long-term contracts and leads to product information exchange, price negotiation, technology sharing and other forms of assistance (UNCTAD, 1990, p. 22). Subcontracting is viewed both as a vital mode of technology transfer and as an enhancement of backward linkages[7] to established local suppliers in order to obtain intermediary inputs. Offsets policy often requires foreign companies to subcontract their activities to local firms as a means of assisting the development of small and medium-sized industries (SMEs) as part of developing a robust supply chain.

Subcontracting is a popular offsets activity and is normally introduced in countries that are preparing to enter into a new manufacturing sector. For example, most of the offsets activity in Malaysia and South Africa was initially focused on the subcontracting of work into the fledgling aerospace industries, as local companies receiving the work were still at the early stages of learning and technical skill. Subcontracting is often criticised as one of the less desirable forms of offsets for a country to negotiate, as it includes little transfer of technical knowledge.

BUY-BACK

Buy-back is a much more complex form of offsets activity, one which tethers sellers and involves long-term commitment and risk. Buy-back is when a seller transfers technology usually embodied in plant and equipment to a buyer country. In this case, seller transfers technology (embodied in plant and equipment) and agrees to buy a proportion of the output over a specified period of time. Buy-back involves the transfer of precise particulars of a product, including the amount, type and delivery mechanisms. The seller and its government agree to provide technical information for the production of all parts of this product abroad. The seller in return agrees to purchase a certain percentage of the plant's output over a given number of years. All production must be carried out in the buyer country, based on the offsets agreement. The buyer will then use the proceeds of sales to repay the seller in hard currency which was borrowed to purchase the equipment. Buy-back arrangements can lead to certain risks for both buyers and sellers. For sellers, risk is associated with products and services produced by buyers which could be of a lower quality, possibly creating a sense of insecurity in supply. For the buyer, a situation of information asymmetry leading to an unequal partnership could arise as sellers could deliberately complicate technology. Buy-back arrangements can also be more costly as they involve sellers agreeing to purchase products from the buyer which may not be the most cost effective or of the best quality. In either case, the seller is tied to an offsets obligation that requires buy-back performance. In light of this, it would be in the best interest of the sellers to guarantee state-of-the-art equipment and after-sales-services to support buyers in producing the best quality products and services (Hennart and Anderson, 1993, pp. 73–75).

CO-PRODUCTION

Co-production activities in offsets permit a foreign government or producer to acquire the technical information to manufacture all or part of a defence item domestically. Co-production can be either government-to-government agreements or between a government and a private manufacturer, but excludes licenced production based upon direct commercial arrangements by prime manufacturers (Hennart and Anderson, 1993, pp. 78–83).

LICENCED PRODUCTION

Licenced production has become an increasingly important activity under the offsets umbrella, though it must cope with multiple challenges. Licencing is defined as the transfer of patents, brand names (including technical assistance), sales of expertise and assembly under a commercial contract which happens across borders. Licenced production can involve the manufacturing of a whole system or just components of a system using technology in the buyer country. An offsets activity that involves a licencing agreement typically has patents, technical know-how, trademarks, marketing expertise, managerial know-how and design incorporated into the agreement (Smali, 1985, pp. 77–97).[8] Licencing is preferred in offsets transactions when transferring relatively less complex technologies with strong, well-enforced and relatively mature patents, with very little reliance on 'user-active' innovation requiring strong links between marketing and product development. Licencing however, must be done with the permission of the supplier government which is often difficult within an offsets arrangement, especially when defence production is involved.

In general, the transfer of licencing through offsets instigates various challenges to both sellers and the buyers holding the licences. Sellers transferring licences are often worried about losing their technological niche if licencees (offsets recipients in buyer countries) do not honour agreements. Sellers jealously guard their licences in technology, as any duplication of competition will drive returns down. Most sellers justify that royalty payments through licencing are an attempt to obtain some contribution towards development costs as well as compensation for exports income forgone. It is unfortunate that many countries still fail to adhere to licencing contracts therefore resulting in duplication of products available at cheaper prices. The lack of strict and reliable enforcement when dealing with copyright and patent infringement has made some sellers lose their cutting-edge technology. These negative experiences have led sellers to impose various restrictions on the usage of technology, including where the output should be marketed and what types of purchases must be made to make the transfer of licences technically effective. This is to ensure that sellers enjoy an advantageous position in the licencing agreement. Sellers also argue that buyers end up paying a fraction of the initial R&D cost, with sellers having to bear the cost of larger research facilities and skilled researchers (Smali, 1985, pp. 77–97).

On the other hand, buyers often complain that foreign technology licencing payments are unreasonably expensive and indeed, they should be cautious about what they are paying for and whether it is a reasonable sum (Pack, 2000, p. 78). Further, it is argued that there is a lack of experts with the adequate technical background in buyer countries to appropriately scrutinise technology costs (Thomas, 1995, pp. 59–61).

TECHNOLOGY TRANSFER, EDUCATION AND TRAINING

In offsets, technology and technology transfer are not well understood by sellers and buyers. The vital issue remains whether technology transfer should also include education and training. I explain technology in detail in Chapter 7. Technology transfer is highly prized and considered to be one of the most valuable benefits of offsets. Technology transfer can take many forms including research and development, technical assistance and training and patent agreements between manufacturers (Hill and Still, 1980, pp. 40–51). For many emerging economies, technology transfer forms an essential part of their offsets arrangement. Technology transfer in the context of offsets is defined as including research and development conducted abroad, exchange programmes for personnel, data exchanges, integration of machinery and equipment into a recipient's production facility, technical assistance, education and training, manufacturing know-how and licencing and patent sharing. Technology transfer can include both product and process technology. Education and training activities have been a central component of offsets activities. Sellers have used offsets to offer hands-on industrial and technical training at their facilities, and also offer educational programmes such as Master's and PhD programmes in critical technology and business management sectors to buyer countries as part of human capital development. Increasingly, government-industry-academia collaboration in offsets is being used for investment in R&D centres, as part of 'triple helix' (Awny, 2005, p. 215; Barnes, Pashby, and Gibbons, 2002, p. 75).

TURNKEY OPERATIONS

Turnkey projects are also called BOT (build, operate and transfer) projects. They involve total construction of a project: product and project design, plant-engineering, procurement and manufacture of equipment, construction management, commissioning and training as well as troubleshooting. The project is handed over to the customer at a future date. The seller normally takes the responsibility of setting up a complete industrial plant. The project is packaged with the provision of skills, services and finance required to deliver a functioning plant to the client. Demand for turnkey projects as part of an offsets activity has become increasingly popular. However, there is a question regarding the viability of setting up a complete plant in smaller developing countries, consisting of a smaller domestic-goods manufacturing base.

OVERSEAS INVESTMENT

Another popular offsets activity involves investment. It is claimed that investments increase foreign currency earnings, human resources, employment and linkages into the economy, such as the development of local suppliers and sales to intermediate goods industries (Hirschman, 1958, p. 27). Offsets is primarily used for investments into commercial sectors such as healthcare, electronics and electrical, transportation and infrastructure (Cable and Persaud, 1987, pp. 76–85; Globerman and Shapiro, 2002, pp. 1899–1919). OEMs[9] have a choice to transfer the appropriate technology into buyer countries based on the product's life cycle (Vernon, 1971, p. 72), through offsets activities (UNCTAD, 2003, p. 32). It is argued , that while sellers may transfer knowledge through outsourcing activities in manufacturing and services, they still attempt to retain tight control of critical technologies (Vitasek, Ledyard and Manrodt, 2013; Bell, 1984, pp. 21–29). This is to maintain competitive advantage and to retain their monopolistic status, to overcome fear or lack of knowledge of foreign markets. By possessing advantages such as scale economies, knowledge advantages, distribution networks, product diversification, and credit advantages to enhance asset power, sellers dominate the business environment and dominate the technology transfer terms and conditions (Cable and Persaud, 1987, pp. 76–85). However, in offsets deals, buyers have some control over the type of investment that flows into a country. Buyers can demand investment flow into sectors appropriate to the country's level of technological absorption capacity, which reflects the available pool of local skills and talents.

Investment is often criticised for its negative impact via pricing (Lall, 1997, p. 111), minimal value-added activities and arguably inappropriate capital-intensive investments in labour-abundant economies. Investment activities can allow sellers to exploit their position in domestic economies, creating beneficial competition, efficiency and jobs; but also tending to be highly exploitative (Howarth, 1994, pp. 243–257). Such investments bought through offsets can also be quickly relocated to another advantageous production site as soon as the offsets obligation ends (Lall, 1989, p. 115). Investments through offsets have been used for activities in commercial sectors such as the enhancement of infrastructure in Spain, fish farming and agricultural activities in the Czech Republic, the electronics industry in Malaysia and aerospace in Mexico and Singapore. The challenge for most nations is to efficiently divert overseas investment flowing in through offsets into strategic industries which require additional funding and resources that otherwise would not be available locally. Investment through offsets should not be treated the same as FDI which can happen anyway through tax relief incentives and Economic Exclusive Zones. Further, when investments flow through FDIs, sellers rather than buyers have the leverage on technology being transferred and the type of job being created.

LOCALISATION

Of late, an increasing number of countries have been strictly enforcing localisation policies as part of international procurement. Sellers exporting their equipment into a host country are strongly encouraged to localise their production through sourcing from local companies within the host country's supply chain (Hines, 2000, p. 27).

Some claim localisation enhances competitiveness, as the foreign company is able to take advantage of the abundant capital, advanced technology and highly skilled labour (Lee, 2004, pp. 97–106) in the host country. Through localisation, foreign companies undertaking international activities are able to understand regional culture, dialects, nuances and other unique aspects of transfer in a way that allows them to create more meaningful materials and communicate effectively with the market (Mackun and MacPherson, 1997, pp. 659–668). However localisation, as a form of protectionism, is seen by some as creating market inefficiencies and hindering the process of globalisation by others. Most offsets activities are subject to localisation rules set by buyer nations. Localisation rules are more stringent in civil sectors.

2.2.3 Understanding international collaboration

The third category of offsets relates to international collaboration. Collaboration in simple terms is when two or more parties work together for mutual benefit (Matthews, 1999, p. 25; Cardell, 2002, pp. 46–49). Collaboration is based on the premise that through formal agreements, technology sharing between firms produces benefits that cannot be obtained by individual firms or through market transactions, as a direct purchase, licencing deal, or in the form of mergers and acquisitions (Dodgson, 1991, p. 92; Herzog, 2001, pp. 28–37). International collaboration in the context of offsets relates to offsets activities that span national boundaries, that are performed as a partnership between buyers and sellers. International collaboration can be structured as a firm legally binding contract that involves equity ownership such as international joint ventures (IJV), or as informal collaborations such as strategic partnerships or alliances (Child, Faulkner and Tallman, 2005). However, international collaboration in offsets is viewed as a collaboration that is not based on distant market transactions but one based on a close relationship between partners that involves substantial and continual contributions of capital, technology and market access. It has to be seen as a 'win–win' for both parties (Mowery, 1999; Chowdhury, 1992, pp.115–133). Collaborative activities through offsets have progressed from low-level manufacturing activities to high-end collaboration in electronics, electricals and systems integration (Balakrishnan, 2015b). The increased value of collaborative activities is aided by new digital activities such machine learning, data mining, developing software and apps, Internet of Things (IOT) and cyber security. In the next section, I explain the various forms of industrial collaboration in the context of offsets.

Strategic partnership (SP)

Strategic partnerships (SP) are another popular activity within offsets. SP is also sometimes referred to as strategic alliances. Most sellers prefer to enter into SPs rather than more formally binding types of industrial partnership. SP is a more flexible and less structured form of international collaboration. A strategic partnership is defined as a relationship between two commercial entities. SP could be formalised through business contracts and can take various forms from just a gentleman's handshake to equity alliances and JVs (Spekman, 1996, pp. Isabella, 346–357; MacAvoy and Forbes, 1996, pp. 346–357). In a strategic partnership, both parties will offer resources or expertise that can help mutually enhance business. SP is seen as having various advantages where companies can take advantage of each other's competency to become stronger in the longer term (Chen and Chen, 2002, pp. 1007–1013). Nevertheless, SP has its own challenges including issues of technology transfer, exclusivity, competition, recruitment of staff, profit-sharing, insecurity in the terms of the relationship, marketing and business development issues (Wheeler, 2012, pp. 94–101). SPs can often be complex, sometimes leading to drawn out and tedious negotiations.

International joint ventures (IJV)

International joint ventures (IJVs) are a popular activity of offsets activity as they offer greater opportunities for the effective transfer of technology and innovation (Peters, 1983, pp. 87–102). There is much argument to the definition of a JV. In this book, I have defined JV more broadly to encompass a distinctive business entity created and jointly owned by two or more owners but still retaining a separate identity (Prime, Gale and Scanlan, 1997, p. 27). IJVs are a form of business association that transcends borders in designing and managing ventures (Woodside and Pitts, 1996, p. 83; BBC News, 2013). In general, overseas companies are driven to engage into IJVs to access new markets (economies of scale) and raw materials, reduce production costs and risks or to conform to trade rules imposed by host countries (Woodside and Pitts, 1996, pp. 88–96; Matthews, 2001, pp. 12–21). Local companies on the other hand engage in JVs to access new technology, and skills. Sometimes companies take part in JVs due to governmental obligation, but JVs are also attractive when certain projects are too costly, involving huge investments, which local firms are not able to solely undertake (Contractor and Lorange, 1988, pp. 115–132; Killing, 2012, pp. 63–68). IJVs are however the most challenging type of international collaboration (Dymsza, 1988, pp. 156–180). There have been cases of troubled IJVs due to a lack of understanding between overseas and local partners, management issues, leadership, organisational and people issues, issues related to trust and secrecy between partners, unequal sharing of responsibilities, monopoly by one dominant party and government policy restrictions on, for instance, equity holdings (Fasel, 2000, pp. 66–68; BenDaniel, Rosenbloom and Hanks, 2002, pp. 223–235; Prime, Gale and Scanlan, 1997, pp. 101–115). IJVs formed through offsets arrangements have had similar benefits and challenges. The only difference between an offsets induced IJV and a commercial IJV is that the performance of the IJV formed through the former is closely monitored by both sellers and buyers through strict offsets contractual agreements (Kleinman, 2017). There are other subtle differences in that offsets induced IJVs receive greater support from host country governments. The shape and type of activity is also influenced by government and sellers show high levels of commitment to the IJV to ensure that their overall offsets performance is not affected (Balakrishnan, 2015b). In recent years, many governments have imposed stringent guidelines on overseas companies operating in host countries, one of which is to form equity partnerships, such as in China, India, Middle East and South East Asia (Gale and Luo, 2004, pp.33–42; Bosshart, Luedi and Wang, 2010; Monaghan, 2012). IJV is becoming increasingly popular in offsets though the overall impact is yet to be seen.

2.3 How have offsets projects evolved?

Offsets projects have evolved over the years from being a simple countertrade activity between buyers and sellers to a complex type of multiparty international collaboration that involves various stakeholders. The idea is for nations to use offsets policy to move up the value chain from being net importers of products and services to building industrial and technological self-sufficiency. Figure 2.3 explains how projects developed through offsets have evolved and are becoming increasingly complex but also innovative. The figure explains offsets evolution in five stages. Stage one is about commodity trading which involves raw products and manufactured goods, defined as a type of countertrade activity. Countertrade is perceived as being simple, straightforward and easy to manage by sellers and buyers. Then, at stage two, nations start demanding offsets for activities like training and education.

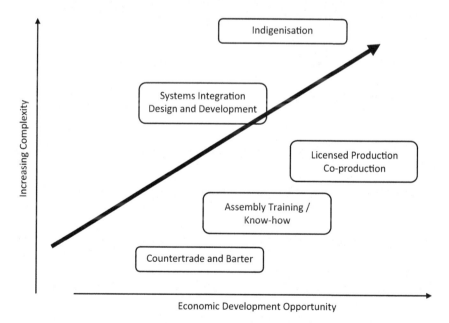

Figure 2.3 How have offsets projects evolved?
Source: Author

The aim is mainly to develop skills in high technology sectors leading to capability building. Most of the activities at this stage are focused on low-level manufacturing like sub-assembly, maintenance, repair and overhaul (MRO).

At stage three once a nation's industry possesses the adequate capability and skill, offsets is then required for activities that relate to licenced production and co-production, activities which involve a higher level of manufacturing. Then at stage four, nations begin to take on more complex activities as part of offsets and enter into systems integration, design and development including some level of research and development. Then finally nations enter into stage five, where they embark on indigenisation by acquiring the capability to produce their own products and services and also penetrate the export market. At this stage, the OEM sometimes becomes a subcontractor to the local company. However, a smooth progression along these five stages is often not easily achieved. The evolution of offsets along these stages is also not linear. Firstly, not all countries are at the same stage of innovation. Countries that adopted offsets earlier have more robust industrial policies, allowing them to more effectively institute offsets strategy and will most likely be at stage three or four. On the other hand countries which are just beginning to industrialise or are contemplating adopting offsets as part of their industrial policy may only be at stage one or two of the cycle. Further, countries can also move back and forth between the stages based on their level of maturity in the industrial sectors. The question is whether every nation has to follow this sequential stage of offsets or whether countries can start at different levels. The answer basically lies with the technological absorption capability of companies in the buyer country and their industrial capacity.

2.4   Origins of offsets

Some argue that the origin of offsets practice can be traced back to the 1870s during the Meiji restoration when the Japanese tried to acquire technological and industrial development without having to undergo an industrial process akin to the British Industrial Revolution (Porter, 1985, p. 72). Offsets practice after World War I occurred when Germany established exchange agreements with some of the old Austro-Hungarian suppliers and clients with the purpose of assisting the involved countries in recovering from monetary crises, by trading manufactured goods for raw materials alongside the partial return of foreign currency where possible (Baptist, 2000, p. 34). Some academics also note the emergence of offsets policies during the reconstruction of Europe and Japan after World War II when the United States wanted to trade agricultural products and services for strategic minerals. The US government created a legal instrument to sustain its policy, the Commodity Credit Cooperation Act of 1949 (Serrao, Ramos and Redore, 2014, p. 2).

However, it was not until the 1940s after the Second World War that offsets were formalised in its present form by the US government within NATO member countries, by encouraging defence contractors to grant offsets to rebuild their allies' defence industrial bases and support the rationalisation, standardisation and interoperability (RSI) provisions of NATO. At the end of the Second World War, nation states were confronted with a variety of problems including domestic economic disarray and international trade crises. During this period, the US became concerned about the Soviet Union's military capabilities and decided to offer offsets to its allies as a means of increasing their allies' industrial capability and modernise as well as standardising military equipment between the allied forces. According to Spears, offsets 50 years ago were a complex blend of national pride, budget concerns, domestic politics and Cold War industrial policy. Offsets, at that time, was perceived as a tool to relieve economic deprivation (Spears, 1997, p. 4).

Subsequently, in the 1950s and 1960s under the Kennedy administration, offsets were used as a commercial tool to increase sales when demand for US defence products declined. Offsets practices during this period, especially amongst NATO members, were clearly aimed at promoting US weapons systems and fostering the reconstruction efforts of US allies. Offsets were then incorporated into international business sales and marketed as a commercially competitive tool used within a strategy designed to win sales (Willett and Anthony, 1998).

Since the 1970s, many US allies and other nations recognising the increasing costs of advanced technology have started demanding offsets as a condition of market access. Eastern European and other developing countries have slowly emulated Western offsets practices aimed at raising their defence and economic capabilities.

The widespread adoption of the neoliberal agenda and the emphasis on globalisation in the 1980s, followed by the end of the cold war in the 1990s, has changed the defence economics landscape forever. The reduction of defence spending followed by pressure to consolidate defence industries through mergers and acquisitions of defence industries within Europe and across the transatlantic has resulted in greater competition. In this environment, offsets started to take centre stage again as a form of leverage to secure new markets and win export sales. This development has been matched with nations seeking to increase the role of offsets, to the extent that offsets has become an integral part of international defence business and public procurement.

At the same time, on the civil side, despite rigorous protest from WTO and other trade bodies for free market and global industrial competitiveness, commercial offsets development has continued to thrive since 1970s. The Keynesian model of state intervention through tools such as offsets is still seen as necessary in many parts of the world where there is an increasing gap in technology and industrial access.[10]

2.5 Understanding offsets terminologies

This section is dedicated to providing a glossary to offsets terminology. These definitions are universal but may be tweaked to suit the context in which a nation or company operates. The aim of this book is to provide a general guideline for the usage of the wider offsets community.[11]

2.5.1   *Offsets quota (value)*

Offsets quota refers to the amount of offsets to be provided in the contract. The amount is usually expressed as a percentage of the contract. Offsets quota can range between 20 and 80 percent of main contract value, of added-value or of foreign content value. For example:

Contract value:	$3 million
Offsets value:	Eighty percent of the contract value with a minimum 50% towards direct offsets
Offsets value:	$2.4 million
Direct offsets:	50% of $2.4 million = $1.2 million (in this case direct offsets is only 50%)
Indirect offsets:	50% of $2.4 million = $1.2 million

For example, the UAE imposes a 60 percent offsets quota, Israel 35 percent, Turkey 70 percent, Norway 100 percent and Spain 100 percent (CTO, 2011).

2.5.2   *Offsets threshold*

Offsets threshold refers to a minimum procurement amount set by buyer governments for sellers to include an offsets package in their sale of goods and services.

Example of offsets threshold is in Table 2.2.

2.5.3   *Eligible offsets transactions*

Eligible offsets transaction refers to activities that are permitted as offsets.

2.5.4   *Causality*

Causality relates to establishing the fact that the project or business would not otherwise materialise without offsets. Sellers or offsets obligors[12] must prove that

Table 2.2 Offsets threshold

Country	Threshold
Canada	$100 million
Saudi	SR400 million
Israel	Above $15 million
Turkey	$5 million
Oman	OR 5 million
Brazil	$5 million (single or cumulative)
Malaysia	RM50 million

Source: Extracted from CTO, http://cto-offset.com/, dated 15 November 2017

Table 2.3 Causality clause

Country	Causality
South Africa	Each project is caused by the seller as a result of the obligation of the seller's direct investment or that investment of an IP had influenced such a project to happen within a shorter time project period that would not have been the case.
Canada	Work must be new work and only Canadian content.
Oman	Work must reflect incremental or new business and be sustainable beyond obligation period.

Source: CTO

they are directly responsible for 'causing' the offsets transaction. Offsets must have created 'new' business. For example, Table 2.3 provides a few clauses of causality in offsets policies.

2.5.5   Additionality

Additionality in the context of offsets refers to projects that are new to the buyer and must create new opportunities such as employment, technology and skills transfer. For example, one project awarded as part of offsets for the development of high quality, organic, high-value exports, focused on specific types of fish species, providing technology transfer on breeding and hatchery. The project has the potential for the creation of 1,500 jobs in a remote island that requires development. The project is also expected to create an export value of more than $300 million per annum in ten years from the start of the project. Belgium and South Africa emphasise additionality in their offsets policies.

2.5.6   Offsets multipliers

Offsets multipliers are a controversial area. Multipliers in offsets are often subjective. Multipliers in the context of offsets are defined as incentives used by buyer countries to stimulate particular types of offsets activities. Multipliers range between 0.1 to 20. Practice among countries varies as to how they implement multipliers. Some countries do not award multipliers, some practise a flexible approach and allow for multipliers to be negotiated on a case-by case basis, others have broad guidelines with specific tables showing multipliers being awarded but these multipliers are negotiable. Finally, there are those with rigid and fixed guidelines that are non-negotiable. Award of higher multipliers is associated with the importance of specific technology or a project to offsets obligations.[13] Offsets policy trends show that higher multipliers are awarded to investments in high tech sectors that create long-term sustainability and employment. Multipliers are also awarded to lure new technologies or capabilities, increase exports, assist in areas of high unemployment and provide specific regional benefits. High multipliers are

Table 2.4 Offsets multipliers

Country	Multiplier
Brazil	1–5
South Korea	1.5–3
Malaysia	1–5
Saudi Arabia	1–4
Oman	1–5
Taiwan	0.25–10
Turkey	1–8

Source: Extracted from CTO, http://cto-offset.com/, dated 20 June 2017

also awarded for knowledge transfers and government-focused projects (Ministry of Economic Affairs Netherlands, 2015).

Table 2.4 lists examples of several countries with multipliers.

2.5.7   Pre-credit offsets

Pre-credit offsets refers to a practice where sellers are allowed to 'bank' credits earned through projects done in advance or in anticipation of a sale. Accumulation of pre-credits can happen in two ways. First, sellers provide offsets projects even before the main contract is agreed or before a sale is finalised. Second, the seller embarks on a project without any anticipation of a future contract but on good will. Some countries allow for pre-credits with conditions attached, such as imposing a shelf life on pre-credit projects, necessitating the seller to obtain approval from relevant offsets authorities when the sellers meet the offsets objectives which are in line with national requirement. Only a certain percentage of offsets as part of a contract is allowed to be claimed from pre-credits and the pre-credits can only be traded with another company or government department with approval from offsets authorities. However, the seller may not be able to claim pre-credits if they have already gone ahead and executed the project before approval. Pre-credits have to be implemented with caution to ensure that the claims and execution does not impact long-term economic benefits. Countries that practise pre-credit offsets include Malaysia, India, Brazil, Israel, Norway and Belgium.

2.5.8   Offsets banking of credits

Banking of credits is slightly different from pre-credits, In the case of banking of credits, sellers are allowed to 'bank' credits earned for projects where they have done over and above their stipulated obligation in an existing contract. There is normally a timeframe for the utilisation of the credits banked, which is usually within three to five years from the offsets credit accumulation date. Credits can be transferred to a third party within their own organisation or another company with permission of offsets authorities. Banking of credits is useful to sellers if they have overachieved, but the onus is on sellers to provide evidence of this achievement. Often, if not implemented carefully, a banking of credits claim may be contentious and disputable. Therefore, offsets authorities need to have clear implementation guidelines as to banking of credit rules and allowable claims. Countries that practise banking of credits include Norway, Malaysia, Oman, the Republic of Korea and Israel.

2.5.9 Offsets penalty

There are two types of practice with regards to penalties in offsets management. First, the penalty is included and is part of the main procurement contract. In this case, the seller is only subject to one penalty for the default of either the main contract or the offsets contract. The penalty is normally in the form of liquidated damages paid in the form of a bank guarantee and deposited with a reliable local bank nominated by the offsets authority, government or purchasing party. Second, a separate penalty is imposed for the offsets contract and the seller has to deposit two bank guarantees, one for the main contract and the other for offsets. The offsets penalty could vary between 2 and 10 percent. Some countries do not impose penalties but publish a list of blacklisted companies in the form of an annual report. Table 2.5 has examples of a list of countries with penalties.

Table 2.5 Penalties

Country	Details
Canada	ISED – liquidated damages and holdbacks, penalties and PG in every contract; 10% of ITB commitment
Columbia	4.5% of contract value from fourth year. This rises to 5% for 5–10 years
Australia	In annual defence report, standard LD attached to contracts that attach clauses as condition to tender. Companies to be excluded from tender if they fail to meet AIC plan objectives; AIC scheduled delays dealt with firmly; A list of companies that breached obligations will be published every year
Israel	2% penalty of any shortfall will be levied at each annual milestone; Example – Obligation of $10 million over five years – 2% penalty if shortfall below $20 million in year one fail to fulfil then blacklisted
Malaysia	ICP bond for 5% of main procurement contract value; penalty deducted in staggering way
Norway	Penalties not less the 10% of standard value
Sweden	Milestone system 5% penalty to unfulfilled obligation of each milestone
Poland	• Liquidated damages of 100% on non-performance/underperformed offsets commitment • Room for negotiation on liability limited and substitute performance not encouraged • Performance guarantee obligatory

(*Continued*)

Table 2.5 (Continued)

Country	Details
Philippines	• 5% of unfulfilled obligation • Performance guarantee and performance bond for non-performance incorporated in countertrade agreement signed between suppliers and PITC • BG submitted with 30 days of contract
Oman	• Corporate guarantee to value + to potential penalty that could be applied on unfulfilled obligation • Staggered based on milestone
Taiwan	• Maximum penalty decided by EC on case by case basis between 3 and 5% of supply contract value
Switzerland	• Case by case basis

Source: Extracted from CTO, http://cto-offset.com/, dated 15 November 2017

2.5.10   *Offsets contract/agreement*

An offsets contract can be in the form of a memorandum of understanding, agreement or contract. A more detailed explanation of an offsets contract is provided in Chapter 4 when discussing offsets implementation. An offsets agreement or contract may form part of a main contract or it can be an independent document. The offsets agreement may be signed before, simultaneously or after the signing of the main procurement contract. There are different levels of offsets agreements. Tier one agreements are normally signed between OEMs and governments. Tier two agreements are signed between OEMs and subcontractors or offsets beneficiaries. Offsets agreements or contracts may cover offsets programmes, detailed projects, roles and responsibilities, details of offsets beneficiaries, costs, value, implementation schedules and timeline, penalty clauses and force majeure. Each detailed offsets project for a programme is normally attached as an annexure to the agreement.

2.5.11   *Offsets milestone or fulfilment period*

The fulfilment period of offsets is defined as the length of the stipulated timeframe in which projects must be completed. There are several methods of offsets fulfilment. First, offsets fulfilment that are the same length as the main contract period. Second, the offsets fulfilment can be longer than the main contract. Third, the offsets contract fulfilment is strictly determined and monitored. Finally, the offsets fulfilment can be flexible and looked at on a case by case basis.

2.5.12   *Offsets obligor, obligee and offsets beneficiary*

An offsets obligor is a company or seller with offsets obligations to be discharged. An offsets obligee is a government or buyer of equipment or services that impose offsets rules. Offsets beneficiary refers to recipients of offsets projects.

2.6 Offsets case study: use of offsets multipliers

The following case study is a hypothetical scenario as to how to calculate multipliers in offsets.

In this case, Country M has signed a contract with OEM B for supply of 12 new multi-role combat aircraft. The value of the contract is $900 million. The offsets quota is valued at 50 percent, which is $450 million.

The offsets activity includes co-production, the setting up of a joint venture company, purchase of parts and training.

Offsets activity	Offsets transaction value	Offsets Multipliers	Awarded Value
Co-production	$40,000	2	$80,000
Joint venture set-up	$100,000	3	$300,000
Purchase of parts	$20,000	2	$40,000
Training	$15,000	2	$30,000
Total offsets awarded			$450,000

Notes

1 The details of the offsets transaction value and determination of offsets multipliers and the final awarded and approved value will obviously be only finalised upon agreement by both offsets obligor and obligee based on a series of negotiations.
2 Conventional financing methods in international trade include Letters of Credit (LC), medium-term capital goods financing and bank guarantees.
3 However, the risk of foreign exchange is determined by the agreement between seller and buyer with a fixed price based on a predetermined exchange rate.
4 GATT produced a study on countertrade in 1984 titled 'Countertrade' condemning countertrade as a commercial policy and practice. The GATT study explained that countertrade is introduced in some countries due to the government's failure to deal with external stocks in a timely manner resulting in the need for foreign exchange rationing or a strategy for disguising real prices in transaction. The study also claimed that countertrade is intended to disguise the real price in a transaction and for dummy and export subsidisation. Refer to 'Countertrade' Consultative Group of Eighteen Twenty-third Meeting 4–6 April 1984 in www.wto.org/gatt_docs/English/SULPDF/92280239.pdf.
5 Most defence companies do not have the experience or in-house expertise to handle counter purchasing. Counter-purchase transactions are outsourced to trading companies thus incurring additional administrative and operating costs for defence companies.
6 Offsets obligors refers to sellers who are offering offsets as part of an international sale. These would include sellers' subcontractors, the seller country or government and other third parties engaged by sellers. Offsets obligee refers to buyers which include the buyer government, offsets agencies, offsets programme recipients and end-users.
7 The concept of backward and forward linkages was developed by Albert Hirschman. The concept grew out of unbalanced growth and describes the relationship between parties involved in supply chain. Backward linkages describe the process of how a company in a given sector purchases its goods, products, or supplies from a company in a different sector and how the company benefits from investments though inputs. Forward linkages describe the process of how a company in a given sector sells its goods, products, or supplies to a company in a different sector and how the company benefits from investments through output.

8 Knowledge that is purchased through licencing includes pre-investment feasibility studies, detailed studies, basic engineering, detailed engineering, procurement, training, construction and assembly, start-up or commissioning, technical assistance agreements, trademarks, copyright licences and troubleshooting. Refer to E. Kaynak, Transfer of Technology From Developed to Developing Countries: Some Insights From Turkey. In: A.C. Smali, ed. *Technology Transfer: Geographical, Economic and Technical Dimensions* (Quorum Books, Westport, 1985).

9 MNCs are global enterprises that manage production establishments with plants located in at least two countries.

10 Article XVI of the GATT's 1979 Government Procurement Code, now known as the WTO's Agreement on Government Procurement accepts offsets for developing countries. This exemption will certainly be maximised by many developing countries to continue pursuing offsets in their international procurements.

11 The offsets terminologies introduced in this book are just a general guideline and may vary between different companies and government offsets policy documents.

12 Offsets obligors refers to the seller or the company that is responsible for discharging offsets obligations as stipulated in the offsets agreement. Offsets obligor is responsible in delivering the offsets contract.

13 Offsets obligee refers to the recipient of offsets or anyone whom benefits from the offsets programme. This includes but is not limited to government, end-users, local companies, SMEs, universities and strategic think-tanks.

3 Theoretical underpinning to the study of offsets

3.1 Introduction

It is hard to classify offsets into a specific field of study due to its pervasive nature. In the field of international relations, offsets would be construed as a strategic tool used by an ally with mutual political and foreign relations interests. This underpinning is based on the fact that offsets is able to transfer the necessary technology and skills into buyer countries as part of international defence and security procurement with fewer restrictions. This would create a complex interdependence between the state and non-state actors informing allies (Keohane and Nye, 1987, pp. 725–753; Keohane, 2002, pp. 632–645; Keohane and Nye, 2011, p. 58) Therefore, offsets becomes an important tool to bridge the political gap and build defence cooperation in the context of international relations between countries. In the field of international political economy, it is argued that offsets are a political tool that is used to derive economic benefit (Crane and Amawi, 1997, pp. 35–42). Offsets are a state-sponsored tool with direct government intervention to ensure that offsets contracts imposed on foreign contractors bring about economic and industrial benefits. This entails a hands-on approach from the state as to how offsets is used and distributed to enhance strategic sectors and communities to fulfil objectives (Escobar, 1995; Karagiannis, 2001, Blinder, 2002; pp. 17–47; Markwell, 2006, p. 53). Offsets analysed as a tool for development would fall into the field of developmental economics (Schumpeter, 1934, 1984; Meier, 1970, pp. 14–18, Preston, 1997, p. 34–45; Bernstein, 1971; pp. 141–160; Hirschman, 1958, pp. 12–18; Hunt, 1989, pp. 42–53; Sachs, 1992; Todaro and Smith, 2006, pp. 666–675; Ziai, 2007; Nafzinger, 2012). In this context, offsets is perceived to create activities for buyer countries that consist of technology transfers, innovation, investments, skills enhancement and export opportunities which could result in greater earning power, jobs that lead to higher earning capacity and highly skilled manpower, thus overall providing greater socio-economic impact. Offsets is also associated to the field of defence economics as the costs and benefits of offsets activities' are evaluated and whether offsets truly contribute to economic growth and development (Kennedy, 1975). Offsets could also be studied as part of public policy, mainly analysing offsets policy formulation, process and implementation (Lall, 1996). Finally, offsets is also an important subject within the field of international business and international trade, especially for companies operating in an export market and entering into international collaboration. Offsets can be used as a strategic tool incorporated by companies into their corporate strategy to gain competitive advantage over their competitors in winning sales and business (Peng and Meyer, 2016, pp. 111–152; Klohs, 2012, pp. 27–34; Hill, 2014, pp. 453–455).

There has not been much attempt to study offsets purely from a theoretical perspective. The arguments put forward in this chapter have been adapted from my primary work which was part of a book chapter titled 'The Rationale for Offsets in Defence Acquisition from a Theoretical Perspective' in *Emerging Strategies Defense Acquisitions and Military Procurement* (Burgess and Antill, 2017, pp. 263–276). In this chapter, I have employed theories from several schools of thought to provide a more comprehensive rationale for offsets.

3.2   Technological self-sufficiency leading to independence in defence and security

The first reason for offsets relates to autonomy in defence and security. Nations create policies that are focused on developing in-country capability to support their industrial and technological bases (Evans, 1986, pp. 361–385; Spears, 2013, pp. 430–445; Arcelia, 2014). Countries want to move up the industrial and technological ladder from being net importers of defence equipment and services to complete indigenisation (Bitzinger, 2017, pp. 22–34; Bitzinger, 2003; Krause, 1992, pp. 14–18). I refer to Herbert Wulf's five-stage model which argues that a nation has to undergo five stages prior to achieving full indigenisation (Herbert, 1985, p. 62). Figure 3.1 explains Wulf's five stage model. According to Wulf, at stage one, countries start off by becoming net importers of equipment and perform minimal levels of repair, maintenance and overhaul on the imported weapon systems. In stage two, the importing country's industry learns to domestically assemble the components and subsystems of the imported equipment. In stage three, local companies obtain the skills to do the domestic production of simple components under licence, though more sophisticated and expensive parts continue to be delivered from abroad. Licenced production and imported contents are then assembled domestically. At stage four, the importing country's industry is licenced to produce near complete weapon systems. While the number of parts is reduced due to local manufacturing, more sophisticated components at this stage still come from overseas for the complete production to occur in-country. Finally, at the fifth stage, local companies embark on indigenous design and production of weapons. This stage can only be initiated, at least for technologically advanced weapon systems, on the basis of many years of production experience and only after sophisticated and diversified R&D facilities are set up. Design and production are often still dependent on know-how and technology input from foreign companies. Few countries are placed on the top of Herbert's five-stage model. The sophistication and complexity of modern weapon systems means that few countries are capable, let alone can afford what is needed for total self-reliance. To have such a

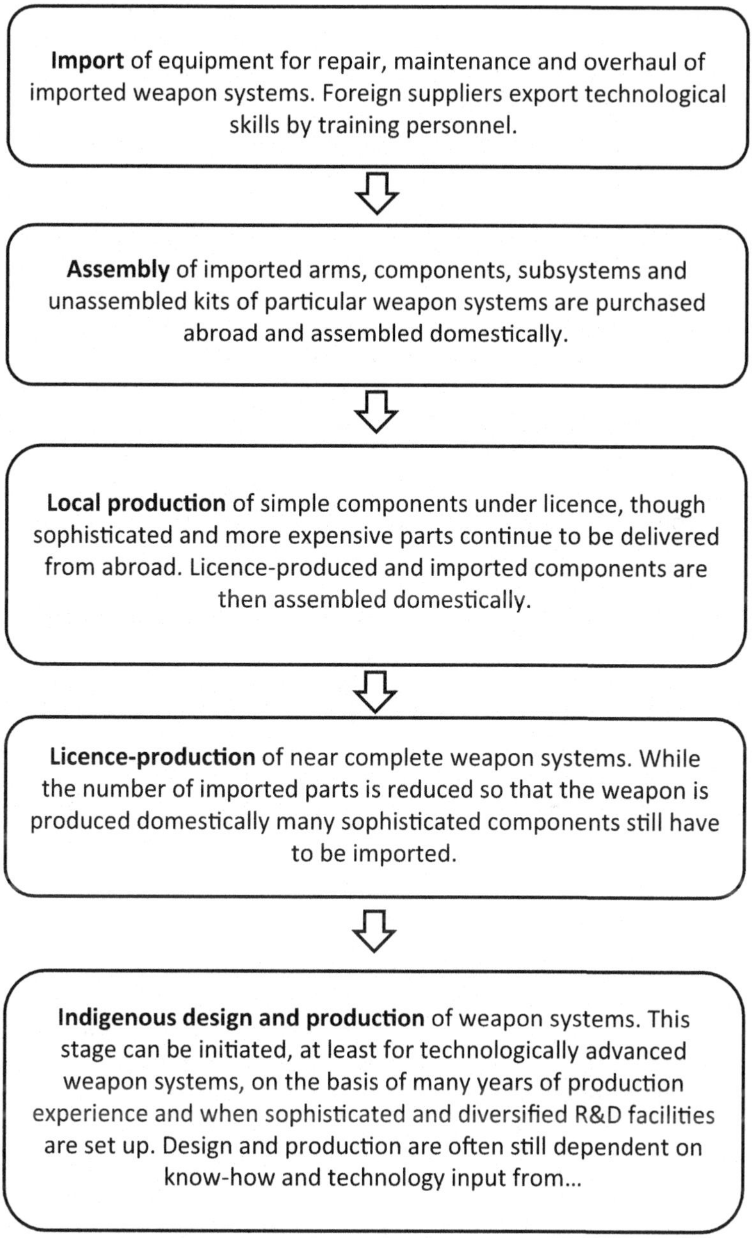

Import of equipment for repair, maintenance and overhaul of imported weapon systems. Foreign suppliers export technological skills by training personnel.

Assembly of imported arms, components, subsystems and unassembled kits of particular weapon systems are purchased abroad and assembled domestically.

Local production of simple components under licence, though sophisticated and more expensive parts continue to be delivered from abroad. Licence-produced and imported components are then assembled domestically.

Licence-production of near complete weapon systems. While the number of imported parts is reduced so that the weapon is produced domestically many sophisticated components still have to be imported.

Indigenous design and production of weapon systems. This stage can be initiated, at least for technologically advanced weapon systems, on the basis of many years of production experience and when sophisticated and diversified R&D facilities are set up. Design and production are often still dependent on know-how and technology input from...

Figure 3.1 Herbert Wulf's five stages of defence industrialisation

Source: Herbert Wulf, Arms Production in the Third World, *In: SIPRI Yearbook*, Stockholm International Peace Research Institute, Stockholm, 1985, p. 330

capability would mean that these countries would possess the full suite of capabilities – design, manufacture, assembly, integration, maintenance and the ability to market the products (a womb to tomb process). Today, only a few countries in the world can be considered as totally self-sufficient, possible exceptions being the USA, Russia and perhaps China.

Further, the sophistication and technological production capability in defence production is explained through Keith Krause's three-tier model of competencies (Spears, 2013, pp. 430–445; Bitzinger, 2015, pp. 453–472). Krause's three-tier structure is based on criteria such as an arms production base, military research and development capabilities, technological sophistication of production and domestic procurement and export dependence. According to Krause, first-tier suppliers are at the highest level of technological sophistication across the entire range of defence production and are not economically reliant on sales. The second tier of suppliers have some form of research and development capability exhibiting some areas of technological sophistication but the majority of defence production is below cutting-edge and states rely on export sales. Finally, third-tier suppliers that have very minimal technological sophistication and often do not progress much beyond slightly modifying products made under licence. All nations would want their defence production capability to move gradually from tier three to tier one (Bitzinger, 2009, pp. 320–365; Spears, 2013, pp. 430–445).

Offsets is sometimes used as a catalyst as part of government industrial and technology strategy in order to acquire capabilities that could lead to greater technological self-sufficiency, finally leading to independence in defence and security (Bitzinger, 2015, pp. 453–472; Bitzinger, 2017, pp. 22–34). The successful transfer of technology coupled by an effective local industrial absorptive capability and ability to adapt foreign technology should lead to local companies in weapons importing countries to move up the stages of technological ladder with the aim of eventually becoming self-sufficient as argued by Wulf and Krause.[1]

3.3   Industrialisation, or 'take-off'

The second reason for offsets is associated with industrialisation. It is long argued that economic growth is influenced by industrialisation (Chenery, 1960, pp. 624–665; Chenery and Syrquin, 1975; Johnson, 1984, pp. 79–89).[2] In this instance, offsets is associated with accessing high technology, such as in defence and aerospace, from where this knowledge is able to diffuse into other sectors of a national economy, in order to achieve rapid national growth and industrial development (Balakrishnan, 2007, pp. 81–83). This idea was popularised by an American, W.W. Rostow, a developmental economist in the early 1970s, through his linear stages of growth model theory (LSG) (Rostow, 1971, pp. 5–6). The LSG model argues that a massive injection of capital (such as foreign direct investment) coupled with intervention by the public sector (through offsets and other government policies) would lead to industrial and economic development of a developing nation.

As shown in Figure 3.2, Rostow also argues that every country should go through these five different stages to break the vicious cycle of poverty and become

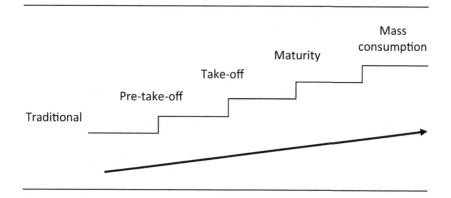

Figure 3.2 Rostow's Five Stages Model

Source: W.W. Rostow, *The Stages of Economic Growth, A Non-Communist Manifesto*, Cambridge University Press, Cambridge, 1960.

a fully industrialised country. The five linear stages are: stage one – traditional (primitive), stage two – pre-take-off, stage three – take-off, stage four – mature and stage five – mass consumption. The first stage is based on traditional society and basic agriculture. The only form of trade that exists is barter or exchange of items required for living. Agriculture is critical to daily life and the only industry that existed at that time. Work was primarily labour intensive as there is very limited technology and little exploitation of raw materials. This restricts the development of other industries and services. In the second stage, which is also labelled as pre-conditions for take-off, agriculture becomes increasingly commercialised as mechanisation occurs. Other industries emerge and resources start to be exploited. TNCs or transnational companies start to invest and further promote the development of industries, also known as foreign direct investment. According to Rostow, the third stage, the 'take off', is viewed as the most important period amongst all the stages, when all the "old blocks and resistances to steady growth are finally overcome" and when "compound interest becomes built, as it were, into [society's] habits and institutional structure" (Rostow, 1971, p. 7). During this stage, there is a rapid increase of economic activity fuelled by equally sudden spurts of savings, investments and radical technological change. A new entrepreneurial class emerges, agricultural productivity improves and resources, including population, begin to be directed into industrial activities located in towns (Rostow, 1971, p. 7). Political and social reforms and improvements occur in conjunction with industrialisation. Infrastructure continues to be developed but growth often remains only in a few regions of the country. At the fourth stage, industries become mature. Rostow claims that during the fourth stage or the drive to maturity stage, nations will invest 10–20 percent of their national income towards new production capacity. Industries will forge ahead, mature and level-off whilst new industries will arrive on the scene. This era witnesses a mature economy and society, supported by technological innovation and the absorption of indigenous technologies (Preston, 1997, pp. 175–177). The population continues to grow and rapid urbanisation starts to decline as manufacturers take dominance and a wider range of industries develop. Finally, in the fifth stage of mass consumption, nations reach a level where their economic system is able to produce a surplus (Rostow, 1971, p. 7). At this juncture, leading sectors of a nation shift from heavy industries towards consumer durables and services. The initially exploitative industries move elsewhere and any remaining industries shift production to durable consumer goods. A rapid expansion of tertiary industry occurs (Rostow, 1971, p. 176).

There are of course many counterarguments to Rostow's theory, especially as nations have learnt methods to shorten the process without having to undergo all five stages sequentially. There are strength and weaknesses to this model as it was piloted on European countries only, not taking other major factors into consideration such as climate, availability of resources and even aspects of colonisation that expedited industrialisation for some countries. Further, not all countries are at the same stage of development. However, this was a good starting point and something that the developing world could rely on for guidance. Many countries especially in the developing world believe in, and have adopted, Rostow's idea. Rostow's model, especially the 'take-off' stage, can be tied to offsets being used as a catalyst by governments (especially with defence and aerospace technology) to industrialise their nations in order to create an environment for greater economic progress (Balakrishnan, 2007, pp. 81–83).

3.4   Reducing the technological gap

The third reason for requesting offsets relates to technology acquisition, where nations aspire to become industrialised without having to go through the five stages as described by Rostow. Technological progress is seen to be crucial for growth and is fundamental for achieving rising per capita income, as it determines the rate at which natural resources can be exploited and capital stock can be expanded, to enhance productivity and maximise output and income (Akubue, 2002, pp. 90–101). It is for this reason that economically developed countries tend to also be those that are industrially and technologically advanced (Krugman, 1979, pp. 253–266; Cheng, 1984, pp. 17–40; Jensen and Thursby, 1986, pp. 269–285; Flam and Helpman, 1987, pp. 810–822; Dosi, 1990).

There are three technology-related theories that can assist in explaining how industries can reduce the technology gap (McIntyre, 1986, pp. 33–39; Lall, 1960; Bell and Pavitt, 1997, pp. 83–137; Pack and Saggi, 1997, pp. 81–98; Dahlman, 2007, pp. 76–82; Fu, Pietrobelli and Soete, 2011, pp. 1204–1212). The first relates to the *technology gap theory* which emphasises technological backwardness and the need to catch up with technology leaders (Posner, 1961, pp. 323–334; Nelson and Winter, 1982). The underlying mechanism of knowledge diffusion in this stream of thought is the mastery of a developed country's technology by developing countries. This theory clearly recognises the need for building sufficient domestic capability through imitation of technological knowledge, but also recognises the huge costs involved in developing such capabilities from scratch (Abramowitz, 1993, pp. 217–241). Without a sufficient level of domestic capability, requiring massive investment, a country is unlikely to benefit from the technological knowledge of developed countries and thus faces the risk of continuously lagging behind advanced countries (Dosi, Pavitt and Soete, 1990, pp. 74–77; Beverly and Kevin, 1995, pp. 222–235; Lall, 1997, p. 11). Many nations decide to acquire technology instead of developing them from scratch for various reasons. Some nations do not have sufficient capital or human resources to develop technological capabilities in certain technological areas. Others have to compromise between allocation of R&D for technological development or to other socio-economic needs. In such cases, the most effective method will be to acquire technological capability from overseas. This can either be done as an outright purchase for technologies that are readily available off-the-shelf, or through procurement for more specific or critical technologies obtained through offsets. For OEMs within the technological life cycle, companies that develop new technology will eventually decide to export when the technology is at the other end of the technological life cycle (Clark, 1986, pp. 43–45).[3] For the technology acquirer, which in this case is the procuring government and offsets technology recipient, FDI, joint ventures or strategic collaborations are more effective methods to leap-frog and obtain technology without wasting too much time and money. This process allows a buyer nation to 'catch up' with the seller country thus reducing the technological gap. Offsets is seen as an easy route to help achieve a technological leap-frog and catch up through the use of the procurement processes.

The second relates to technology appropriation. This school of thought, named the *endogenous growth theory* or *new growth theory*, argues that technology is appropriated and monopolised by its innovators (Romer, 1994, pp. 3–22; Parente, 2001, pp. 49–58). Once technology has been mastered, it is difficult for others to catch up due to economies of scale in both physical and human resources and the geographical localisation of technology. Today, technological leaders attempt to restrict transmission of their most advanced technologies to foreign competitors and protect their intellectual property rights, especially from the encroachment of developing countries. Recipient governments and firms, however, attempt to obtain control of these advanced technologies, as these have become factors in economic growth and international competitiveness. There is a greater emphasis on innovative investments, human capital accumulation and externalities as the dominant factors that determine long-term economic growth. Again, offsets is seen as a vital tool to assist in achieving these goals. Procuring governments and their industries realise offsets can be used to demand some of these state-of-the-art technologies in defence and aerospace which otherwise could not be obtained off-the-shelf. In the case of defence, the issue of national security and maintaining battle-winning technology adds even greater complexity which works against economic logic (Jones, 2001, pp. 108–118).

Third, technology theory relates to the protection of an *infant industry* (Chang, 2002, pp. 2–7; Glass and Saggi, 1998, pp. 369–398; Kim and Dahlman, 1992, pp. 437–452; Bell, 2002, pp. 44–50). The increasing rate of interconnectivity between different parts of the world is constantly changing the dynamics of how international business is conducted. Transnational corporations (TNCs) and states are constantly operating within a volatile industrial and technological environment in a space and time shrinking era. There is an increasing pressure from TNCs to open and liberalise regional markets through economic forums. This has been the case in South East and East Asia for example. Many trade theories on foreign direct investments argue that OEMs operate on a 'fly by night' model whereby they move their company to the most cost effective and business-conducive location to set up their operations. It is claimed that OEMs have neither commitment nor loyalty towards national industrial and technological development in the countries where they operate, but do business on a purely commercial basis without any long-term commitment. Past evidence has shown how nations have lost their industrial base overnight due to the adverse impact of foreign direct investments (FDIs) flowing out of the country together with the technology. For these reasons, national governments attempt to build and preserve local industries and technological bases. Many local industries are still sheltered largely through 'infant industry' protection schemes and other local content requirements. Such policies are enforced to ensure that local industries are not completely wiped out in the process of globalisation where only the best and most competitive industries survive. Offsets is claimed to negate this effect through the enforcement of long-term commitments in business projects. Both industries and governments work towards ensuring a sustainable partnership by working through joint ventures, collaboration and partnerships. Offsets is used to first gain quicker access to industry knowledge and best practice in order to close the technology gap and help local industries face a more competitive environment once on a level playing field. Second, offsets is used to help seek foreign companies' expertise to build the capability of local industry in order to properly enter the global supply chain, gain expert assistance for skills development, increase product and process innovation, facilitate exports and increase the intellectual capital of the nation through activities such as advanced training and education.

3.5   Building dynamic capability

The fourth reason for offsets relates to building dynamic capability. Dynamic capability is discussed as part of strategic management theory in international business management. Dynamic capability is a firm's ability to integrate, build and reconfigure internal and external competencies to address rapidly changing environments. The basic assumption of the dynamic capability framework is that companies use core competencies to modify short-term competitive positions that can be used to build longer-term competitive advantages (Eisenhardt and Martin, 2003, pp. 124–135; Helfat, Finkelstein, Mitchell, Peteraf, Singh, Teece and Winter, 2007, pp. 152–159; Cetindamar, Phaal and Probert, 2009, pp. 45–58). Governments can use offsets as a catalyst to create and develop dynamic capability within their industrial environment. Offsets can be used as a short-term measure to build capability in certain emerging and high technology sectors which can then lead to adding competitive advantage in the long-run if utilised effectively. As for suppliers, the primary motive is to leverage offsets as a tool to outperform competitors. Providing new technology especially in defence and aerospace can be a major pull factor for countries favouring one OEM against another. The competitive advantage theory by Michael Porter clearly describes differentiation as an advantage against rivals (Porter, 1985, p. 232). A firm is said to have competitive advantage when it is implementing a value-creating strategy (Clulow, Gerstman and Barry, 2003, p. 34; Abdalla Alfaki and Ahmed, 2013, pp. 4–13). In this instance, offsets being introduced as a business strategy to win contracts is perceived as providing competitive advantages for one company over another based on the content, quality and benefits offered by the offsets programme to a nation.

3.6 Industrialisation through clusters

The next reason for offsets is associated with cluster development. This concept has been discussed in strategic management and international business circles and yet is also an important aspect of technology policy (Jenkins, 1991, pp. 197–231; Porter, 2000, pp. 15–34). A cluster in the context of industrialisation is defined as a "geographic concentration of competing and cooperating companies, suppliers, services and associated institutions grouped according to their technology and networking characteristics". Clusters must compete and grow through innovation to be able to increase sustainability (Mowery and Oxley, 1995, pp. 67–93). Industry tends to cluster geographically due to the need to exchange information, transmit tacit knowledge about business formation and product development, the localised concentration of skilled labour, lifestyle amenities, and research facilities associated with research universities, large corporations and labs. Industrial clustering has been identified as an effective way to nurture SMEs in developing and developed countries so that they survive and stay competitive on a regional, international and global level (Bell, 1986, pp. 1715–1734; Morosini 2004, pp. 305–326). Clusters are also said to increase the productivity and quality of local suppliers, focusing on specialised local research and training providers (Bell, 2002, pp. 122–132) and stimulating new business formations that support innovation (Lawton-Smith, 1991, pp. 403–416). This is possible as the proximity of firms encourages the development of highly skilled workers for the specific needs of a particular industry (Lall, 2000, pp. 337–369). Firms in need of this skill will have easy access. These firms can experience economies of scale in developing and using common technologies, tending to promote a maximum flow of information and ideas. Products, markets and technological knowledge can be easily shared and effectively turned into valuable innovations. These factors together contribute towards industrial competitiveness (Lall, 1999, pp. 230–247).

Clusters can be formed through local knowledge and industrial networks or through cross border externalities, with the increasing internationalisation of economic activities such as FDIs, foreign patenting, international R&D,

collaboration, international trade and knowledge flows. MNCs relocate their value chains into specific clustered areas to exploit the potential of coverage. There is evidence that firms relocate to one geographic area to improve their comparative and competitive advantages. Information technology clusters, such as in Bangalore and Singapore, have been extremely successful in producing globally competitive IT firms. Countries such as Malaysia and Thailand have followed similar routes in developing industrial clusters to support their SMEs (Schmitz, 1984, pp. 1503–1514).

Offsets is seen as a tool by governments mainly to facilitate defence and aerospace clusters (Balakrishnan, 2011, pp. 216–230). Offsets is identified as a proactive strategy to develop late-comer clusters through linking with foreign partners and sources of technology and knowledge. Such defence and aerospace clusters borne out of offsets exist in the United States, Canada, France, the United Kingdom and Spain, among others. In recent years, developing countries in the Middle East, such as the UAE, and in Asia, including China, India, Japan, South Korea, Singapore and Malaysia, have taken a similar approach of using offsets to develop their defence and aerospace clusters (Balakrishnan, 2011, pp. 216–230; Niosi and Zhegu, 2005, p. 42; Carrincazeane and Frigat, 2007, pp. 260–284; Dreher, Fuchs, Parks, Strange and Tierney, 2017).

3.7   Sustaining firm competitiveness through technological absorption capability (TAC)

An important argument is that offsets is often used to enhance the technological absorption capability of industries in buyer countries. A highly technologically able company is able to attain high levels of competitiveness[4] leading to sustainable industrial development (Junni and Sarala, 2013, pp. 19–23; Archibugi and Coco, 2004, pp. 629–654). Figure 3.3 suggests four drivers for effective industrial technological absorption capability. The model has been modified from Porter's National Competitive Advantage Framework.[5] The TAC model highlights four drivers in an offsets environment that are crucial to ensure effective technological absorption within local companies in buyer countries. This occurs with an end goal of increasing industrial competitiveness, leading to long-term economic growth and increased productivity. First is the role of local firms, their strategy and structure in term of employment, training, skills development and their positioning in the global market (Huq, 2004, pp. 151–171). Local firms must build capability in order to effectively absorb technology. In recent years, much has been written about the importance of technology capability building (TCB) within local firms especially in developing countries (Lall, 1992, pp. 165–186; Lall, 1998, pp. 645–654; Lall, 1975, pp. 799–810). TCB involves a mixture of information, skills, interactions and routines that firms need in order to develop technology. Routine TCB involves the capability to use the technology as much as resources to produce goods and services at a given level of efficiency, using a combination of factors such as abilities, equipment, products and production specifications, organisational systems and methods.[6] TCB is vital for firms to be able to effectively absorb technology and build

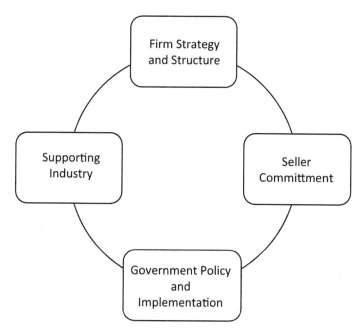

Figure 3.3 Drivers for technological absorption capability (TAC)
Source: Author

industrial competitiveness. This means local firms selected to participate in offsets programmes must be willing to invest in infrastructure, human resource development, training and research and development to build its TAC. The question is whether these local companies have the right strategies to enhance their competitive edge in order to penetrate the global market (Jomo, 2003, pp. 78–89). Eventually, the local firm should be able to use offsets to build its capacity to the extent that it is able to compete on a level playing field on the basis of price, quality and product characteristics (Cohen and Levinthal, 1990, pp. 232–240; Kim and Nelson, 2000, pp. 12–18; Keller, 1996, pp. 90–92).

The second driver behind effective TAC in offsets relates to vendor commitment and attitudes towards technology transfer. A transparent and positive technology transfer process by sellers should increase the competitiveness of local firms and enhance TAC through 'learning by doing', where firms will be exposed to a multifaceted technological learning curve, including problem-solving, managing technology processes, internal and external firm interactions and the ability to market and export their products (Fu, Pietrobelli and Soete, 2011, pp. 1204–1212). Continuing access to emerging technologies including new products, new processes, management techniques from sellers and tighter relations between technology and science are all essential for building local firm TAC.[7] These include sellers' willingness to transfer technology, the level and type of technology to be transferred, whether the technology is commercially viable, the cost of technology, intellectual property rights and patenting issues, the willingness to give away licences, the ability to find suitable partners to collaborate on specific projects and the issues of cost-sharing (Marton, 1986, p. 91; Zahra and George, 2002, p. 75; Das, 2008, pp. 67–92). An interesting example of a supplier's commitment is the 2004 BAE-SAAB Gripen programme in the Czech Republic. The offsets programme which ran from June 2004 to December 2014, was worth 25.5 billion CZK, which represents 130 percent of the value of the lease payments for Grippen aircraft. By December 2004, the project had officially accumulated an offsets value exceeding 4.2 billion CZK, which represents 16.5 percent of the total offsets obligation. BAE and SAAB have jointly committed to attracting offsets projects, mainly indirect work, related to automotive component manufacturing, electric tools, export-based investments, such as the production of power generation equipment, the supply of medical components, the export of spark plugs, nitro-cellulose and investment into producing a brake disc foundry and forging equipment for Saudi Arabia. These initiatives have largely benefitted the Czech manufacturing industry. In the Gulf States however, contractors claim that they are unable to deliver offsets projects effectively due to complicated and underdeveloped commercial laws, government bureaucracy, underdeveloped investment infrastructure, as well as cultural issues.

However, it is also argued that that foreign suppliers are not making sufficient efforts to transfer actual knowledge and develop a learning curve. It is argued that less technologically developed countries should break loose from this chain and reduce their total reliance on foreign technology if the partnership becomes impossible. Instead, these countries should practise a strategy of forming technological alliances with individuals and firms who are willing to become technology partners. Often, these forms of challenges emerge in offsets programmes as well.

The third driver for effective TAC in offsets relates to policy and implementation by buyer country governments. State intervention is argued as being necessary in an imperfect market environment of information asymmetry, especially to ensure the successful transfer of technology between firms (Bell, Martin and Pavitt, 1984, pp. 124–132; Keller, 1996, pp. 199–227; Lall, 1960; Bozeman, 2000). In any examination of successful TAC, the role of government must be considered (Lall and Morris, 1998, pp. 1369–1385). For example, local content rules are imposed to ensure that buyer country firms are included in industrial projects in order to increase their TAC. However, intervention is also criticised, as the act of controlling, regulations, restrictions, special privileges, and subsidies are at the expense of others (Von Mises, 1998, pp. 10–12). In this case, offsets is imposed by governments as part of international procurement to pave the way for local firms to be provided with the necessary exposure and experience for effective TAC.

Finally, the fourth driver in offsets that relates to effective TAC is attributed to the role of supporting industries. Supporting industries, especially in critical infrastructure sectors including defence and aerospace, are vital to ensure high level of specialisation (Chowdhury and Islam,1993). This for instance includes work such as painting, drilling, welding and wiring. A successful TAC also includes having a robust and sufficiently strong base of supporting industries to assist main contractors in offsets work. In the case of South Korean offsets, for example, the uneven growth of the country's defence industrial base was linked to the monopoly dominance of a small number of large conglomerates – the chaebol – providing little diffusion of production work to small and medium-sized industries. At the end of 1995, 82 Korean defence contractors produced 308 types of defence equipment but the top ten chaebol accounted for 75 percent of production. It is argued that chaebol dominance of the Korean industry minimised the multiplier effect from technology transfers and necessitated continued dependence on foreign firms through the procurement of spares and maintenance (Kim and Lee, 2015, pp. 42–53). This has also been the case in other countries such as India, Malaysia, Poland and South Africa where SMEs are often sidelined by prime contractors. On the whole, a suppressed SME base with fewer opportunities cascading down from prime contractors in buyer nations can lead to weak overall technological absorptive capability.

Notes

1 Technology transfer alone will not lead to economic progress, instead the ability to maintain and fully maximise the appropriate technology may be the key to long-term economic development. Successful technology transfer can only occur if the recipient nation has the capability to adapt or improve the technology. Governments can stimulate the achievement of technology and knowledge transfer only if they create the necessary conditions for enhancing both the absorptive capabilities of local firms and the connections between foreign investors and local organisations.

2 The linear stage model assumes that economic growth is achieved through industrialisation.

3 The technological life cycle is associated with the product life cycle theory, developed by Raymond Vernon. The model is based on the comparative advantage of nations and discusses three categories of products – new products, matured products and standardised products. The products go through five stages in the life cycle: introduction, growth, maturity, saturation and decline.

4 Technology capability building, or TCB, can be divided into four levels. At the first level is the operational function involving basic manufacturing, demanding troubleshooting, quality control and maintenance and procurement skills. The second level involves duplicating skills investment capability to expand capacity and purchase and integrate foreign technologies. The third level involves gaining adaptive skills involving activities such as importing technologies, adapting and improving them, and design skills for more complex engineering. Finally, the fourth level involves innovative skills, including R&D, to keep pace with moving technological frontiers and to generate new technology. For most developing countries, TCB is at the first or second level with a few at the third level. The Far East region, some Latin American countries and South Africa are at the third level, and they are making strong efforts to move into the fourth level. Countries like Malaysia are somewhere in transition between the second and third level.

5 Michael Porter's five forces model discusses the demand conditions, factor conditions, related and supporting industry strategy, structure and rivalry, all important aspects of national competitiveness.

6 Innovative capabilities include the capability to carry out technological change to encourage the use of distinctive resources to generate and manage technological activities.

7 Firms define competitiveness as the ability to compete in world markets with a global strategy. Governments define competitiveness as a positive balance of trade. Economists argue that competitiveness is all about achieving low unit costs of labour adjusted for exchange rates. Indicators of competitiveness include sponsorship of R&D, measuring profit levels, management practices, labour unions, balances of trade, labour productivity rates and export market penetration. Drivers for competitiveness include foreign direct investment, skills, domestic R&D, licencing, economic strength, government, exchange rates, finance, infrastructure and management. A macroeconomic level of competitiveness is focused on issues such as monetary and fiscal policies, a trusted and efficient legal system, a stable set of democratic institutions and progress in social conditions. Microeconomic levels of competitiveness depend on the sophistication with which foreign sub-operators or domestic companies in the local country operate, and the quality of the microeconomic business environment in which firms operate. In the context of industrialisation and economic growth, competiveness would include effective investment into research and development leading to invention and innovation, profit, management competency, trusted and efficient legal systems, stable exchange rates, transparent governance processes and the availability of human capital possessing appropriate skills. Industry and firm competitiveness is vital in the microeconomic business environment at which local companies operate.

Phase II

4 Role of government: offsets strategy and policy formulation

Development phase

4.1 Background

This chapter focuses on the role of government in formulating offsets policy. Most of my thoughts on offsets policy are based on my own experience of having been involved in offsets policy formulation, comparative research on various written and unwritten offsets polices worldwide and in my government advisory capacity on offsets policy formulation. This chapter is only a general guide to how offsets policy is formulated and does not claim to be an all-encompassing solution. This chapter should provide a sound understanding of key factors and characteristics of government in offsets policy formulation.

Two components are vital in viewing offsets with a long-term vision: first, deciding on a national offsets strategy, and second, based on the strategy, to formulate an offsets policy. The offsets policy can be written or unwritten. The offsets strategy and policy are both not cast in stone and can continuously evolve based on dynamic internal and external political, social and economic changes that may have direct or indirect impacts on a nation's industrial and technological landscape. Many countries around the world undertake policy formulation and implementation through a policy transfer process[1] (Rose, 1991, Parsons, 1995; Evans and Davies, 1999; pp. 3–30; Cairney, 2012, pp. 75–77, Bardach, 2006, pp. 92–99). This chapter first elucidates the features of offsets in international procurement and in the bid process. The chapter then discusses offsets strategy and development, how offsets policy is formulated, offsets objectives and the role of stakeholders in offsets management (Balakrishnan, 2007, pp. 155–182).

4.2 Role of offsets in international defence procurement

Defence acquisition is a very complex activity that deals with purchasing of products and services that are highly differentiated and multidimensional (Kincaid, 2002, pp. 36–40; Kincaid, 2008; Weiss, 2005, p. 5; Kaur, 2013). Regulations surrounding defence acquisition and support services are extremely complicated, diffuse and decentralised (Markowski and Hall, 1998; Boyce, 2000; Weiss, 2005, pp. 61–71). The UK's Acquisition System Guidance (formerly the Acquisition Operating Framework) defines acquisition as:

> Acquisition is how we work together with industry to provide the necessary military capability to meet the needs of our Armed Forces now and in the future. It covers the setting of requirements; the selection, development and manufacture of a solution to meet those requirements; the introduction into service and support of equipment or other elements of capability through life, and its appropriate disposal.
>
> (Ministry of Defence, 2015)

In many countries, defence acquisition is simplified to only cover procurement activities which involve acquiring capability, goods and services from the letting of a contract through to receipt of payment (Kiely, 1990, pp. 7–9; Weiss, 2005, pp. 60–81; Keith, Vitasek, Manrodt and Kling, 2016). Defence organisations and industries are the principal parties involved in defence acquisition transactions. Local content and domestic sourcing normally feature as a prerequisite in defence procurement in order to meet the aspirations of achieving 'self-reliance' in defence capability (Singh, 2000, p. 43; Markowski, Hall and Wylie, 2010, pp. 22–24). Offsets is used as leverage within procurement activities, by governments seeking to enhance their industrial and technological capability in-country (Braddon, Dowdall, Kendry and Reay, 1992; Toru, 2003; Taylor, 2004).

There are several unique features to offsets within defence acquisition. The first is that the tool sometimes becomes the deciding factor in procurement decisions as opposed to price and technical specifications. Although there is a lack of evidence on how significantly offsets features as a deciding factor in procurement decisions, many governments nonetheless claim that offsets has been the primary reason for certain procurements. This can occur especially in sectors where technology is critical and cannot be obtained off-the-shelf, or where the forecasted economic benefits and multipliers derived from offsets projects outweigh the actual procurement itself (Nackman, 2011; Taylor, 2012).

The second feature refers to differences in how governments incorporate offsets in defence acquisition. Generally, there are three types of practice by governments. The first type refers to mandatory requirement by offsets authorities or government. This means the offsets requirement is set as prescriptive, stated as a law or written guideline and is mentioned to bidders at the outset. This is the case in countries such as South Korea, South Africa, Malaysia and Turkey. The second type of offsets incorporation involves nation states requiring OEMs to fulfil offsets obligations on a voluntary basis, separate from the procurement exercise. This practice is done to stress that acquisition and offsets are two separate activities, implying that the former activity does not depend on the latter. This is practised widely in countries such as the United Kingdom, Australia and China. The third type of incorporation is when offsets requirements are not explicitly mentioned in policy and is not mandatory, but there is a subtle requirement that offsets or local content be included in the acquisition exercise. This is a common practice in countries such as Japan and Singapore. There are also variants with regards to the selection of the technology recipient for offsets. In some countries, the government determines where and to whom the offsets technology should be transferred, mainly to protect government-linked companies or national champions. In other cases offsets technology transfer is left to market forces, leaving OEMs with the decision of choosing the most competitive and capable recipient company with which to partner (Verma, 2009, pp. 21; Taylor, 2003b, pp. 338–356).

The fourth feature is found in the terms of the acquisition contract document. In some instances, offsets will form part of the main procurement contract whilst in other cases, a separate offsets contract is signed in parallel or before the signing of the main procurement contract. There are many reasons for a separate offsets contract. These include emphasising the importance given to offsets obligations, ensuring that there is a separate penalty for non-performance of offsets and sometimes as offsets obligations take longer to complete than the main contract, for simplicity of execution.

The next section briefly discusses the government offsets management cycle in countries where offsets is made mandatory as part of international defence procurement. This model can be applied and extended to non-defence sectors with some modification.

4.3   The offsets management cycle (OMC)

Figure 4.1 depicts a flow diagram of how governments can manage offsets (Balakrishnan, 2013). The OMC is divided into two phases. Phase one, the development stage, is discussed in this chapter. Phase two, the implementation phase, is explained in detail in Chapter 5. The development phase furthers consist of two stages – phase 1 which focuses on strategy and phase 2 which focuses on policy formulation.

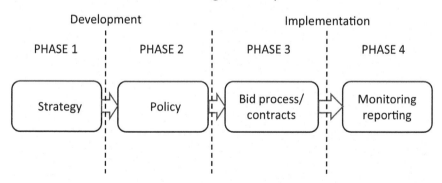

Figure 4.1 Offsets management cycle
Source: Author

4.4   Offsets strategy development

Offsets strategy involves setting long-term visions and planning at a national level. Offsets strategy is closely linked to setting direction and scope for a nation's industrial, technological and economic development; recognising and using available resources; and meeting stakeholder requirements (Grant, 2010, pp. 72–83). A simple rule in offsets is to identify opportunities and align objectives and goals that could deliver effective offsets programmes for maximum results. A successful offsets strategy is when a government is able to identify national industrial and technological strengths and weaknesses, recognise the available resources and incorporate these factors into the national offsets strategy to obtain maximum benefit (Balakrishnan, 2011, pp. 321–341) .

4.4.1   Considering the choices

In formulating an offsets strategy, it is important to take note of existing offsets strategy. There is a dearth of literature that discusses offsets strategy and strategic management. Matthews' offsets strategy matrix expounds the four most globally popular types of strategy. The matrix consists of four quadrants: defence offsets for defence projects, defence offsets for civil projects, civil offsets purely for civil projects only and finally civil offsets for defence projects (Brauer and Dunne, 2004, pp. 92–102). This model provides a good foundation, but has its limitations. It fails to take into account the variations when countries undertake a two-pronged strategy of using defence offsets for defence and civil projects at the same time or vice versa and that offsets strategy can change. It also does not consider the possibility of moving from one quadrant to another.

Table 4.1 provides examples of offsets strategies from countries that impose defence offsets, civil offsets and a combination of defence and civil offsets (CTO, 2017). The table is divided into two axes where the horizontal axis shows the types of offsets – direct, indirect or both – while the vertical axis shows the offsets category, either defence, civil or a combination of the two.

Table 4.1 National offsets choice according to type and sectors

Sector/type	Direct	Indirect	Direct and Indirect
Defence offsets	United Kingdom, South Korea, Singapore, most EU countries, United States	Japan	Oman, UAE, Canada
Civil offsets	Nigeria		
Defence and civil offsets	China, India		Malaysia

Source: Extracted from CTO, http://cto-offsets.com, accessed 15 November 2017

In summary, nations should take four key steps before finalising offsets strategy leading to policy formulation:

- Commission a feasibility study to establish the need for an offsets policy. Study various offsets strategies, policies and international best practices. Analyse the impact of case studies. The study may be undertaken internally, through an independent third party, or through an interim committee consisting of government, industry, academia and independent consultants.
- Consider whether to proceed with an offsets policy and if so, consider the available offsets strategy options based on the established report.
- Understand that offsets strategy is not a universal fit. Strategy choice is often based on the resources available such as skilled human capital, financial resources, raw material and the technological absorptive capacity of a buyer country, amongst others (Moore, 1995; Mintzerberg, Ahlstrand and Lampel, 1998; Vaughan Evans, 2013).
- Communicate the strategy effectively to internal and external stakeholders (Gulati, 1998, pp. 293–317).

4.4.2   *Flexible versus obligatory*

Past practices have shown that a nation can adopt a range of practices in executing offsets strategy. Some nations have in place formalised and mandatory offsets policies, which form part of the tender document. The policies are fully developed with very detailed offsets requirements. Other nations have in place a more flexible approach, where offsets requirements are mentioned in procurement guidelines but are left to market forces to implement projects and fulfil requirements. In other instances, offsets are not mentioned anywhere in the procurement bid or in contract documents, but sellers are aware that host governments will impose some form of offsets as part of the procurement exercise. A specific model on the flexibility of the offsets strategy spectrum was created by Matthews, where he clustered offsets strategy into three categories: case-by-case, best endeavour and obligatory (Brauer and Dunne, 2004, p. 92). Some criticism stems from the fact that the model has associated partnership and trust strongly with best endeavour, questioning whether such an environment can exist in a case-by-case or obligatory offsets strategy.

I have illustrated the offsets strategy spectrum differently, by categorising offsets strategy as either being flexible, obligatory or being instituted under exceptional circumstances. A flexible offsets approach is when offsets requirements are not mandatory. However, buyer nations may impose offsets when there is a need to acquire certain types of technological capability, industrial know-how or expert knowledge, that will provide strategic and long-term benefits for the nation. Countries such as Singapore, Japan, Australia and the United States focus on such a strategy. Then, on the other end of the spectrum, is where offsets requirements are made obligatory and are highly prescriptive. Obligatory strategies focus on structured delivery and also include punitive measures for

Development
Phase 1 – Offsets Strategy

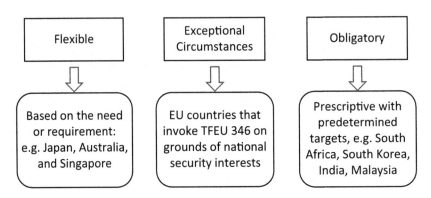

Figure 4.2 Offsets strategy spectrum: flexible versus obligatory
Source: Author

non-performance. This practice is prevalent in developing countries. Examples of countries with obligatory offsets strategies include South Korea, Brazil, Malaysia and India. The third category of offsets strategy is those employed only in exceptional circumstances. This practice emerged mainly due to the European Commission's decision through the European Defence Agency (EDA) to ban offsets practice, except in situations favourable to national interest invoked by Article 346 of the Treaty for European Union (TFEU). All EU countries fall under this category.

4.5   Offsets policy formulation

It is important to take note of a few general rules when formulating offsets policy. Like any other general policy formulation, offsets policy formulation sets the agenda for how offsets is later executed (Cairney, 2012, p. 4; McConnell, 2010; Anderson, 1975, p. 56). The offsets policy should be crafted so it is pragmatic, flexible and consists of features that are easily applicable in real world contexts. Overcomplicated offsets policies that are littered with too much technical jargon and complex formulae lead to a scenario where both offsets obligors and obligees are unable to understand or execute an effective policy. Policies should be revisited from time to time in order to realign the policy with contemporary national economic requirements (Linder and Peters, 2006, pp. 19–40; Marsh and McConnell, 2010, pp. 564–583).[2] Some governments review their policy every five years whilst others do it every two. In the case of India, the Indian offsets policy was reviewed six times (Behera, 2012a, online).

The following should be considered in offsets policy formulation:

i   First, the organisations and individuals that will be responsible for drafting of the offsets policy.

ii Second, the nature of the policy – whether the policy will be a legally binding document such as a decree, statute, enactment or a government circular or guideline. For example, countries like Indonesia, Oman, the Philippines and Poland have in place offsets policy in the form of statutes. Others, like Malaysia, UAE and South Africa, have offsets guidelines.

iii Third, the offsets policy objectives – whether the objectives are aligned with the wider national agenda and ensuring they are not formed in isolation.

iv Fourth, the policy content – to determine details such as the threshold value, multipliers, penalties and the banking of credit.

v   Fifth, identification of the multiple stakeholders involved and obtaining their input in the policy drafting process.

vi The sixth and final stage is to present the final draft policy document to stakeholders for approval followed by implementation.

4.6   Responsibilities for offsets policy formulation

There are various options as to who should be responsible for formulating and drafting offsets policy (Fischer, 2003, pp. 112–114; Page, 2006, pp. 90–94; Hogwood and Gunn, 1984, pp. 12–17). The cardinal directive is in ensuring that any organisation being appointed to craft the offsets policy is independent of the organisation that is implementing the policy. The separation of function between the former and latter is to ensure that there exists impartiality in offsets policy formulation and implementation (Howlett, Ramesh and Perl, 2009, pp. 223–228; Jenkins-Smith and Sabatier, 1993, Dolowitz, 2003, pp.101–108; pp. 109–115; Eliasson, 2010; John, 2012, pp. 19–22).

The offsets policy team could form an interim committee that consists of different stakeholders, including the offsets management office that implements the policy. The policy committee can also appoint external experts or reputable consultants who could provide impartial views and tips on best practice. It is important that the policy committee be headed by someone with a good level of offsets knowledge. Otherwise, the committee can engage experts who have sound knowledge of the subject and are able to provide reasonable advice. Several governments around the world have taken the approach of developing in-house offsets capability for continuity, but have also engaged external experts who are able to provide greater insights into offsets through their international engagement and exposure.

4.7   Determining offsets objectives

Finalising offsets objectives is an arduous task. As mentioned earlier, offsets objectives should not be formulated in isolation but must be developed in tandem with other national policies. This is because offsets policy exists to support wider

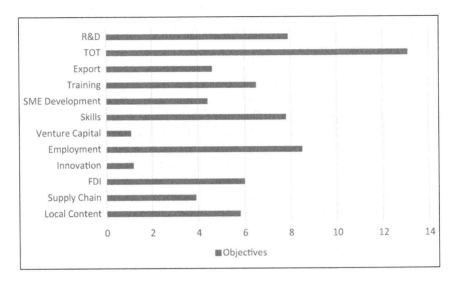

Figure 4.3 Offsets policy objectives

Source: Author

national industrial and technological aspirations. For example, when I was involved in formulating Malaysia's offsets policy, I had to refer to many other national documents such as the Malaysia Five Year Plan, the Vision 2020, the Industrial Master Plan and the Science and Technology Policy. These documents helped me appreciate the strengths and weaknesses of Malaysia's science and technology as well as industrial policy. Thus, it is critical to identify overlaps between other national policy objectives in order to eventually draft effective offsets policy objectives in line with the overall national agenda (Balakrishnan, 2007, pp. 154–160).

When I was invited to speak at the IRB workshop in Ottawa, Canada, in 2009, I investigated around 40 written offsets policies which I had obtained from CTO and mapped out their objectives. Referring to Figure 4.3, I found that the majority of offsets policies specified technology transfer as their main objective but had not clearly defined what is meant by technology. The other objectives were employment creation, local content, skills enhancement, FDI, research and development, training, SME development, exports, enhancement of supply chain, entrepreneurship and innovation (Balakrishnan, 2012). Based on the distribution of offsets projects to 14 Malaysian companies from 1992 to 2005, my PhD thesis provided evidence that Malaysian offsets policy objectives during this phase focused on technology transfer, employment creation and skills development.

Nonetheless, policy objectives have evolved in the past ten years to incorporate new national goals, especially focused on high-income employment creation and

Table 4.2 Examples of offsets policy objectives

Country	Objectives
India	• Develop defence industry • Development of civil aerospace and internal security sectors • SME development • Electronics sector
Malaysia	• Local industrial capability and capacity development • Requiring technology transfer • Market access • Participation in global supply chain • Commercialisation • Through life support • Human capital development • Collaboration in R&D • Strategic and local content
Norway	• Competitive defence industry in line with procurement needs of armed forces • Strategic cooperation with foreign suppliers
Israel	• Long-term cooperation leading to competitive production of Israeli production • New market for high-quality goods • Regional job creation and local content • R&D grants available

Source: Extracted from CTO, http://cto-offsets.com, accessed 20 November 2017

the opportunity for Malaysian companies to enter the global supply chain through exports and R&D. These changes reflect the way in which offsets policy objectives must constantly evolve in order to cater to current national industrial and technological needs.

Table 4.2 provides a summary of countries with offsets policy objectives.

4.8   Identifying stakeholders

Stakeholders play a major role in offsets policy formulation (Cairney, 2012, pp. 63–69; Baumgartner and Jones, 2002, pp. 77–79; Sabatier, 2007; Henry, 2011). However, the complexity of offsets leads to the existence of multiple internal and external stakeholders. Although the existence and role of stakeholders is crucial throughout the offsets management cycle, it is important to anticipate who these stakeholders will be and then ensure that their requirements have been considered. These parties must be provided with the opportunity to contribute from an early stage in policy formulation or else the policy will not succeed. This is also advantageous when implementing the policy as there will already be a buy-in from all stakeholders concerned.

Table 4.3 Internal and external stakeholders of offsets

Internal stakeholder	External stakeholder
Offsets Management Office	Original equipment manufacturers (OEM) Subcontractors to OEMs
Ministry of Defence	Local prime companies in-country
Armed Forces	SMEs
Ministry of International Trade/Economy	Consultants/external academic and research organisations
Ministry of Finance	
Other governmental agencies	
Research think-tanks/universities	

Source: Author

When involving stakeholders, the following considerations are important:

1 Who are the stakeholders?
2 What is the role of each stakeholder, their influence and interest in making the offsets policy work?
3 How will you engage with stakeholders?
4 When is the appropriate time to involve stakeholders?
5 What is the mode of engagement?
6 Evaluation of stakeholder input.

Table 4.3 provides a suggested list of potential internal and external stakeholders that should be considered when formulating an offsets policy. The choice of stakeholders and their involvement will depend on the type of procurement. For example, in defence procurement, it is vital that the armed forces, the Ministry of Defence and defence industries are consulted on offsets matters. If the procurement activity involves purchase of civil aircraft then the Ministry of Transport, Ministry of Trade and Economy, the airline and its MRO services and other supporting industries should be consulted on offsets matters.

Most countries however receive limited input from external stakeholders when formulating offsets policy, with contributions coming predominantly from the offsets obligor. However, some governments do obtain external input after the execution of offsets policy and during the policy review process. This is mainly done to ascertain the difficulties that external stakeholders face when implementing offsets, which can then be used to enhance existing offsets policy. This is often done through OEM conferences and forums.[3]

In summary, the discussions on offsets strategy and policy formulation in this chapter aim to be a useful guide for governments worldwide in crafting or reviewing offsets policies. Although the preceding discussions are based in a defence environment, this model could easily be applied to a civil procurement context.

For offsets obligors, this chapter seeks to unravel the government's role in offsets strategy and policy formulation. This understanding should set the basis for offsets obligors to analyse the mechanics of offsets policy, explain why it is important to closely monitor offsets objectives and clearly appreciate offsets stakeholders and their influence in offsets policy formulation.

Notes

1 Policy transfer refers to the use of information gathered on current problems, lessons from the past and lessons from experiences of others in order to inform current policy decisions. Often the decision whether or not to transfer a policy is done after learning from the experiences of another country.
2 The frequency of policy review is subjective and is based on an individual country's requirements. However, a general guideline will be to review the policy once every five years. Any interim changes to adapt to new industrial and technological requirements should be done administratively by offsets authorities. Frequent changes to offsets policy can create confusion and the inability to measure impact.
3 For example, GOCA organised a forum in 2013 in Abu Dhabi to provide feedback to the Tawazun Economic Council (TEC) of the UAE government as to why OEMs are facing difficulty in implementing existing policy. Based on this feedback, TEC did consider some of the feedback and incorporated the suggestions into a new reviewed policy document.

5 Role of government in offsets implementation

Pre-, during and post-contract phase

5.1 Background

This chapter is dedicated to the role of government in implementing offsets. There are no fixed rules as to how governments should implement offsets. Most of what I have imparted in this chapter is a collection of my research work, discussions with offsets authorities worldwide and specific observations. The context for offsets implementation in this chapter refers to the defence sector. However, this model and application can be easily adapted to civil sectors.

Policy implementation phase is critical but one that is normally overlooked (De Leon, 1999, pp. 311–338). Through my years of involvement in both policy formulation and implementation I have realised that there is plenty of effort and attention into policy formulation but there is lack of commitment and follow-through when it comes to the actual implementation of policy (Cairney, 2009, pp. 355–377; Hill and Hupe, 2009). Often, a feedback loop to feeding issues that arise at the implementation stage back to revaluating and realignment of policy does not happen (Sabatier, 1986, pp. 21–48; Matland, 1995, pp. 145–174; Massey, 2001, pp. 134–265; Lindquist, 2004, pp. 19–40; Barrett, 2004, pp. 215–255; Hay, 2006; Sabatier, 2007).

A dedicated organisation to offsets policy implementation is vital. The offsets management authority or OMO is an important organisation that is responsible in managing offsets. An OMO is not always set up as a separate entity with an independent role in most organisations to manage offsets. However, in defence, the role of an OMO is visible (Balakrishnan, 2016b). In this chapter, first, I discuss the role and function of an OMO. I then discuss the government offsets implementation process and how OMOs handle the process.

5.2 Role of offsets management authority (OMO)

OMO has a significant role in offsets implementation. Having had the experience of heading an OMO for several years, I realise that a well-organised and staffed OMO is able to translate offsets policy and deliver effectively. There are differences as to where an OMO is located in each country. In the case of defence, OMOs typically reside at the Ministry of Defence. However, in some instances OMOs may reside at the Ministry of Science and Technology, Ministry of Innovation and Entrepreneurship, Ministry of International Trade and Industry, Ministry

Table 5.1 Offsets management authority

Country	Offsets authority
Finland	• Ministry of Employment and Economy (MEE)
Korea South	• Defence Acquisition Programme Administration (DAPA) including agency for Defence development and defence technology quality board • Policy is developed by DAPA's Acquisition Planning Bureau
India	• Authority: India Joint Secretary • DOMW reports to Department of Defence Production (DODP) • DODP responsible for formulation of offsets guidelines and all matters pertaining to post-contract management • Monitoring, administration of penalties • Credit banks and assists vendors
Indonesia	• Defence Industry Policy Committee KKIP (Komitee Kebijakan Industrie Pertahanan) • KKIP – management for IP in defence and security sector
Turkey	• Under Secretariat Industry (SSM) • Civil procurement agency under MND
South Africa	• DTI manages NIP programmes in the commercial and non-defence sector • Broad Based Black Economic Empowerment Competitive Supplier Development Programme (CSDP) • DIP managed by ARMSCOR

Source: Extracted from CTO, http://cto-offsets.com/, dated 15 November 2017

of Finance or as an independent offsets organisation directly under the head of government. Table 5.1 lists several examples of OMOs and where they reside within a government.

OMO role includes:

• development of offsets specification as part of a bid process;
• evaluate and discuss the value and impact of offsets projects suggested by offsets obligors;
• negotiate offsets projects with offsets obligors;
• develop offsets contracts and sub-tier agreements for approval;
• build relationship with offsets technology recipients;
• build relationship with prime and subcontractors to ensure project is implemented successfully;
• actively engage with stakeholders and politicians and sometimes the public in providing feedback on effectiveness of offsets and challenges;
• monitor offsets projects jointly with offsets obligors and offsets obligees;
• collate and present reports on offsets projects to stakeholders.

This list is not exhaustive and some OMOs take on broader responsibilities including developing their own capability to undertake industry audit, investment portfolio and other consultancy services.

OMOs are normally funded through government funding or treasury budgets but some OMOs are self-sustainable and are funded through offsets budgets, consultancy and investment returns gained through offsets.

What are the basic skills required of OMO officials? OMOs should plan and develop a structured training module that will provide the essential tools necessary for an offsets manager to function effectively. The suggestion I have listed here is just guidance and this list is not exhaustive. Further, it is not possible that one has all these characteristics. Often, the expertise is built through training and years of experience and exposure. The attributes and skills required of an offsets manager include technological understanding, evaluation and decision making, planning and control skills, knowledge of offsets terminologies, ability to analyse offsets proposal and business plans, contractual skills, financial awareness, negotiation skills, general knowledge of procurement, cultural awareness, leadership skills, calmness and patience. It is an advantage for an offsets manager to be multi-skilled in several subjects such as in engineering, finance, economics, technology management, business management and legal. It is also advantageous for an OMO to have offsets managers from various backgrounds who can form an effective negotiating team, as an individual may not have all the required skills to negotiate effectively. Sometimes this specialisation can be sourced externally through consultancy by OMOs on a case to case basis which could be more effective.

5.3   Offsets implementation process

The offsets implementation stage falls neatly into three stages. The first stage is the 'pre-contract phase', which consists of tendering and offsets proposal evaluation. The second stage is the 'during contract phase', which consist of contract finalisation and contact negotiation. The third stage is the 'post-contract stage', which involves offsets monitoring, reporting and performance evaluation. Figure 5.1

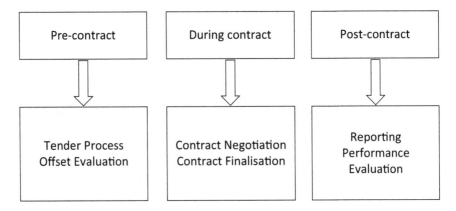

Figure 5.1 Stages of offsets implementation process
Source: Author

illustrates in detail the sequence of activities for each stage in the implementation process. An important aspect to note is that the three stages are not linear (Yang and Wang, 2006, pp. 101–109). This chapter discusses each stage of this implementation process in detail.

5.3.1 Pre-contract phase

The pre-contract phase includes activities that happen before an offsets contract or agreement is developed. The activities, which include bid process in procurement tendering and offsets evaluation, are discussed next.

Tender and bid process

A traditional offsets process[1] is where the offsets requirement is stated explicitly in tender document. In non-defence context, this could be labelled as 'local content'. There are several types of procurement tendering practices worldwide. Although it is not the intention of this book to discuss these practices in detail, a brief explanation is provided in the context of setting the background to how offsets is incorporated into this process.

There are several types of procurement tender. First, an open tender is one where the end user (armed forces) decides on acquiring a specific capability and the requirement is channelled through the appropriate organisations to acquire those capabilities. The procurement department of a ministry is normally responsible for sourcing and procuring product and services either locally or internationally. When the requirements cannot be met locally, then the said organisation has to develop and announce an international tender to source for product or services globally. As it is an open tender, any international company that is able to fulfil the criteria spelt out in the tender document can apply. After the closing date, tender document is evaluated, short listed and a tender committee evaluates and decides on the best offer based on price, quality and performance. Second, in a restricted tender, a similar sequence of activity, such as an open tender, occurs except that the bid is restricted to only a handful of bidders. Restricted tender is often applied to procurement that involves high standards of delivery, national security and to critical infrastructure projects. A third type of procurement involves direct negotiation between two parties, either between two governments or between a government and a company or two companies. Direct negotiation works in a controlled environment where decisions are made between two organisations on procurement activities, including price, quality and performance. Negotiations are restricted to pre-agreed terms and conditions. Direct tender normally involves procurement relating to defence and security and critical infrastructure projects that may involve transfer of sensitive technologies or equipment or services which otherwise may not happen under normal circumstances. Each type of tender has its pros and cons. Government procurement decisions on the type of tender to choose is mainly dependent on the product or services being purchased, political and international relations decisions, cost and technology requirements. Often it is the case that restricted and direct tenders are much preferred for international procurement especially in the defence and security sectors (Kiely, 1990, pp. 28–31; Russin, 1994, pp. 65–88; Hambleton, Weiss and University College London, 2005).

Based on the explanation earlier with regards to the different types of procurement, offsets can feature as part of tender document in a procurement bid. However, offsets will only be applicable when the procurement value hits the offsets threshold value. In some countries, several procurement activities from the same seller are combined to meet the offsets threshold value in order to request for offsets. Offsets requirement do differ based on the type of tender. In the case of open tender, offsets requirement is incorporated into main tender document. Sellers have to develop a competitive offsets proposal alongside price and technical proposal. Offsets proposal will be evaluated and graded separately from price and technical proposal. As there are many contenders with different offsets proposals in an open tender setting, the offsets offering is claimed to be more attractive and competitive in an open tender environment. This is said to allow buyers a wider choice when making decisions on which offsets package to choose. At the same time, too many proposals can also be time consuming and complicated, resulting in a buyers not getting what they want. In the case of restricted tender, similar practices apply except that the offsets proposal is evaluated against a restricted number of competitive bidders. The benefit is that the overall exercise is much more focused, less time consuming with a tighter control over the proposal submission and evaluation. However, there is less choice now with regards to what sellers are offering for offsets which can limit the options for buyers. Finally, in the case of direct tender, offsets is decided between two parties irrespective of the main contract. As the tendering is not carried out in a competitive environment there is a huge possibility that buyers will lose negotiation power and leverage to obtain the best possible offsets package. However, direct tender could also be an advantage where buyer is given the best possible offsets on the pretext of seller gaining 'selective instead of elective advantage' on procurement bid. In some other circumstances, offsets activity is conducted in complete isolation from main procurement contract. Offsets is treated independently. When a tender exercise triggers, an independent action is taken where offsets requirement is sent out separately by OMO to sellers and the offsets proposal evaluation and contract finalisation is kept completely independent of main procurement and offsets is said to have no impact on procurement decision. All the preceding types of procurement and the associated offsets execution have advantages and disadvantages. Each nation has to decide the most suitable and preferred method to incorporate offsets as part of tender process based on the context and national requirements, maturity of their procurement system and offsets management (Taylor, 2003a, pp. 985–998).

Offsets proposal evaluation

The second step in the offsets implementation process involves evaluating the offsets proposal. Normally, seller develops an offsets proposal based on the offsets policy input, discussions with the OMO and stakeholders over a period of time. When a seller is made aware that a buyer country has an offsets requirement and that the value of the sale requires offsets obligation, the seller then develops an offsets proposal which is submitted as part of the main procurement tender document.[2] In the process of developing a proposal, sellers actively engage the OMO and other stakeholders with the intention of understanding whether the proposal meets the national offsets policy requirements. Therefore, in most cases, the offsets proposal being submitted as part of the bid during tender does not come as a surprise to the procurer or the offsets authority which is evaluating the proposal (Sunders, 2009, pp. 71–80). However, the official offsets evaluation can only begin once the offsets proposal is submitted as part of tender document during a bid. The offsets component of the proposal is normally evaluated by the OMO together with relevant stakeholders and technical experts by forming a special interim offsets evaluation committee.[3] The function of this committee is to evaluate and grade each proposal and later present the results to the procurement tender committee that will determine the overall winning bidder based on price, technical specification and offsets. This is a typical offsets evaluation workflow that is applicable in an open or restricted tender process. It is however not possible to follow such a guideline in the case of direct negotiation. The interim offsets committee can still be formed to scrutinise the submitted offsets proposal but the leverage over to what extend the proposal can be changed to meet policy requirement is questionable.[4]

I used to teach offsets to students on the Advanced Management Programme organised by the Offsets and Countertrade Academy at the ESSEC Business School. One of the topics often discussed is 'what is a winning offsets proposal'. How do offsets authorities evaluate an offsets proposal and what are the measures used in deciding a winning bid. Based on feedback from governments who evaluate proposals, Table 5.2 outlines a list as to determinants to a winning offsets proposal (Balakrishnan, 2016b, lecture presentation).

Table 5.2 Determinants to a winning offsets proposal

No.	*Determinants to a winning offsets proposal*
1	Are the projects listed in the proposal aligned to offsets objectives highlighted in the offsets policy?
2	Is the offsets proposal aligned to the overall country strategy and vision, including economic, industrial and technological need?
3	Does the proposal include a detailed business plan?
4	Does the proposal itemise projects, details, value of each project, description of project, suggested technology recipient, justification for selection (industry audit results if a company has been down selected), track record, milestone, multipliers, proof of additionality and causality where applicable?
5	Sustainability of the project
6	What are the deliverables? The expected output, outcome and impact to recipient and to the larger community

(Continued)

Table 5.2 (Continued)

No.	Determinants to a winning offsets proposal
7	Commercial viability of projects such as profit, buy-back arrangements, equity ownership in joint ventures, engagement into international supply chain, marketing and export assistance into new markets
8	Has risk to suggested offsets project been factored in or considered? Is there an additional cost or issues to be considered in implementing the suggested offsets projects?
9	Element of capacity and capability building through technology transfer (local content, know-how, training, education leading to skills enhancement, salary increment, and better job prospects that has been highlighted)

Source: Author

5.3.2 During contract finalisation phase

The second phase of offsets implementation is the during contract finalisation phase. This is the phase where the details of offsets project, multipliers, offsets project value, type of technology, offsets beneficiaries and other critical factors in programme execution are determined. This phase includes offsets contract negotiation and contract finalisation. Both of these activities are discussed in the following sections.

Offsets contract negotiation

There are plenty of academic writings, journal papers and business magazines available on the art of negotiation (Thompson, 2012; Graham and Lam, 2003; Cavusgil, Ghauri, and Agarwal, 2002). It is not my intention in this book to discuss the basics of negotiation or how to negotiate. My aim is to highlight the different features and complexity of negotiation in an offsets environment. Negotiation is one of the most critical components of offsets implementation. Offsets managers require a set of specific skills to be able to negotiate effectively (Alfred and Cungu, 2008, pp. 112–125. This chapter is focused on the importance of negotiation in the context of offsets practice. In this chapter, I discuss the three stages of offsets negotiation and the skills required of an offsets manager in offsets negotiation. Although I have approached the topic of negotiation from a government angle, this discussion is applicable to anyone including companies that are negotiating offsets.

There are several features that must be noted in offsets negotiation. First, offsets takes place as a consequence of main procurement of product or services, therefore offsets negotiation often takes place in parallel with main procurement negotiation. Often, this can lead to issues such as pressure to conclude offsets negotiation within the timeframe in line with the main contact negotiation although the offsets contract has not been finalised. This is an important factor to consider as often offsets managers can agree to a lesser quality proposal due to time constraint.[5]

Second, offsets negotiations normally involve multiple stakeholders (Taylor and Balloch, 2005; Maude, 2014, pp. 167–175). These would include technology recipients, procurement agency, other governmental organisation that may have an interest in the programme, the user group (specific to whom the equipment or services are being procured for), research or technology assessment team, local contractors and sellers and their team. Thus offsets negotiation becomes much more complex as feedback from multiple stakeholders must be considered. Third, due to various stakeholders, offsets negotiations involve multiparty negotiation involving smaller groups. The benefits of a multiparty negotiation would be that the decisions made could be more accurate judgement and information could be more readily available. However, social interaction could become complex and information-demand processing increases exponentially. Also, there could arise communication breakdown ending in formation of smaller groups for strategic purposes. Multiparty negotiations can also take a long time and is tedious (Weiss, 1994, pp. 35–39; Maude, 2014, pp. 167–175; Karass, 1996). In such instances involving multiparty negotiations which are usually the norm for offsets, it is important to know who will be attending the meeting and their interest in the project, create a matrix to manage information and to propose suggestions and brainstorm extensively before and during negotiation. Also try and reach a point of agreement even if it is only at the preliminary stage of the process. Fourth, offsets negotiation involves extensive offsets technical terminologies. Therefore, both buyers and sellers should be exposed to offsets terminologies for ease of use during offsets negotiations. Fifth, there are chances for offsets negotiation to continue even when the main contract has been concluded. There are instances where offsets negotiations were extended beyond five years from the signing of the main contract.

The next important aspect involves the phases of offsets negotiation. For the purpose of discussion in this book, I have divided offsets negotiation into three phases. Figure 5.2 illustrates the three phases of offsets negotiation – phase one

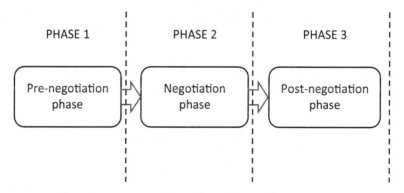

Figure 5.2 Offsets negotiation process
Source: Author

which is the pre-negotiation phase, phase two which is the negotiation phase and phase three which is the post-negotiation phase.

During the negotiation phase, offsets managers should set clear objectives and targets as to their intended outcomes. It is vital to spend some time preparing for the negotiation; to study the offsets rules and know one's opponent and the various stakeholders. At this stage of negotiation, it is also important to prioritise issues and interests. At this stage, for OMO, it is important to clearly understand what is being proposed. For sellers, during the negotiation it is important to obtain buy-in from offsets authorities as to the projects being proposed and to be able to confidently defend the suggested projects.

During phase two of the actual offsets negotiation, it is about building relationship, getting to know one's opponent better and learning to build trust. At this stage of negotiation both buyers and sellers should discuss details of the negotiation process, such as who will chair the meeting for both sides, setting the agenda, who are the others attending the meeting, frequency of the meeting, duration of each meeting, location of the meeting, who will pay for the cost if any incurred, language being used and if any interpretors are being used during negotiations (duration) (Graham and Lam, 2003, pp. 44–49). Using an interpretor could have implications if the translations are not acurate. Also, if the meeting is held in an overseas location not condusive to one of the parties this could also have implications on the outcome (Alfred and Cungu, 2008, pp. 108–112). Sometimes, food and beverages served during negotiations may also have to be considered in case these are not suitable to the negotiators and may cause illness or other side effects during negotions which may impact on negotiation outcome (Alfred and Cungu, 2008, pp. 108–112). Also, bring along your subject matter experts. You will need them to provide you with technical details. You need not rush through facts and details to conclude the negotiation. Take frequent breaks if needed to discuss and evaluate proposals made. Break the negotiation if there is a stalemate and resume the next day or once you are confident that there is sufficient information to be able to continue with the negotiation. It is not reasonable to take too much time and to drag out negotiations, as this involves costs to both parties especially if it involves overseas travel. The longer the negotiation takes, the more the cost will increase. Therefore, it is important to negotiate within a reasonable time and be prepared (Karass, 1996, pp. 257–265).[6]

Finally, during the offsets post-negotiation phase, parties entering into negotiation should aim to end on a positive note. At the post offsets negotiation relationship and trust amongst the parties is crucial. The post-negotiation phase denotes a collaborative approach for ongoing relationship building in moving to the next stage where offsets programme implementation be carried out successfully as it involves the commitment of buyers, sellers and the rest of the stakleholders who have an interest in the offsets projects.

What does it take for successful offsets negotiations? It is hard to address this question but there are general rules to successful negotiation that can be extended to offsets practice. A successful offsets negotiation can be defined by one where both sellers and buyers end the negotiation with a 'win–win' feeling where they have both obtained what they wanted (Karass, 1996, pp. 405–411; Maude, 2014, pp. 420–428). A successful offsets negotiation should lead to understanding and respecting the different objectives, business goals and cultural differences between the sellers and buyers. This feeling of mutual cooperation is crucial in offsets negotiation to create a sustainable offsets programme. There should exist a feeling of trust and lasting relationship between sellers and buyers in managing offsets. This is because the offsets contract finalisation is only the beginning of an offsets programme delivery and sellers and buyers have to continue to work together for many years to come based on the project timeline. Any ill feeling left from the offsets negotiation will not be healthy for the relationship moving forward (Thompson, 2012, pp. 122–136).

Offsets contract finalisation

Once an offsets proposal has been accepted and projects agreed, the actual execution of the programme in terms of the type of offsets contract depends on buyer government. Generally the practice varies within countries as to the type of contract they choose to have. Table 5.3 explains a few choices of countries and their preference for offsets contracts.

Figure 5.2 explains that an offsets agreement can take a few forms. First, an offsets agreement can form part of a main procurement contract. A clause is inserted within the main contract implying offsets and annexures to explain details of the project. The second type of offsets contract is where offsets agreement becomes a separate contract and is independent of the main procurement contract. In such instances, the offsets agreement will incorporate a separate penalty clause and performance bond. In some cases, the main offsets agreement will be substantiated with tier two agreements between sellers and individual offsets obligees. The third type of offsets contract is when offsets agreement is accepted as a Memorandum of Understanding (MOU) and may not be legally binding. However, the MOU will have details as to how to execute the programme, governance and project details. The MOU may not include penalty. The fourth type of offsets contract is one where the offsets agreement is a volunteer agreement, not legally binding, and

Table 5.3 Examples of types of indicators to measure offsets outcome

Local content value (material, man hours, logistics)	Number of jobs created in targeted sectors
Small business participation (support to SMEs)	Number of people trained in specific targeted sectors or new/emerging technologies
Proof of upskilling and reskilling of workers for targeted economic sectors	Investments into R&D (applied research) leading to commercialisation
Volume of FDI inflow into targeted sectors	Value of export
Value of buy-back	Value of business in new market
Licensing agreements	Patents

the onus of implementing the programme resides with sellers. There is no penalty imposed on the contractor for non-compliance to the offsets policy.

Each type of offsets agreement has advantages and disadvantages. A more legalistic offsets agreement could be harder to execute. Also, two separate penalty clauses, one for offsets and the other for main procurement contract could increase the administrative cost for offsets obligors which could eventually lead to an increase in the overall contract cost. A binding and complex offsets contract may also seem punitive and not favourable to sellers during implementation of the contract. Some countries prefer to judge sellers' performance based on track record as opposed to imposing a harsh penalty. The basis of track record and removing penalty is only applicable in circumstances where sellers are well established and have a strong presence in-country. On the other hand, the risk to buyers is that a non-binding contract could mean that sellers could evade their offsets obligation. The buyer government will not be able to to recover loses if the offsets projects are not implemented as promised. It is even more risky for one-off offsets contracts where sellers know that they may not end a future sale. Most often sellers and buyers can choose to have a combination of contractual methods and progress the contracts as their relationship and trust matures. This may be a better option than a 'one size fits all' type of contract for every country. The policy guidance document should be able to provide this flexibility in order to make offsets management more cost effective (Cohen and Zysman, 1986).

A basic offsets agreement will include:

- background referring to the obligation under the main procurement contract that requires offsets
- background to offsets agreement
- objectives of the offsets programme
- threshold value
- brief description of the programme and projects (details to be described in the annexure)
- value of the project/amount of offsets obligation
- composition of direct and indirect offsets
- eligible parties
- eligible transactions
- effective date
- termination date
- governance
- penalty and performance bond/guarantee
- force majeure
- performance milestone
- offsets implementation schedule
- dispute resolution clause
- reporting requirements
- modification to contract
- confidentiality

- anti-bribery and corruption clause
- applicable law
- any other offsets clauses.

5.3.3   Offsets post-contract phase

The offsets post-contract phase is equally as important as the offsets pre- and during contract phases. Most often, once the offsets agreement has been finalised and signed, the execution of the contract is then left to the devices of the same team or another team of offsets managers.[7] The post-contract phase is equally challenging when projects are being executed. During the post-contract phase, this is also the stage where the offsets team is able to witness the project coming to fruition and the challenges that come with it. During this phase it involves execution, monitoring, reporting and managing performance.

Offsets contract execution and monitoring

During the offsets contract execution and monitoring stage, both sellers and buyers are expected to work closely in delivering the project. A dedicated project team composed of members from offsets obligors and obligees is assembled to monitor progress of various projects within the offsets programme. Like any other project management delivery, the offsets projects should be delivered on time, there should be sufficient resources and they should be appropriately allocated. The dedicated offsets project team should be involved in on-site project visits to view project progress and ensure an up-to-date progress report is submitted periodically as outlined in the contract.

Offsets programme reporting and performance evaluation

An offsets report is usually prepared by sellers in line with the timeline mentioned in the implementation schedule. How frequently should such a report be prepared? The offsets report is churned out more frequently during early stages of contract implementation and this task reduces over time. The offsets report should include progress of individual projects according to milestone, any shortfalls and reasons, feedback from technology recipients along with credits being claimed. Supporting documents or other evidences should also be submitted along with the offsets report. Besides, the progress report should also highlight any other issues or challenges that may hinder the project from being completed on time. The report is then submitted to OMO for approval and for credit claims. OMO should determine and be transparent in terms of the timeline for offsets credit approval. In some cases, when OMO have queries related to the report, sellers are invited for a face to face discussion on how to resolve the issues to ensure successful completion of the offsets project. Most offsets authorities have automated systems in place such as Enterprise Resource Planning (ERP) and web-based systems which manages offsets monitoring and reporting processes.[8]

Finally, the aspect of offsets performance evaluation is becoming increasingly important to justify offsets activity. OMO have the responsibility for evaluating the impact of offsets projects; measure the overall success of offsets programmes and individual offsets projects based on offsets policy objectives.[9] What indicators are used to measure offsets success? This question was seriously discussed at the offsets workshop organised by IRB Canada in 2012. During the workshop, a comprehensive list was later put together which captured most of the indicators that could be used to measure the success of an offsets programme (Balakrishnan, 2012, Conference presentation Ottawa). Table 5.3 explains the different types of indicators used to measure offsets. This included local content value, technological level, research and development success where either a product or process has been developed from the R&D, number of jobs created from offsets projects, salary and type of jobs created, export value due to offsets, buy-back value due to offsets, FDI in-flow value due to offsets, SME involvement and how the project had benefited the company like profits, jobs created, value-creation, part of international supply chain, transfer of know-how in a university or research think-tank and value of business in a new market (Balakrishnan, 2012, conference presentation Ottawa).

5.4   Common issues in offsets implementation

5.4.1   *Tension in buyer–supplier relationship*

One of the most common issues during implementation is the tension in the relationship that arises between offsets obligor and obligee. This tension escalates during offsets negotiation when both parties are manoeuvring to maximise each other's offsets value. Sellers aim is to reduce cost and aim for the highest possible credits and multipliers for each offsets project. Further, sellers have to show evidence to claim technology transfer value, project credit value and multipliers. On the other hand, buyers have an interest in maximising economic and industrial outcome for each offsets project through award of minimal offsets credit and multipliers. The diverging interest between offsets obligors and obligee often results in increased tension during negotiation.

5.4.2   *Managing multiple stakeholders*

I discussed the role of stakeholders in Chapter 4 and mentioned the complex nature of offsets as it involves multiple stakeholders. During implementation, it is challenging to manage stakeholders as each one of them differs in their perspectives to their expectation on the outcome of offsets projects. OMO and sellers have the responsibility of managing these stakeholders who could range from offsets technology recipients, subcontractors, other governmental organisations, user community and so on. For example, during implementation, the seller who is the prime contractor may not receive adequate support from the subcontractor in transferring technology to an offsets obligee (technology recipient), a problem which may not have been anticipated by the seller earlier.

5.4.3 Cultural issues

As offsets is practised in an international trade environment within international business, offsets practice will involve overseas and domestic stakeholders. In such an instance, culture becomes of central importance in offsets management. Those handling offsets should be exposed to intercultural issues. Sellers and buyers should understand and appreciate each other's different cultural values, attitudes and experiences. During negotiation for example, culture determines our expectations. For example, dividing the pie may depend on the balance between self-interest of winner take it all (individualistic) and collective culture (Cohen, 1999, pp. 9–15; Baesu, Bejinaru and Iordache, 2015, pp. 148–156). At times, ethnocentrism can be an issue in negotiation, where one group believes that they are more superior in their value and behaviour than another. It is vital to understand that different cultures react differently to situations. For example, in some cultures, people are very loud and expressive. This behaviour in a meeting can be misunderstood as either being rude or argumentative when that is not the real intention.

Offsets implementation is as equally important as policy formulation though this is an area that is often neglected in offsets management. The role of an OMO is critical in ensuring effective implementation of offsets through the various stages of contract development and finalisation. This has to be substantiated with suitable offsets managers who have the capability and knowledge in offsets management to undertake offsets implementation activity. Offsets implementation is not free of challenges. The list is not exhaustive, but the complex nature of offsets management with multiple stakeholders, tension in buyer–supplier relationship and cultural differences form several of these challenges.

Notes

1 A traditional bid process is referred to as one where offsets is considered part of procurement and the tender would incorporate an offsets component. It does not matter if the offsets proposal is not submitted together with the main procurement proposal during the bid as long as there is a requirement for offsets that has been clearly spelt out in the procurement tender document. In some instances, the offsets requirement is not mentioned anywhere in the tender document or it is labelled as a 'local content' requirement.
2 The seller either sets up an internal team within the company, engages experts to assist in developing an offsets proposal or outsources offsets proposal development to a third party consultant who is an expert in delivering offsets projects.
3 The offsets evaluation committee can consist of members that are identified and appointed by the offsets authority. Numbers do not matter as long as the members have the expertise and sound knowledge to the projects being evaluated. Further, the members should not have direct interest in any of the offsets project being suggested.
4 My own experience has shown that when it is a direct negotiation between the government and seller without competition, it is much harder for the buyer country to obtain the best offsets programme. This is mostly the case as the buyer loses the leverage over procurement decision making.
5 This is often the case when a procurement contract is ready and the pressure is mounting on the offsets manager to conclude the offsets contract in order for both agreements to

be signed in parallel. This could be detrimental to the offsets contract. There have been various occasions during my offsets negotiations where I am under pressure to conclude the negotiation and finalise the contract due to pressure from procurement. This had led to appeal for offsets contract to be signed at a later stage and not in parallel with the main procurement contract thus giving offsets managers sufficient time to negotiate offsets contract.

6 I have had several awkward situations during offsets negotiation. Without mentioning any specific names of countries or sellers, there was once a company that brought in interpreters for the negotiation. The interpreter did not have much understanding on offsets matters and thus the whole negotiation fell apart. In another situation, the negotiation was held in the seller country. My team consisted of three people and the seller's team consisted of 20 people. This was very intimidating and put me and my team in an awkward position as the negotiation team was unbalanced.

7 My experience in the past has been that some companies prefer to use the same offsets team for offsets contract negotiation phase and offsets delivery phase and others like to keep the two teams separate. There are pros and cons to both approaches but the bottom line is that there must be continuity in the offsets management and the spirit behind the contract must be crystal clear for an effective offsets programme delivery.

8 When I was involved in offsets implementation in 2002, there was hardly any systematic reporting system for offsets. Offsets obligors usually submit a simple report which is normally taken at face value. In fact, even in the year 2008, I was still struggling to create an online system within the department to monitor offsets projects. Most of the exercise was done manually, which made it hard to obtain a comprehensive data on offsets.

9 In 2009, I was invited to present at a workshop conducted by the Canadian government, specifically the Canadian Regional Benefits Authority (IRB). The objective of the workshop was to gather all government offsets authorities to discuss how to measure offsets success. At the workshop the conclusion that we came to was that the success has to be measured based on the objectives set in the policies.

6 Sellers' offsets strategy and implementation

6.1 Background

Sellers have a major role in ensuring successful offsets programme delivery. This chapter is solely dedicated towards the role of a seller in managing offsets. My knowledge in writing this chapter on sellers' perspective and how they manage offsets comes from my first-hand experience of having closely worked with OEMs through training and consultancy sessions.[1] This knowledge was further enhanced through my association with Roger Bulgin of Offsets 2000, Greg Glugston (former Raytheon), Michael Thome (Rockwell Collins) and Dov Hyman who were all part of the GOCA offsets training team. They were all instrumental in coaching me as to how OEMs develop and implement offsets. Further, the section on factors that influence sellers' successful offsets strategy in this chapter is written based on work that I did with Christian Sylvian (past Chairman and President of ECCO). Christian invited me to present a paper on factors that influence a contractor's offsets strategy. I then contacted 15 OEMs who were members of ECCO in a survey questionnaire, which then helped me with the finding. From this exercise, I understood that strategy is an important aspect of a company and in this case, all these companies have taken offsets seriously (Porter, 2004).

In this booksellers refer to large corporations with offsets obligations. These sellers have similar features where they are normally the primary contracting party; they act as manufacturers of large platforms or systems integrator; they have responsibility for overall project management and delivery of complete systems to customers and they are also legally responsible for overall contract delivery and associated risks. This chapter covers the sellers' view to offsets, company offsets management cycle, factors that influence sellers' offsets strategy and issues for sellers in delivering an offsets programme.

6.2 Sellers' perception of offsets

Fundamentally, it is argued that sellers are not in favour of offsets. It is claimed that sellers view offsets as a burden, troublesome and to be avoided if possible. However, considering that offsets has become a core part of competition in the international defence trade, sellers tend to strike a balance between trying to 'minimise the adverse effects of offsets' in exports while ensuring that the ability of their firms to compete for military export sales is not undermined. In the US for example, the law might be said to take a see-no-evil-hear-no-evil policy and leaves it to the private sector to work out any offsets arrangements without government support or hindrance. Yet, as offsets is an area so important to most seller governments, it is impossible to take a completely hands-off approach.[2] Sellers tend to have their views to offsets (Advanced Electronic Company, 2012).

First, to sellers, offsets is contractual obligation that is imposed on them as part of an international sale. Sellers have to perform offsets as stipulated in procurement guidelines and as part of the bid process. Sellers view offsets as mandatory in accordance with the law and as something that must be carried out in order to be able to do business in a country. Second, most sellers also see offsets as a differentiator that could deliver competitive advantage to them. Most companies strive to offer excellent products and services at the most competitive price. However, sellers realise that when quality and price of products and services offered is par then additional benefits in the form of offsets can become the deciding factor in winning a sale (Vitasek, Manrodt and Kling, 2012; Kirchwehm, 2014, p. 20).[3] Third, some sellers view offsets as a business opportunity to alternative sourcing for efficient and cost-effective supply chain base. Sellers use offsets as a catalyst to realign the company supply chain and as a source for suppliers that are cost effective and efficient (Aillianos, 2015, pp. 173–179). In the process, sellers could end up moving some of their manufacturing or other activities to buyer countries where resources are abundant. At the same time, incorporating buyer nation supply chain also provides sellers with the opportunity to claim long-term partnership and growth as part of their business model[4] (Root, Contractor and Lorange, 1988; Hall and Markowski, 1994, p. 33; Kremer and Sain, 2012, p. 62; Kimla, 2013). Fourth, offsets is also viewed by sellers as a 'cost centre' which means adding costs to the product or services being rendered as part of procurement. This cost is difficult to justify. The costs are unpredictable and often vary for each programme in every country on a case-by-case basis. The issue of who takes on the offsets costs, how much and how it is administrated is highly debatable. Hence, sellers are tempted to develop offsets projects that can minimise costs and at the same time bring in profit. Often, activities such as joint ventures and subcontracting are lucrative offsets business that can deliver a 'win–win' solution to both buyers and sellers. Fifth, sellers view offsets activities as risk. The risks are often associated to offsets projects, technology recipients and their absorptive capacity and capability to take on highly sophisticated or technical projects, financial risks, government policies, etc. Sellers also find it difficult to operate in highly regulated market environments where buyers and their governments solely dictate projects, type of technology being transferred and technology recipients. I discuss offsets risks in detail in Chapter 9.

6.3   Essential features of offsets in a company

6.3.1   *Importance to function of offsets*

The role and function of offsets is still new to many companies. Although offsets work is carried out by many companies but the function itself is not recognised as one that warrants much attention or resources within the organisation. . Even companies with huge overseas offsets obligations do not sometimes have a dedicated department with trained staff to work on offsets projects. Offsets is often viewed by these companies as an 'after thought' and less important. In most cases, offsets function will be lumped into sales or business development. Smaller companies prefer to outsource offsets function to third party contractors or consultants as this is felt to be more cost effective as opposed to developing their in-house capability in offsets management. However, in recent years the function of offsets has become increasingly important to companies. Many companies have taken the effort to set up offsets divisions within their strategy, corporate or business units. Offsets is given much more emphasis, as these companies realise the importance of a good offsets package in winning a contract. Having been involved in offsets management for many years, I note the increasing number of company personnel being trained on offsets.

6.3.2   *Where does offsets reside in a company?*

There are many considerations as to where offsets function should reside within a company. Each company may take a different approach to offsets function based on the company's overall strategy, importance given to offsets activities, availability of resources to manage offsets and allocation of funding for offsets. Most importantly, it also depends on the buy-in to offsets from the various internal stakeholders in the company.

There are several options to where offsets may reside in a company. Offsets could be centralised into a company's corporate department and viewed as part of corporate diplomacy. The benefit of this strategy is that offsets is then recognised as a corporate activity, will be given further promotion during marketing campaigns. In this case, offsets will receive recognition and visibility within the company as the directive to undertake offsets is being delivered through the company chair and CEO. This directly helps sanction funding for offsets activities with greater ease. However, this could also mean that the project management office (PMO) then views offsets as a separate activity and not as part of the project management team.

The second option is to decentralise offsets activity and to incorporate offsets into every PMO as and when offsets requirements exists. This means a new budget is allocated for every offsets programme under individual PMO. The benefit of this option is that then the offsets activity falls directly under the responsibility of a PMO concerned. As the PMO has more knowledge and understanding of the overall contract and the in-country requirement, the PMO will take extra interest in offsets to ensure that the overall project, including offsets, is successfully delivered. However, the cost of this option is that offsets is then not part of the company's vision and strategy. The role of offsets is subsumed within PMO duties and may even risk the danger of being eliminated or over looked.

Figure 6.1 Offsets interface in companies
Source: Author

The third option is to include offsets as part of business development, contracts or supply chain activity. Offsets as part of business development (BD) would mean offsets gains momentum and visibility from the initial marketing and BD campaigns. If offsets resides within contracts, offsets will be seen as a risk and cost to the sales activity. Sometimes, contracts department may suggest that offsets activity be outsourced to a third party consultant to manage the risk. Finally if offsets resides within the department for supply chain and procurement, offsets activities may focus on production type of activities thus neglecting other projects that could be incorporated as part of offsets.

Figure 6.1 illustrates the different departments with which offsets managers have to deal with. This includes marketing, business development, corporate and communication, procurement and supply chain, legal, finance and human resources.

6.3.3   *What are the essential traits of an offsets manager?*

An individual is required to have two levels of skills when dealing with offsets – one, basic traits, and the second, specialised knowledge. Basic traits include negotiation skills, interpersonal skills, analytical and critical thinking skills, communication skills as well as an understanding of legal and finance.

At a more advanced level, an offsets manager is required to acquire the following knowledge to be able to handle offsets projects:

- knowledge of host country and industry such as economic, industrial and offsets policy;
- understanding of the geopolitics, international relations and strategic business issues in host countries;
- how to develop a good relationship with embassies, consulates and ministries of economy, industry and defence as well as trade unions in host countries;
- how to develop relationship with industry and trade associations in customer country and in-country supply chain including SMEs;
- identify internal and external stakeholders;
- work with PMOs in scoping and putting an offsets programme together;
- evaluate the risks involved in managing offsets;
- understand customer needs and interest;
- implement the offsets projects with the offsets recipients and authorities;
- prepare periodical reports and submit for credit clearance;
- ensure compliance with company's ethical code of conduct.

In the next section of this chapter, I explain in detail the sellers' offsets management cycle. This is just a guideline, and the offsets activities do vary for each company.

6.4 Sellers' offsets management life cycle

Companies may differ in how they manage offsets projects. Figure 6.2 is an illustration of how offsets is intertwined into a company's sales life cycle. As soon as a company decides to enter into an international sales competition, the PMO set

Figure 6.2 Sellers' international sales activities
Source: Author

What is the role of a prime contractor?

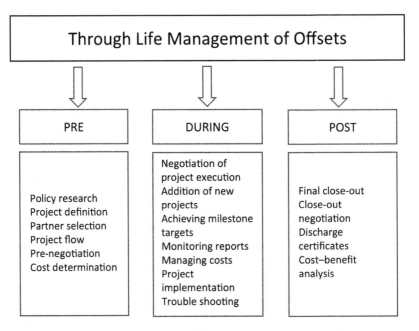

Through Life Management of Offsets

PRE	DURING	POST
Policy research Project definition Partner selection Project flow Pre-negotiation Cost determination	Negotiation of project execution Addition of new projects Achieving milestone targets Monitoring reports Managing costs Project implementation Trouble shooting	Final close-out Close-out negotiation Discharge certificates Cost–benefit analysis

Figure 6.3 Company offsets management life cycle
Source: Author

up for this purpose has to be aware of offsets requirements and capture offsets as part of the overall international sales strategy. If the sales triggers offsets, then the offsets proposal is developed at the marketing and bid phase, finalised at the contract phase and offsets obligation is discharged at the delivery phase.

PMOs usually manage offsets activities in three different stages (Figure 6.3). Stage one is during the pre-contract phase that involves marketing and bidding activities. At this stage, the PMO introduces offsets function to the bid team and a dedicated offsets manager is appointed. During this phase, the PMO and the offsets manager should consider offsets budget and cost of delivering the overall offsets project, which is then fed back into the sales bid. It is also vital to consider risk and mitigation strategies at this stage. At this stage, it is also the responsibility of the offsets manager and his team to consider and recommend offsets strategy and approach together with possible projects (Mintzerg, Quinn and Ghoshal, 1998; Johnson and Scholes, 1999). Offsets managers also discuss their proposal to gauge the appetite of various internal and external stakeholders to proposed projects in order to align the proposal with national requirements. This process is vital to obtain a buy-in for the proposed offsets programme as part of sales. An OEM that is able to undertake this exercise objectively without external interference and influence is then able to deliver expected outcomes to offsets technology recipients and the buyer nation. The offsets manager and the PMO will also have to engage with the company's internal purchasing and supply chain, legal, engineering and quality assurance team. Besides, the offsets manager is to conduct extensive due diligence to check the reputation of local companies where the technology is being transferred, Often the offsets manager and his team will also assist in conducting quality assurance and ethical compliance with companies with which they will be selecting as offsets partners. At this stage, it is important to have calculated the cost of executing each offsets project and to view whether the allocated budget is sufficient for the programme to be conducted successfully. There may be a need to review the cost at this stage and either scale back on the projects or bid for additional budget.

Stage two is the contract and delivery phase. Upon winning the bid, the offsets manager and his team as part of the PMO will be involved in drawing up the offsets contract and the detailed individual offsets projects. The draft contract and projects will be discussed and negotiated at various levels and for a period of time until all parties to the contract including the offsets technology recipients are satisfied with the draft contract and project details. The documents are then vetted by the legal team of both the sellers and buyers before the contract is finally signed for execution. The PMO and offsets manager will at the same time set up an offsets delivery team. This team could be the same team that was involved at stage one or could be a completely new team that is more specialised in the technical aspect and supply chain. This may be the case if the projects have a critical mass of technology transfer actvities. The PMO will also develop and focus on reporting structure and discuss with OMOs on how and when the reports should be submitted for credit claims. These details are often spelt out in the offsets contract but in cases where there are no offsets contracts then it is vital to discuss and agree on a reporting structure.

Finally, it is the post-contract phase that involves offsets reporting and closure. At this stage the offsets team, through the PMO, will prepare and submit a complete final report to OMOs on the performance of the contract, outcomes and delivery. This is also necessary to indemnify the bank guanrantee and obtain discharge certificate if the programme has been completed successfully. In some cases, an offsets conference is held by the PMO and OMO with stakeholders to detail out the outcome and impact of the offsets programme.

6.5   Five forces that influences sellers' successful offsets strategy and delivery

What influences a seller in delivering a successful offsets programme? Figure 6.4 explains the five forces that could assist a seller in managing an offsets programme effectively. The model was modified from Porter's five forces model where the

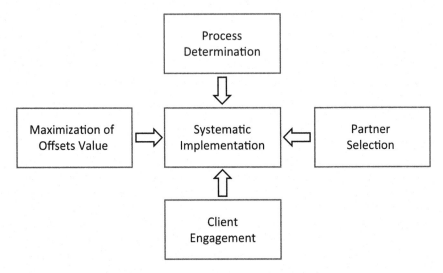

Figure 6.4 Five forces that influences successful offsets delivery
Source: author

determinants were derived from a semi-structured interview that was conducted with 15 companies across Europe and the USA. The finding from this interview was then corroborated, analysed and presented at the ECCO offsets conference in Paris (Balakrishnan, 2015a, ECCO Conference). Figure 6.4 explains the five determinants for successful offsets project delivery being project determination, maximisation of offsets value, partner selection, client engagement and systematic implementation. I shall explain each determination in detail in the following section.

6.5.1   *Project determination*

The first determinant for successful offsets delivery involves project determination. Offsets managers should develop a systematic plan on defining the scope and breathe of the project. During the planning stage, it is important for the offsets team to study and understand buyers' offsets policy and other related policies that influence the economic, industrial and technological environment of buyer nations. Project determination should also involve an estimated cost determination for the overall offsets programme and for individual projects. At the project determination stage, the offsets team should also identify and influence stakeholders on the offsets proposal. And take measures to analyse in-country industry strength, the strength of the supply chain base and technological absorptive capacity of buyer nations' industries (Bower and Doz, 1979, pp. 152–166; Edwards, 1977, pp. 13–27; Eisenhardt and Sull, 2001, pp. 107–116; Freeman, 1984).

6.5.2 Partner selection

The next important factor for successful offsets delivery involves partner selection. The offsets team should consider suitability of partners being selected to undertake any form of industrial collaborative activity such as joint venture, licenced or co-production. The selected partners should have complementarity and compatibility of goals (Fasel, 2000). Another factor to consider is the financial capacity of the partner. It is also important to know the reputation of the partner and whether the company has had a good record of accomplishment in good performance and fulfilling contractual obligations (Bishop, 1996, pp. 171–222). Finally, the organisational culture of the partner company is important and the offsets team should ensure that the culture is compatible and one that encourages long-term partnership and trustworthiness (Yang and Lee, 2002, pp. 98–109; Tsang, 1994, pp. 4–21; Tatoglu and Glaister, 1998, pp. 635–656; Hamel and Prahalad, 1989, pp. 63–76).

6.5.3 Maximisation of offsets value

The next important success factor for offsets delivery involves maximisation of offsets value. This requires the offsets team to acquire good negotiation skills and tactics, the expertise to use the offsets technical tools to leverage reasonable benefits. The offsets team should have sufficient skills in developing and justifying technology transfer value to OMOs. In order to claim banking of credits or pre offsets, proposed projects should be convincing and transparent to OMOs. Most sellers' mention that offsets projects which are awarded reasonably good offsets credit and value are often executed much more efficiently.[5]

6.5.4 Systematic implementation

The fourth aspect to successful offsets delivery involves systematic offsets programme implementation. The seller has to ensure that there is continuity in the project team and in executing offsets programme during pre- and post-contract. Often there is lack of enthusiasm after a contract is signed and if a new offsets manager is assigned to undertake the role of delivering offsets there is the danger of not understanding the spirit of the contract and why certain decisions were made. Other important factors in delivery include preparing a good offsets report that covers project performance, issues, challenges and outcome. This would also include periodical meetings to discuss project outcome and preparation of impact analysis report.

6.5.5 Client engagement

Finally, the fifth factor in successful offsets delivery involves client engagement. The first task is to recognise and differentiate between internal and external clients. Then to closely analyse each client's position and perspective to the project concerned. The process of understanding clients results in relationship building which contributes to delivering offsets projects to the specific needs of the clients (Canada Department of Business and Industry, 2013). For example, in defence procurement, speaking to the user community (armed forces) is important to understand the type of training and technical expertise that should be offered as part of offsets which is then not covered in the main contract to ensure that sufficient maintenance of the equipment can be undertaken in-country. Considering that the preceding five factors are important for sellers to deliver a successful offsets programme, the sellers do face several challenges when managing offsets.

6.6   Issues to consider for sellers when managing offsets

We need to appreciate the potential challenges faced by sellers when managing offsets, though I cover most of these issues in detail in Chapter 9 when I discuss offsets risks. Some of the most common challenges include transferring technology through offsets programme as requested by buyers. Technology is the most controversial subject in offsets and projects that involve technology can be the most difficult to fulfil. Sellers interest is in sales but when buyers make it a condition that technology must be shared as part of the sale this request than becomes complex. Sellers have to then garner for internal shareholder approval, apply for export licence and obtain government approval to export technology. Nevertheless, sellers are adopting export strategies that could lead to a 'win-win' approach to technology transfer for them and buyers as part of sustainable business model. I discuss technology transfer issues and challenges in detail in Chapter 7.

Next, sellers also face immense challenges in partner selection. As the defence industry market is one that is either a monopoly or oligopoly, sellers have limited choice as to whom they can work with in-country. This often can mean that they may end up working with a partner that is not compatible or even not interested in the partnership. Further, sellers face the challenge of being directed to specific partners in-country that do not have the right level of capability or technological absorptive capacity. Sellers then have to invest a considerable amount of time and resources to bring the partner to a level where they can work with them. Often, there is a risk that partner selection is based on merits when determining an offsets project recipient.

The other challenges include dealing with OMOs and bureaucratic channels that can be problematic. This is difficult in an environment where offsets processes and approvals are less transparent. Sometimes sellers are unsure as to the internal OMO approval processes such as how and who makes the decisions and approval timeline. Such inefficiency may cause delay to the overall offsets programme and result in unexpected cost escalation.

Finally, sellers could also face challenges when implementing offsets projects. This includes not having sufficient cooperation from offsets technology recipients, being unsure of credit claim processes, lack of access to OMOs to discuss issues that arise when implementing projects, constant moving of the yardstick by OMOs in terms of delivery and difficulties in claiming offsets banking of credits, pre-credit offsets and bank guarantees.

Notes

1 I am unable to disclose the names of the companies that I have worked with and have provided offset advice due to non-disclosure agreements that have been signed with these companies. However, the experiences and knowledge gained from interaction with these companies who are mainly based in the United States and Europe have been extremely useful in understanding how sellers manage offsets.

2 For instance, the 1994 Feingold Amendment prohibits US contractors from making incentive payments to subcontractors to induce the subcontractors to purchase from abroad in satisfying the prime contractor has offsets obligations.

3 Most of the OEMs that I have spoken to are keen and interested to deliver offsets if required by their customers. OEMs realise that offsets is being taken seriously by buyer nations and given additional weight in procurement. The commitment from OEM to offsets is obvious when I compare the seriousness that they give to understanding and delivering offsets as opposed to a decade ago.

4 Sellers may not necessarily move their state-of-the-art activities overseas or to a buyer market as this is viewed as creating direct competition and taking away jobs from the home market. Most sellers are willing to transfer activities that is less attractive to be undertaken in-country or of which the technology has become less lucrative.

5 From discussions with OEMs, it is often mentioned that a 'win–win' offset solution to claiming of credit is much more positive to the buyer–seller relationship, as both parties do not feel shortchanged.

Phase III

7 Technology, competitiveness and offsets valuation

7.1 Background

> Technological gap between nations has led to international political controversies as nations seek to access control over science and technology. This control is achieved through the costly and sustained investment in a national or military R&D establishment that has the ability to generate, develop, and disseminate new inventions and innovations. Nations that lack such an autonomous capability must rely on technology transfer process, and eventual diffusion and assimilation of foreign technologies, usually less than state of the art and in most cases with strings attached.
>
> (McIntyre and Papp, 1986, p. 22)

With this opening quote, I have dedicated this chapter to focusing on the practicalities of technology in offsets. I find issues relating to technology and technology transfer being the most challenging in offsets management. Technology becomes the epicentre of offsets for many governments. In this chapter, I focus on the practical aspects of technology in offsets management. The chapter provides a brief definition of technology, discusses the role of technology leading to national competitiveness advantage, then analyses technology in the context of offsets and finally how technology is valuated. In this chapter, I have also provided a critical discussion on success factors for transfer of technology in offsets practice and concluded with a few brief examples on how to calculate technology in offsets management.

7.2 Defining technology

It is quite common that offsets managers in government and industry lack knowledge and appreciation to technology and technology valuation. Defining technology is not straightforward. Definitions of technology can be drawn from multiple disciplines, each with its own idiosyncrasies to suit the characteristics of that particular discipline. Table 7.1 is an extraction of a few definitions of technology. Simply, technology is defined as the application of science to industry or for commercial objectives. Technology consists of technical data (manuals, drawings, electronic media-software and source codes); expertise (information, assistance,

Table 7.1 Definitions of technology

General: Dictionary definitions:

Webster's Dictionary (2001)
1 The science or study of the practical industrial arts
2 The terms used in a science, technical terminology
3 Applied science. In simple terms, the definitions stress on the study and application of science
(*Webster's Third New International Dictionary of the English Language*, 1986, p. 2348).

Collins Dictionary (1991)
1 The application of practical or mechanical sciences to industry or commerce
2 The methods, theory and practice governing such application
3 The total knowledge and skills available to any human society
(*Collins English Dictionary*, 1991).

Oxford Dictionary (2000)
Science or industrial art; literally, the science of technique is systematic knowledge of technique. Technique: the interaction of people/tools with machine/objects which defines 'a way of doing' a particular task (*Oxford English Dictionary*, 2000).

Eveland (1986)
Defined technology as "information that is put to use in order to accomplish some task" technology includes hardware and software and therefore acquiring technological capability is a cumulative process and not a one-off process, where learning is gotten from the development and use of technology (Bennet and Vaidya, 2005, pp. 112–153; Shrivastava, 1995, pp. 183–200).

The Open University, UK (2006)
"Technology is the. . . " application of scientific and other knowledge to practical tasks by organisations that involve people and machines. There are three important aspects to this definition – technology is about taking action to meet human needs rather than merely understanding the workings of the natural world, which is the goal of science. It uses much more theoretical knowledge; technology involves organised ways of doing things. It covers the intended and unintended interactions between products (machines, devices, artefacts) and the people and systems which make them, use them or are affected by them through various processes (Lane, Andy. The Open University, UK., 2006).

Abetti
Technology as a body of knowledge, tools and techniques, derived from science and practical experiences that is used in the development, design, production and application of innovations as well as new processes or methods by which outputs are generated (Beverly and Kevin, 1995, pp. 43–70).

Baranson
Gives a similar definition of technology as consisting of product designs, production techniques and managerial systems to organise and carry out production plans. (Baranson, 1978, pp. 82–85).

Goulet
Specifies the results of the application as asserting control over nature and over human processes of all kinds (Goulet, 1989, pp. 141–142).

Meissner
Goes one step further by defining technology as the configuration of processes, plans, techniques, knowledge and skills and that the configuration of this structure is to effectively produce, process and market a product or service (Meissner, 1988, pp. 53–58).

Djeflat

Technology marketed as a complete entity: all technological components tied together and transferred as a whole: capital goods/ materials/know-how/qualified and specialised manpower. (Djeflat, 1988, p. 149; Rebentish and Feretti, 1995, pp. 1–25).

Technology is defined as any form, material and knowledge, this includes software, hardware, rules, products, procedure, and technical know-how. This is because knowledge is "repetitive actions that are codified into forms which reduces processing effort or cost in the future".

Source: Author

technical training); licences (design, development, markets, fees, intellectual property rights, production) and research and development (Reissman, 2005, pp. 189–202; Eveland, 1986, pp. 303–322). Technology is considered as a complete package, including both soft and hard technology involving the production, processing and finally commercialisation of the product.

Based on these definitions, the distinctive elements of technology include process technology, product technology, method, techniques, human skills, management techniques, industry structure (suppliers, users, promoters) and commercialisation (Webster, 1994, pp. 189–202; Bell, Hobday, Abdullah, Ariffin and Malik, 1995; Balakrishnan, 2007, pp. 94–99; Drucker, 2011, pp. 162–170). Technology in an industrial context has evolved over several decades from mechanisation to automation and now digitisation (Wahab, Rose and Osman, 2012, p. 61). Both 'soft' and 'hard' technology components are critical in the transfer process. Hard technology is confined to the material aspects of the technology, such as jigs, tools, machines and equipment that is used in the production process. Soft technology includes knowledge, manuals, management, work organisation and marketing. In the context of offsets, technology is defined in a very broad sense to encompass various aspects of the technology and the technology transfer. In this instance, technology is deemed as a complete package – both soft and hard technology, including product technology, process technology, method, techniques, human skills, management techniques, expertise and industry structure and commercialisation (Eaton and Kortum, 1999, pp. 537–570).

7.2.1 Dual-use technology

Dual-use technology is a term often used in offsets. Dual-use refers to products and technologies that have both civil and military purposes, such as computers, chemicals and advanced telecommunications, encryption, radar and laser technologies. Dual-use technology has today become a strategic technology development choice for many countries. Dual-use products can be applicable to defence and civil uses without any modifications (Molas-Gallart, 1997, pp. 260–285). Dual-use technology transfer is very popular in offsets activities as it has wider application, meets economies of scale for product or process being developed and has greater impact on society (Molas-Gallart, 1997, pp. 260–285). Dual-use activities can be output or input oriented. Output relates to output of the research or production activities. In the case of offsets, output, relates to the type of technology transferred through offsets. This output can produce dual-use products applicable to defence and civil use without modifications, such as general-purpose computers, electronics or dual-use products that need adaptation, such as radar, numeric control machines, transport containers and microwave ovens. Many military systems are not dual-use as they cannot be adapted to carry out a task other than the specific job for which they have been designed (Molas-Gallart, 1997, pp. 260–285). However, the subsystems and components are generic components and could be dual-use. Other types of dual-use output identified include codified knowledge, such as licences and management principles. In terms of dual-use inputs, these are most likely to represent capital and labour. Capital can be in the form of equipment, machinery, tools, plants and other production facilities. Skills refer to knowledge embodied in the technology from researchers, managers and employees.

7.2.2   Technological 'spin-off' and 'spin-on'

In offsets, technology spin-off is another frequently used terminology. Technology spin-off relates to technology developed for the military or used by firms to fulfil the specifications of military projects which might have applications for non-military customers and suggests that military spending could promote favourable human capital spill over through education and training (Askari and Glover, 1977, p. 194; Benoit, 1978, pp. 221–280; Deger and Sen, 1983, pp. 67–83; Kennedy, 1983, pp. 232–245; Biswas, 1993, pp. 223–235). The antithesis to technological spin-off from defence to civil is that the military expenditures on defence technology could hinder economic development by reducing savings and misallocating resources away from more productive use in the public or private sector (Deger and Sen, 1983, pp. 67–83; Deger and Smith, 1983, pp. 335–353; Deger, 1986; Sivard, 1989, pp. 79–96; Ram, 1993, pp. 20–39; Landau, 1994, pp. 205–202). Although technological spin-off is present in offsets deals, the outcome from spin-off projects have had less success in offsets deals due to the high cost and technology transfer complications (Balakrishnan, 2007, pp. 94–98). On the other hand, spin-on is defined as technology developed for the civil or commercial sectors that might have applications for military use. Spin-on has been highly popular in certain countries such as Japan that had used civil technologies gained through offsets to build military capability (Michael W. Chinworth in Brauer and Dunne, 2004, pp. 233–254).

7.2.3   High technology sector

Another terminology frequently used in offsets is high technology. Oxford English Dictionary defines high technology as advanced technology. High technology is also popularly called the 'Third Wave', 'new industrial' and 'entrepreneurial' initiatives (Jenkins, Leicht and Jaynes, 2006, p. 267). High tech industry can be defined as

> the design, development and introduction of new products and innovative, manufacturing processes, or both, through the systematic application of scientific and technical knowledge.
>
> (U.S Congress, Office of Technology Assessment, Technology, Innovation and Regional Economic Development Government Printing Office, 1984, pp. 8–9)

There are various arguments to the factors that contribute to development of the high technology sector. The most crucial factor in high technology development is scientific intelligence harnessed to technical problem-solving. This sector been largely supported by direct state intervention in the creation of new enterprises, products, markets and technologies (Harrison and Samson, 2002; Murmann, 2003, pp. 337–369; Ministry of Defence, UK, 2012). It is claimed that offsets is a useful tool for governments to request for high technology. This relates directly to the purpose of offsets, which is to bring in technology that cannot be obtained off-the-shelf.[1]

7.2.4   *Geographical cluster*

A prominent feature of high technology industry is associated geographical cluster effect. Industrial clustering has been identified as an effective way of nurturing high technology industries to stay competitive (Porter, 1990, pp. 346–352; Chandra and Kolavalli, 2006, pp. 19–22). Government support is crucial in trying to push forward risky but potentially productive projects that would not otherwise materialise. Governments assist in identifying market opportunities, fostering local innovation capacities, and making public investments in new technology and private enterprises – the very reason why governments use tools such as offsets as a means to fund such high technology projects (Mowery and Rosernberg, 1989; Singh and Jain, 2003, pp. 249–262). Offsets is an attractive mode to lure overseas contractors to share and transfer high technology into local companies that require cutting-edge products and advanced state-of-the-art techniques, sometimes offsets can be used to raise joint expenditure on research and development and hire a higher percentage of workers from technical and engineering fields. There are many successful offsets projects in the high technology sector, mainly in aerospace and defence, such as the aerospace cluster in Wharton in the UK, Marsaille and Toulouse in France, Seville in Spain, Missouri in the United States, Bangalore in India and Ankara in Turkey (Balakrishnan, 2011, pp. 223–224). These high technology clusters have been heavily government led and directed projects.

7.3 Elements of transfer of technology in offsets (TOT)

7.3.1 *Defining technology transfer*

Many nations have developed policies and encouraged open trade around encouraging international technology transfer as they see the benefits of such policies on the development of their industrial and technological base (Patel and Pavitt, 1993, pp. 85–101; Reissman, 2005, pp. 189–202; Fu, Pietrobelli and Soete, 2011, pp. 1204–1212). Transfer of technology[2] is a term frequently used in offsets management. In this context, I refer to transfer of technology as the acquisition, development and utilisation of technological knowledge by a country other than that in which this knowledge originated. This means moving the technology from one country to another through procurement activity between buyers and sellers that include offsets agreement. The nature, magnitude and mode of technology transfer can be influenced by various factors such as geopolitical conditions, culture, economic circumstances, political ideology, production possibilities, research and development (R&D) policies and profitability (Centre for Exploitation of Science and technology (CEST), 1991). These factors are highly influential in determining the effectiveness of the transfer process (Soete, 1985, pp. 409–422; Madu, 1989, pp. 115–124; Hill and Richard, 2001, pp. 40–51; Ashok and Kharbanda, 2003, p. 234; Jegathesan, Gunasekaran and Muthaly, 1997, pp. 96–214).

In offsets, normally technology transfer process happens either as inter-firm, across borders to subsidiaries, joint ventures or to a very new firm. In addition, horizontal type of technology transfer where technology used in one place, organisation or context is transferred and used in another place, organisation or context is a more common type (Mansfield, 1975, pp. 372–376; Norman, 1985; Nahar, 2006).[3] Transfer of technology through offsets can happen at several phases. The material transfer which involves transfer of new material or products to a country; transfer of designs and blueprints that facilitate the manufacturing process of the new product or material and capacity transfer which involve adapting the new item to the specific conditions of the recipient country. Technology related offsets projects involve transfer of technology at all phases and the transfer highly depends on the context, place and market. Transfer of technology through offsets involves tangible technology such as equipment, machinery and documents and intangible technology in the form of design, patents, licencing agreements, know-how engineering studies and manufacturing, training as well as consulting services (Stiglitz, 1987, pp. 125–153).

7.3.2 *Objectives of technology transfer in offsets*

In offsets, there are two dimensions to analysing the objectives of technology transfer, those of the seller and the buyer. Sellers normally transfer technology for several reasons. First and most importantly because it is part of the offsets policy requirement. Second, a seller will be willing to transfer technology in conditions where the offsets project involves commercial activities between the seller and a local company that requires support to enhance their technological capability to be able to undertake the designated work. The seller would want to be seen as making an effort towards establishing a good reputation in the local market, which hopefully creates a positive feedback, which paves the way for future sales (Bellais and Guichard, 2006, pp. 273–286). However, the supplier will still attempt to retain control over the use of the technology transferred even after the expiration of the contract period. Despite the huge technological gap that often exists between sellers and buyers, suppliers are still worried about competition in international markets from their customers as there have been instances where offsets technology has been successfully used by buyer nations to eventually create similar products that are cheaper and technically on par with sellers (Rosenberg, 1982, 1970). Therefore, the transfer of technology process often forms part of the negotiation in order to prevent the recipient country from exploiting the technology and breaching IPR (Oman, 1989, pp. 212–216). Third, technology transfer is also encouraged as a method of cost-sharing, as technology production is very expensive. Offsets technology recipients cannot afford a high start-up cost and huge investments into buying equipment and training their staff (Wills, 2012). In this case, the seller provides such support as part of the offsets arrangement thus creating a break for the offsets recipient to enter the market and catch up with some level of support provided by the seller through government policy directive (Roman, 1986, pp. 132–158). Fourth, technology transfer in offsets is also undertaken especially in defence offsets, as a means of providing allies with superior technologies. The US, for example, during the Cold War, transferred technology to other NATO countries and its developing country allies to defend themselves against the Communist threat. Suppliers also transfer certain technologies through civil offsets, such as those linked to health and education, to enhance the social-economic development of developing countries.

By contrast, in an offsets environment, buyers request for transfer of technology to build indigenous technology capability. Technology is seen as fundamental to wealth creation, contributing to growth and to developing talent required to compete at a global level (Ogunade, 2011, p. 1.24; Fozdar, 2015, pp. 9–16). It is too costly and time consuming for buyers to develop the same technology independently, especially if the technology is one that is valuable and costly to develop from scratch. Buyer countries, therefore, will try to obtain technology through various modes including offsets, which they can use to operate, establish new production units and expand existing ones, develop new techniques, and innovate. However, there are various examples to prove that using new technologies is not an automatic or simple process (Rosenberg, Landau and Mowery, 1992, pp. 93–99; Sunil, 2002). New technology can be very complicated, involving complex processes and continuous learning cycles. In fact, the issue is whether the identified offsets technology recipients are willing to invest into technology capacity-building to develop indigenous expertise. The absence of this spirit and to consider offsets as a mere 'gift' or 'free lunch' by technology recipients cannot lead to a successful transfer of technology process in offsets programme (Choi, 2009, p. 40).

7.3.3 Technology collaboration (TC)

Technological collaboration (TC) is one of the most popular aspects of technology transfer within offsets activities mainly due to the nature of offsets that emphasis partnership. TC is defined as any activity where two or more partners contribute differential resources and technological know-how to achieve agreed complementary aims.[4] This mode of transfer includes collaboration in product development, manufacture and marketing that spans across national boundaries, is not based on arms-length transactions and includes substantial and continual contributions of capital, technology and other assets.[5] TC has become more popular than other modes of technology transfer due to its emphasis on long-term partnerships as well as the sharing of management responsibilities amongst partners. TC is most appropriate in an offsets environment, as it is both broader and more in-depth than joint ventures, requiring strategic alliances and cooperation from every angle, including sometimes the involvement of the governments of both transferor and transferee country. The success of the technological collaboration however could vary depending on the degree to whether it is a legally binding contract or a loose form of partnership. In offsets, however, technological collaboration involving downstream activities is more popular than collaboration focused on activities further upstream, involving product development, manufacture and marketing (Tyler and Steensma, 1995, pp. 43–70; Beard, 2002, pp. 242–253).

7.4 Technology acquisition and offsets – justification for national competitiveness

Having defined technology and discussed elements of technology transfer in offsets, it is critical to evaluate technology as an important factor that contributes to national competitiveness. What is competitiveness and why is competitiveness important to a nation? The word competitiveness is highly debatable (Krugman, 1994, p. 28; Miozzo and Walsh, 2006, pp. 162–173). The World Economic Forum (WEF) defines competitiveness as "the set of institutions, policies and factors that determine the level of productivity of a country" (Global Competitiveness Report, 2018, p. 68). Competitiveness is the ability to compete in world markets with a global strategy; to governments, competitiveness is about a positive balance of trade, while economists argue that competitiveness is all about achieving low unit costs of labour adjusted for exchange rates (Athreye and Cantwell, 2007, pp. 2019–2226; Feurer and Chaharbaghi, 1994, pp. 49–58; Foray and Freeman, 1993, pp. 22–28; Blunck, 2006; Dahlman, 2007, p. 29). Competitiveness, either at the macro or micro level,[6] is said to be driven among others by foreign direct investment, skills, domestic R&D, licencing, economic strength, government, exchange rates, finance, infrastructure and management (World Industrial Development Report, 2002/2003, pp. 118–193; Lall, 2001, pp. 189–213. Traditionally, competitiveness is measured based on sponsorship of R&D, profit levels, management practices, labour unions, balance of trade, labour productivity rates and export market penetration (Porter, 1990; Bennett and Vaidya, 2005; Dhalman, 2007, p. 29; Blunck, 2006). This traditional measurement is of course highly questionable in an era of digitisation but that is not a discussion I will pursue here. The most often quoted work in this field is by Michael Porter when he wrote about the competitiveness of nations in 1990 (Porter, 1990).[7]

Governments realise that there is increasing competition globally for a wider market share, changing structure of world trade and finance, availability of more advanced technology and uneven distribution of global value chains and integrated production systems. Due to this development, inherent technological development is necessary to maintain competitiveness in order to attain sustainable industrial development (Dunning, 1988, p. 19; Singer, 1999, p. 12; Jomo and Felker, 1984, pp. 95–107).

Against this backdrop, technology is identified as a *sine-qua-non* for maintaining national competitiveness. Technological progress is crucial for the growth process and is fundamental for achieving rising per capita income (Betz, 1993, pp. 78–82). Technological progress determines the rate at which natural resources can be exploited and capital stock can be expanded to enhance productivity and maximise output and income (Solow, 1956, pp. 65–94). It is for this reason that economically developed countries tend to be those that are also industrially and technologically advanced. It is said that a competitive nation is one that can succeed via high technology and productivity, with accompanying high wage and income. At the height of globalisation, technology was seen as a key element in attaining national competitiveness (Lall, 1992, pp. 165–182; Mowery and Oxley, 1995, pp. 67–93; Dahlman, 2007); for firms to attain competitiveness, they must process both hard and soft technologies in the form of equipment, patents, design and know-how. Firm level competitiveness can be obtained through 'learning by doing' where firms are exposed to a multifaceted technological learning curve, including problem-solving, managing technology processes, inter- and intra-firm interaction and the ability to market and export their products. Sustainable competitiveness can only be achieved through continuing access to new technologies, including new products, new processes, management techniques, forms of linkages between buyers and sellers and tighter relations between technology and science (Evenson and Westphal, 1995, pp. 2209–2299).

Technology features as an essential objective in most offsets policies. Technology and 'know-how' are both critical objectives within offsets policies of many nations. For those nations that have written offsets policies, technology transfer activities are explicitly awarded high multipliers. Table 7.2 explains a few examples of countries where their offsets objectives are tied to technology requirements and multipliers awarded for technology transfer.

However, there is lack of uniformity to how governments understand and translate technology and technology transfer in offsets. Each country has its own interpretation of how it defines technology and what is accepted within technology transfer activities. The critical factor is to be explicit about the context of

Table 7.2 Offsets objectives focused on technology

Country	Offsets objectives	Multipliers
UAE	Enabling domestic industries with know-how, technology transfer, training of nationals	On a case by case basis based on input-output model but general rule is 1
Saudi Arabia	Technology transfer, training, talent development	Up to 5
Oman	Transfer of technologies and technological know-how through training	Up to 10
Norway	Technology transfer	Multiplier up to 5
Malaysia	Technology transfer	Multiplier up to 5 but higher multiplier awarded for exceptional cases where technology is critically required

Source: Extracted from CTO, http://cto-offset.com/, dated 20 June 2017

technology and the boundaries in order to develop clarity in the overall offsets management process. Further, in offsets-related technology transfer, there is certainly a lack of focus on soft technology environments such as on issues of laws, rules and regulation, the internal environment and market conditions as opposed to the hard technology environments such as infrastructure, industrial base, economic strength and capacity to provide capital investment. The overemphasis on the latter can sometimes cause low efficiency in technological absorptive capacity leading to sustainable development (Lall, 1992, pp. 165–182; Dunmade, 2002, pp. 461–471; Zhouying, 2005, pp. 35–46).

7.5   Technology valuation, process and approach

Technology valuation in offsets is the most challenging exercise for an offsets manager. Technology valuation is often the key factor that can derail or complicate an offset negotiation and delay finalisation of an offsets contract. Technically, each nation has acquired a different level of maturity in defining technology, appreciating technology issues, valuation and process. Countries that have had a longer history of offsets practices have a more established offsets technology valuation capability and capacity. For example, in South Korea, technology valuation is carried out by the Department for Technology Assessment and Quality (DTaQ). Other countries with established technology valuation practices include Turkey, Malaysia and Brazil. In Argentina, a technology committee reports to the Institute of Scientific and Technological Research for Defence (CITEDEF), a federal agency that reports to MOD. All contractors are required to liaise with CITEDEF when negotiating technology transfer. In Austria, an evaluation cost of 0.3 percent of offsets credit value is levied on the seller if an expert is required and the expert is normally appointed by MOEA to assess the value of offsets projects. Obligors can waive if they can prove that this is inappropriate or not needed.

A few important questions that should be considered in offsets technology valuation include:

- What are the transactional and non-transactional types of offsets?
- What are the considerations in offsets technology valuation?
- Which organisations valuate technology content of offsets programmes?
- Whether there are formulas on how to valuate technology offsets.
- What are the valuation processes?
- How is technology valuated? Critical versus non-critical technology; existing capabilities and how much will the new technology being transferred bridge the gap, is the technology linked to direct or indirect offsets – purpose and how will it be transferred; to whom and the audit process involved? Consideration to other issues such as technology life span and the intrinsic value of the technology such as spin-on and dual-use as well as the market value of the technology.

7.5.1   *What is technology valuation in the context of offsets?*

Technology valuation is defined by business dictionary as valuing technology acquisitions which, in addition to the purchase price and start-up costs, also include current market value adjustments and the risk premium of the acquisition (businessdictionary.com). Technology valuation is used to estimate the value within an activity which includes to review technology, aspects of commercialisation and marketability factors with tangible and intangible technology itself and the intellectual property rights which involves royalty amount (Hsiung, 1998, pp. 11–15).[8] Thus, the value of technology is 'fair market value', which is different from the price itself.

In the context of offsets, technology valuation is defined as evaluation of activity of defence and non-defence technology itself to describe monetary values with a review of technical, economical and strength effects especially in the context of defence and security (Gupta, 2015, pp. 45–60; Jang and Joung, 2007, p. 33). Technology valuation in offsets is not limited to IPR but may also be based on the purpose for the technology, usage, point of view and intention of managers. In offsets, there are two types of technology valuation. First, transactional offsets value, which includes labour to prepare and provide training, cost of drawing transfer, travel to perform technical transfer, management and administrative costs. Second, non-transactional offsets value, which includes estimated investment in the design, value of patent, trademarks, trade secrets and know-how (Jang, Chul, Kim and Joung, 2007, pp. 91–101).

The technology value is one that is agreed between buyers and sellers in which case both parties have to negotiate to agree to a fair price to the technology. The most important aspect of technology valuation is to find a method of valuation which both buyers and sellers are most comfortable with and are willing to base their technology calculation on that particular model. A few valuation methods are discussed in this section as options that may be available to buyers and sellers in their technology valuation exercise. These models are generic technology valuation models that are applicable in the context of offsets (Benkenstein and Bloch, 1993, pp. 20–27; Autio and Laamanen, 1995, pp. 634–664; Mohamad, 2005, p. 215). Buyers and sellers managing offsets can choose to apply any or all of the models based on the suitability of the project.

7.5.2   Cost-based approach

Cost-based approach is the most commonly type of calculation used for technology valuation in offsets. This approach is based on covering costs of developing a new product. This involves calculation of actual amount of an asset or cost of reproduction and replacement of assets. A cost-based approach takes into account depreciation and obsolescence of assets. The cost of technology involves development costs, basic research, applied research, prototype, integration, validation, verification, pre-production and production, suppliers estimated cost of technology based on number of years that it takes to develop the technology, cost of hiring engineers and researchers, cost of prototypes and other indirect costs such as travel, third party subcontracting, etc. This method is good to price an article that is being produced but not the most suitable method when calculating IPR that is embodied in the asset or technology being transferred nor capture benefits and future potential of technology. However, knowing cost of technology is useful when calculating relative inputs of parties into a joint venture or partnership deal.

7.5.3   Market-based approach

Market-based approach may be more complex and difficult in the case of offsets. This method requires finding a similar or comparable technology to the one being evaluated. In the case of civil products, it may not be as simple as finding out the cost of technology transfer in the production of cars of similar capacity and capability as these may involve local content, joint production and other factors. Similarly, it may not be possible to find out the cost of technology transfer for production of one single unit of submarine between Brazil and India. This approach would require finding sufficient data about similar transactions to arrive at an accurate estimate of the value of a product. This approach could often end in misunderstanding and mistrust if not dealt with carefully. Market-based approach is much more difficult to be applied in sectors where data is not available publicly, such as in defence and security (Boer, 1999, pp. 115–132; Cho, Han, Park, Yang, Lee and Ahn, 2006, pp. 15–22).

7.5.4 Income-based approach

In an income-based approach, value of technology is measured by net-present value of associated economic benefits over the lifetime of the technology. This approach can only be applicable for a profit-based project as part of offsets. Considerations must be given to product costs, projected profit margin for a certain number of years, annual production and cash flow, incorporate real value of technology, patents, trademarks and copy rights plus other technology-related factors. It takes into consideration the type of market, technology, entrepreneurial and management factors. The setback with this method is that there may not be any sales in the future market or cost data to predict the future. The method also relies on distribution of risks between buyers and sellers and who should take the risk and apportionment (Boer, 1999, pp. 115–132; Cho, Han, Park, Yang, Lee and Ahn, 2006, pp. 15–22).

7.5.5 Hybrid approach

In a practical situation, as I mentioned earlier, buyers and sellers may have to employ more than one approach towards technology valuation. This will most often depend on the purpose, intent, content, parties involved and usage of the technology. A training programme in offsets, for example, may employ a cost-based and market-based approach whilst a joint venture project may employ a market and income-based approach. It is dependent on buyers and sellers to agree to which of the hybrid models suits their offsets programme best and valuate technology based on those approaches (Boer, 1999, pp. 115–132; Cho, Han, Park, Yang, Lee and Ahn, 2006, pp. 15–22).

Table 7.3 summarises all of the technology valuation approaches.

Table 7.3 Summary to technology valuation approaches

Approach	Cost approach	Market approach	Income approach	Real option approach
Definition	Valuation based on reproduction or replacement costs	Valuation based on the comparable market price	Valuation based on the present value or future flow of benefits	Valuation adjusted to factors of risk and uncertainty
Advantages	Easy to use and calculate if cost data are available	Easy to rationalise if the market data are available	Makes use of the well-developed concept of net-present value	Takes uncertainty and risk into account, rendering valuation more flexible
Disadvantages	Difficult to obtain the data	Lack of comparable market data	Chance of error due to subjective estimation	Difficult to calculate

Source: Author

7.6 Critical factors for successful transfer of technology through offsets

Figure 7.1 illustrates critical factors that contribute to the transfer of technology in offsets management. The four factors described here are seller strategy, buyer absorptive capacity and capability, focused and incentivised offsets policy and robust buyer–supplier relationship. Each of these factors is explained in detail.

7.6.1 Seller strategy

Success of technology transfer in offsets transactions is dependent upon several factors. First, 'seller strategy' where sellers have to decide on technologies that have to be transferred; costs and benefits of such transfer; whether technology sharing could lead to a complementary or competitive environment; long-term impact to sellers' supply chain, especially if it involves manufacturing activities; where in the technology life cycle[9] does the technology being transferred reside; technology gap; protection to technology being transferred[10] and finally what are the restrictions–export control and governmental regulations that need to be addressed in the technology transfer process. These considerations are crucial for sellers when incorporating technology as part of an offsets programme (Bartlett and Ghoshal, 2002; Zeng, 2012, p. 280).

7.6.2 Buyer absorptive capacity and capability

The second important success factor to technology transfer in offsets is dependent on the capability and the capacity of technology recipients to absorb technologies being transferred. This, I discussed at length in my earlier chapter. In

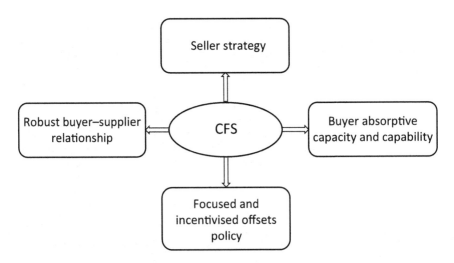

Figure 7.1 Offsets technology transfer CSF diagram

Source: Author

this case, selected technology recipients must have a reasonable level of existing technology capability with equipment, skilled workers and financial strength to expand if needed. Technology recipients should also have the right attitude and enthusiasm to grow and invest in new technologies being transferred through their partners. These companies should have an organisational culture that embraces innovation and is motivated to learn step by step in order to become competitive (Jomo, 2001; Jomo, Felker and Rasiah, 1999).

7.6.3   *Focused and incentivised offsets policy*

The third important factor for successful technology transfer in an offsets environment involves thrust and focus of offsets policy. I discussed in an earlier chapter the importance of a robust policy formulation that could effectively be used to enhance industrial capability (Lall, 1992, pp. 165–182; Lall, 1993, pp. 72–103; Lall, 1995; Lall and Morris, 1998, pp. 1369–1385). Offsets policies that clearly spell out the importance of technology transfer attract more of such activities from sellers. Further, higher offsets multipliers and other incentives motivate contractors to undertake technology-focused projects. For example, countries like Turkey, Brazil and Taiwan offer very high multipliers to attract technology-related projects. Taiwan for example awards up to a ten multiplier for technology transfer, whilst Turkey awards up to an eight multiplier for technology transfer.

7.6.4   *Robust buyer–supplier relationship*

The fourth and final aspect of successful technology transfer in offsets environment relates to the interdependency and relationship that is built between both buyers and suppliers. As the nature of offsets practice involves large international procurement that could last for many years, buyers and sellers should build a relationship around trust with a view to long-term partnership. Such a relationship allows for open and honest discussion around any issues that may affect the performance of the project, including technology transfer. There is a greater chance of problems being solved when parties to the project have a good relationship and are willing to find solutions through discussions and negotiations rather than being confrontational (Sinha, 2001, pp. 127–151; Beverly and Kevin, 1995, pp. 43–72).

In the final section of this chapter, I provide a few case studies on how to valuate technology. These case studies should be useful for offsets managers to use in offsets technology valuation.

7.7   Case study

7.7.1   *Hypothetitical case study 1*

This offsets project involves the seller helping a local contractor, an offsets technology recipient, expand their existing capability by manufacturing aircraft parts for the seller. This is an indirect offsets project. The value of the project is estimated at USD 300 million. The breakdown given for the project consists of

1	Technology transfer	USD 100 million
2	Purchase of parts and tools	USD 70 million
3	Export value	USD 130 million
4	**Total**	**USD 300 million**

In this case, item 2 involves the seller having to purchase additional parts and tools that are required for manufacturing activities by the technology recipient. The export value is the estimated export value by the technology recipient. Although there will be issues and negotiations around item 2 and 3, the the most contentious issue is likely to arise as to how did the seller value item 1 technology transfer at USD 100 million? The seller has to provide a detailed breakdown to what is meant by technology transfer, what does item 1 consists of and the value for each activity.

7.7.2   *Hypothetical case study 2*

Project two involves a training project as part of an offsets programme. The value of the project is USD 100 million. The breakdown of the project is as follows:

Technology transfer	**USD 100,000**
1 Documentation	
(10,000 pages × USD 200/pg)	USD 2.0 million
2 Training 20 weeks	
Instructor fee USD 500.00 hr (40 hours per week)	
Prep 5 × 10 = 50 weeks	
Classroom = 10 weeks	
Subtotal = 80 weeks	
40 hrs/wk × USD 500	USD 16.0 million
3 Factory familiarisation 10 persons	
(accommodation, airfare, subsistence)	USD 0.3 million
4 Internship for 10 local engineers in factory	USD 81.7 million
• Salary	USD 0.12 million
• Know-how	USD 81.58 million
5 Total	**USD 100 million**

In this case, items 1, 2 and 3 are clearly defined and the value is less contentious though there are still opportunities for parties to negotiate. The main area for disagreement between seller and buyer will arise as regards to item 4 on the component of know-how. For the seller, know-how is the most valuable aspect of technology transfer. This is tacit knowledge that is being transferred which may result in handing over the seller's 'crown jewel' or even establishing a competitor in the long-run. Therefore, the seller would want to maximise this value and ensure that the investment made on the know-how is covered. The buyer on the other hand would be keen to minimise the cost of know-how by seeking for justification on the proposed cost. Both parties will eventually have to come to a rational decision based on technology agreed approach to technology valuation but also based on trust, relationship and what each party expects out of this partnership.

7.7.3   *Hypothetical case study 3*

Offsets project three involves direct offsets where the seller is providing support to a local MRO company in setting up their capability in terms of supporting the combat ship that is being procured by the buyer government for their navy. Total value of the project is estimated at USD 131.96 million. The breakdown of technology transfer claim for the project is as follows:

1	Purchased tools and machineries	USD 50.0 million
2	Documentation	USD 10.0 million
	50,000 pages × USD200/pg	
3	Technical assistance	
	Instructor fee USD 700/hr (40 hours per week)	
	Prep 5 × 10 = 60 weeks	
	On-site specialist = 10 weeks	
	Subtotal = 70 weeks	
	40hrs/wk × USD 700 × 70 weeks =	USD 1.96 million
4	Know-how =	USD 25.0 million
5	Familiarisation/internship for 5 engineers	USD 45 million
	Sellers MRO site for 90 days	
	(accommodation, airfare, subsistence)	
6	**Total**	**USD 131.96 million**

In case 3, the seller and buyer would have to negotiate and agree to most of the value that has been quoted by the seller. Some of the items, such as items 3, 4 and 5, have not been clearly spelt out and a detail cost breakdown has not been provided to the buyer. In such instance, the negotiation could take longer if the seller is unable to provide the cost breakdown to the satisfaction of the buyer.

Above are three hypothetical cases of how technology offsets projects are valued. The valuation may differ according to activities, content of the project and other external and internal factors that may influence the valuation process. It could be argued that there is subjectivity in the valuation process and the need to make valuation more transparent. Having a structured approach with justification may assist in achieving a more objective technology valuation outcome agreeable to both buyers and sellers.

Based on the preceding discussion, there are no absolutes to technology valuation. In fact, due to the complex nature of offsets transactions and the variety of technology transfer activities, defining and valuating technology becomes much more complex than in a normal business environment. Further, technology transfer in defence requires anticipation of the strength of the technology for future use, other factors such as alliances and friendly nation status. The technology valuation method is highly dependent on type of project within each offsets programme. Negotiating for the best technology value becomes central to buyers and sellers as both parties want the best deal for themselves. Eventually, the criticality and success of technology transfer and valuation depends on whether both buyers and sellers agree to the technology valuation assumption that has been agreed upon and walk away with a sense of satisfaction that they have obtained the best deal.

Notes

1 Several studies highlight the importance of location as the critical factor that facilitates high tech development. Others argue that the success of high tech industry is not based on location and traditional competitiveness but rather on factors such as the low cost of labour and the low cost of commodities. Some analysts argue that high tech development is a path-dependent process that cannot be influenced by public policies. Further studies dismiss the location factor and argue that high tech industries may achieve development through building business partnerships and extensive interpersonal networks among distinct firms to exchange technical and market information.

2 Technology transfer can occur in two forms. First is process technology transfer, which includes procedures, documentations, manufacturing processes, software, production equipment, etc. Product transfer includes the materials, components and design details of a product. However, both product and process technology transfer are interrelated and include the transfer of documentations, procedure, use of equipment, technology, software and humans as in know-how and skills or tacit knowledge.

3 First is the vertical technology transfer where information flows from basic to production level.

4 JVs are categorised into three main types: dominant parent ventures, shared management and independent ventures. A dominant parent manages dominant parent ventures, as if they were wholly owned subsidiaries. Shared management is where both parents play a meaningful management role, with functional managers drawn from both parents. Independent ventures are where both firms in the joint venture operate their own strategies.

   OECD, Economic Integration: OECD Economies, Dynamic Asian Economies & Eastern European Countries, Paris, 1993.

5 There are four types of technology-focused collaborative ventures: research collaboration amongst firms; exchange of proven technologies within a single product line or across multiple products, such as microelectronics and robotics; joint development of one or more products, these ventures typifying international collaboration in commercial aircraft, engines and segments of telecommunications equipment, microelectronics and biotechnology industries; and collaboration across different functions, with one firm providing a new product or process for marketing, manufacture or application in a foreign market.

6 Competitiveness can be viewed from both the macro and micro levels. The macro level of competitiveness is focused on macroeconomic issues such as monetary and fiscal

policies, a trusted and efficient legal system, a stable set of democratic institutions and progress in social conditions. Micro-level competitiveness, on the other hand, depends on the sophistication with which foreign sub-operators or domestic companies in the local country operate, and the quality of the microeconomic business environment in which firms operate.

7   Michael Porter in the chapter on Business Competitiveness index under the Global Competitiveness index 2006 discussed the variants for business competitiveness and the importance of micro-level competitiveness. See Michael Porter, 'Building the Microeconomics Foundation of Prosperity: Findings from the Business Competitive Index' in *Global Competitiveness Report 2006–2007*.

8   The royalty amount is normally affected by level of market demand, improvement the technology can bring to the final product, whether or not other investments will be needed to develop the final product and the predicted rate of uptake in the marketplace.

9   Technology life cycle (TLC) describes the costs and profits of product from technological development phase to market maturity to eventual decline. TLC has four distinct stages: research and development, ascent, maturity and decline (DAMD). TLC I primarily focused on time and cost of development as it related to projected profits. As product life cycle span varies, understanding and effectively estimating technology life cycle allows for a more accurate reading of whether and when research and development costs will be offset by profits. For example, products such as electronics and pharmaceuticals are more vulnerable to shorter life cycles compared to steel and composites.

10 Various ways are used to protect technology and the technology that is being transferred. These include copyright, patents, non-disclosure agreements, International Traffic in Arms Regulation (ITAR).

8 Transparency in offsets

8.1 Is offsets a corrupt practice?

The chapter on offsets and transparency has been the most difficult chapter for me to write. The frequent question thrown at me is whether offsets is a corrupt practice. It is a complex and multi-faceted question. While it has been said that some offsets practices have been mismanaged. In this book i make the case that if correctly applied, offsets has immense potential to deliver economic development.[1] Offsets, which forms part of defence business can be susceptible to corruption like any other business practice (Tirole, 2005; Matthew, 2016).[2,3] Offsets, which is mainly tied to defence and security sector, is claimed to be the second most corrupt business sector by TI UK's 2002 Bribe payer's index and that 40% of all corrupt practise happens in arms trade (SIPRI, 2010, p. 1) (Transparency International, 2002; Committees on Arms Export, 2013).

Offsets attracts bad press and negative stories in the media and academic publications. Often the success story of offsets is not discussed because it is shrouded in secrecy. Many label offsets as 'dark art', non-transparent and that the offsets activity itself is elusive (Economist, 2013, pp. 69–71; Financial Times, 2017). Although there are widespread allegations to offsets being corrupt, there has been lack of empirical evidence to prove the case (Platzgummen, P., 2013, p. 17). Further, the definition of corruption in itself is plagued by controversy and confusion. United Nation's Development Programme defines corruption as the 'misuse of public power, office or authority for private benefit – through bribery, extortion, fraud, speed money or embezzlement' (UNDP, 1999). Offsets is not spared from the controversial definition and perception of corruption between the west and the east (Hoyos, Tsar and Aman, 2013). This is extremely obvious from my dealings with sellers from the USA, Europe, Asia and other parts of the world as to their company policies on corporate governance. In addition, what one government will label as a corrupt practice is acceptable to another government due to cultural differences (Holmes, 2015, pp. 3–6; Platzgummer, 2015, pp. 17–38).

Offsets projects are normally not announced or published due to commercial and security reasons, especially if the project relates to transfer of critical technologies to allies. In such instance, this may create an impression that such offsets transactions and projects are less transparent. As having had the opportunity to practise offsets first-hand, my stand is that offsets in itself is not corrupt and offsets as a policy tool if formulated and implemented appropriately can deliver huge benefits to both buyers and sellers. Hence, in this chapter I argue that the practice of offsets itself should not be eliminated due to its intrinsic value but to develop a structured offsets implementation process that promotes greater transparency. In this chapter I introduce Transparency International's (TI) view on offsets, discuss briefly several of the allegations of corrupt practice made on offsets using case studies, highlighting areas where offsets can be susceptible to corrupt practice, and finally suggest actions that stakeholders can undertake to mitigate corrupt practice in offsets.

8.2 What does Transparency International (TI) say about offsets?

> Transparency International calls on Governments and Defence Industry to work collaboratively to raise integrity and reduce the corruption risks in all offsets contracts.
> (Transparency International, 2010, p. 33)

The above quote was picked from a TI report.

I would like to specifically highlight the report produced by TI in 2010 titled 'Defence Offsets: Addressing the Risk of Corruption and Raising Awareness' (Magahy, Vilhena da Cunha and Pyman, 2010, pp. 40–47). I recall Mark Pyman[4] and his team had worked effortlessly on this report and travelled to many offsets-practising countries to interview offsets authorities and companies on offsets and perceived corruption risks. This report is probably the first and only of its kind that had debated the issue of offsets and corruption openly.[5] Platgummer in his article on Arms Trade offsets and corruption had also developed a structured method to demonstrating levels of corrupt practise in offsets (Platzgummer, P. 2013; pp. 17–38). I applaud TI for such an effort and to have made several recommendations that could be carried through by governments and companies. The 2010 TI report had identified three main categories to corruption risks in offsets: first, it is alleged that offsets could be improperly used to influence a decision; second, that offsets could be used as a conduit to bribe government officials and third, that offsets could allow for a competitive decision to contract award be made in a non-transparent way. However, these risks are not unique to offsets and are common to any government procurement environment. The 2010 report also identified three possible opportunities for key vulnerabilities for offsets corruption to occur being political corruption, bureaucratic and private sector corruption which are all again vulnerabilities that are possible in not just offsets but in a defence procurement or other contract scenario (Magahy, Vilhena da Cunha and Pyman, 2010, pp. 40–47). However, the report should be highlighted for its recommendations made specifically to reduce corruption in offsets, to increase awareness and to develop business ethics around offsets (Fluker, Muravska and Pyman, 2010).

Nevertheless, some aspects have not been addressed by the 2010 TI report. The report mentioned that offsets as part of an activity in defence procurement is prone to corruption[6] but it failed to highlight that offsets in itself could not be corrupt unless the overall defence deal is corrupt. Therefore, in this instance, the issue is not to address offsets, business ethics in isolation but to impress on buyers and sellers those issues of offsets governance is equally important, and that should be incorporated into main procurement discussions (Pyman, 2013, ECCO presentation). One cannot single out offsets in isolation but consider that a corrupt practice is an act of corruption and an opportunity for bribery that can occur at any phase of a procurement contract including during technical and commercial negotiation, bid process, contract award and during the overall implementation of the contract (Organization for Economic Cooperation and Development (OECD), 2011; Kottasova, 2014). The important aspect to stress based on the TI report is that governments and industries should take note and consider offsets as part of the overall ethics and compliance process.

8.3   Possible malpractice in offsets dealings

I mentioned earlier that offsets in itself is not corrupt but that offsets gets mentioned when the whole defence contract is subject to allegations of corruption (Garyard, Barney and Thompson, 2012, GOCA presentation). There are several opportunities to where offsets could be misused. I intend to briefly discuss several of these aspects in this section. My views are not targeted at any specific governments or industries but from my extended observations and research on offsets governance.

First, offsets practice becomes unclear if the overall procurement process and contract is unclear. This would include the tendering process, bid process, guidance to tender submission and proposal and guidance to offsets proposal submission. In some cases, the procurement workflow, approval processes, stakeholders and their responsibilities become unclear. In such cases, it can become fuzzy as to when to introduce and incorporate an offsets proposal and the approval timeline, especially if the offsets contract is tied to a main procurement contract. In some instances, an offsets programme that is substandard and that has not met the offsets guideline has been approved (Muravska, Pyman and Vilhena da Cunha, 2010; Pyman, 2013, ECCO presentation; Platzgummer, P., 2013; Markowski and Hall, 2014, pp. 148–162).

Second, offsets could also be subject to malpractise when a contract involves an intermediary or an agent in the procurement exercise. In many countries, the use of an agent or intermediary is widely practised when dealing with large international procurements, especially in defence and aerospace. FSPA reports 80–90 percent of bribery involves a third party (GOCA, 2016). In such instances, the agent, normally a local person in-country, brokers the deal. Middlemen or agents are seen as facilitators, often someone reputable with a good track record and social standing who is appointed to represent the OEM. However, sometimes agents can be susceptible to corrupt practices or even be pressured to do so under certain circumstances to win a sale. It is possible for agents to use offsets as a conduit for corrupt practices such as creation and award of bogus projects with a large value attached or awarding of offsets projects to cronies or individuals who have a direct interest in approving the procurement contract Schultz, T. 2016.

The third option of malpractice in offsets involves project determination. This includes why such a project was chosen, the relevance of the project and the impact that such a project could have on industrial and technological development. Fourth, dispute as to how an offsets programme is evaluated and how one proposal is weighted against the other. The transparency of the evaluation process is questionable including the evaluation and decision-making process; how offsets multipliers are awarded and the value of technology being approved. Fifth aspects of offsets malpractice relate to offsets implementation. These include whether there is an internal mechanism that has been developed to track, manage and report offsets (Hoyos, 2013); oversight on non-performance; approval of completion for unsuccessful project without being charged a penalty and for submission of invalid supporting documents. Most of the malpractices in offsets that I highlighted earlier are also common in most project management environments and are not specific to offsets practice. As offsets is new and often not recognised within procurement, it is much more susceptible to corrupt practice. Therefore, much more commitment from the senior management within governments and companies is required to ensure that there is a robust governance structure for offsets that is recognised and one that is practical and works (United States, Government Accountability Office (GOA), 2004).

It is a much more complex argument around offsets practice and transparency in the context of other countries such as China and Russia (Transparency International, 2002, 14 May). Next I have listed a few case studies of alleged corrupt practices that relate to offsets. These cases were picked mainly because they have been reported on mainstream English based media publications though there are other cases available for review. (Plutzgummer, P. 2013)

8.4   Defence sales and allegations of corrupt practice in offsets

8.4.1   South Africa

The first case is of South Africa where the allegations of corrupt practice in defence sales was associated to the 1999 arms sales by the UK government through BAES to South Africa. There were controversial allegations of corruption involving European firms and senior South African politicians, including the President of African National Congress (ANC). It was reported that the South African defence minister had secretly received shares in Log-Tek electronics group, which benefitted from the arms deal (Daily Maverick, 2016). Another case involved Thyssen-Krupp, which was under investigation by South Africa's elite serious crime squad over allegations of corruption for the sale of the frigates (McCorkell and Gillard, 2010; Daily Maverick, 2016) as the success of the projects under this sale had been difficult to establish. In both cases in South Africa, the entire defence sales and arms trade was alleged to be corrupt and not just offsets alone (Munusamy, 2016). Hence, offsets may have also been used for wrong reasons but it is unfair to single out offsets when the overall sales activity was blemished (Jarrett and Taylor, 2010).

8.4.2   Czech Republic

The second case relates to the Czech Republic government, which was under investigation for alleged corrupt practice as part of the contract for the purchase of Gripen fighters 24 JAS 39 from BAES in replacement of the ageing fleet of MiG-21s. There was an investigation as to allege overpayments being made to senior Czech officials in 2001 and on the structure of the tender that was apparently drawn up for purchase of Gripen fighters. Again, in this case, the whole corruption allegation was associated to the main defence procurement contract and there was a lack of evidence or direct relationship to offsets. Nevertheless, ten years later it was reported that offsets commitment was delivered two years earlier, over 50 Czech companies benefitted through either inward investment or local export support value over $1.4 billion (Guardian, 2009; McCorkell and Gillard, 2010). Prague State Attorney's office later decided to shelve the case (Leigh and Evans, 2010; Perlo-Freeman, 2017a).

8.4.3   Saudi Arabia

The third case involves Saudi Arabia. One of the biggest arms trade scandals ever discussed is the Al Yamamah contract. Al Yamamah was negotiated between the UK government on behalf of BAES and Saudi Arabia in the 1980s. The deal was alleged to be corrupt and an investigation into this matter was initiated in July 2004 when Serious Fraud Officials (SFO) showed evidence that BAE set up 'slush funds' worth $120 million for Saudi Royal families in order to gain the contract. The investigation was however ditched later by the Blair government on the pretext of national security concerns (Leigh and Evans, 2009). The UK National Audit Office (NAO) investigated the Al Yamamah programme but the report was eventually withheld. The UK MOD stated that the report was sensitive and disclosure would harm international relations and UK's commercial interest. It was stated that the investigation had to be discontinued to 'safeguard national interest and national security' (Thompson, 2010). However, the outcome of this scandal was the Woolf report. Lord Woolf was commissioned to study and produce a report on this matter (Woolf Committee, 2018).[7] Based on this report, the BAES Board of Directors announced the creation of an external, expert committee to review and evaluate the company's policies, processes and application relating to ethics and business conduct. Under a plea bargain with the US Department of Justice in March 2010, BAES was found guilty of false accounting and making misleading statements in connection with the Al Yamamah contract and was ordered to pay $400 million, one of the largest fines in the history of the Department of Justice in connection with its investigation into the Al Yamamah contract in Saudi Arabia. Again, apart from a minor reference to offsets in the *Financial Times*, 2 July 2007, with regards to this contract no other major references or evidences related to offsets was specifically mentioned as being corrupt in this deal. Again, the point to take note of is that the whole defence contract was under investigation and not offsets per se (Perlo-Freeman, 2017; Steinberg, 2009, pp. 1–60).

8.5   Recommendation on best practices for greater offsets transparency

In this section, I have aimed to provide several suggestions on how the different stakeholders can help create a more transparent offsets environment underpinning good governance. These recommendations are not exhaustive. The offsets sector has to be more accountable for an end to end process.

8.5.1   *Role of buyer government and offsets authorities*

First, the role of the host government, especially offsets authorities, is critical to introduce transparency in offsets management. This can only happen when the government concerned has clear offsets policy and guidelines that explicitly spell out the intended objectives, stakeholders and expected outcome. The guidelines should cover offsets approval process, timeline, governance structure and project selection criteria. The offsets guidelines should also be supplemented by an 'Offset Code of Conduct'.[8] Another important aspect for offsets authorities is to have a well-managed offsets office with trained officials who are well informed of the rationale for offsets and how it works. Organisations that invest in training and education on offsets management often have staff that understand offsets and work towards a much more structured offsets management practice. This educational enhancement can be hands-on and lectures but they should not be a one-off but rather a continuous education that also caters to the high turnover of staff in an offsets environment. Offsets education should be extended to other than offsets authorities including internal and external stakeholders who are directly or indirectly involved in offsets. The education programme should cover aspects of transparency and governance in offsets. Offsets authorities should also aim to compile and publish yearly reports that reflect on offsets performance, mainly output and outcome but also the wider socio-economic and development impact derived from offsets activities for a nation. Finally, offsets authorities should carry out a post independent offsets audit to measure the success of an overall offsets programme. This report should be made public such as through distributed ledger without having to expose any commercially sensitive information.

8.5.2   *Role of industry*

A seller or OEM is an important stakeholder in offsets business. The major challenge to an OEM is often translating the cost of an offsets programme. 'Offsets is not free'. Unlike what most believe and what is mentioned in some offsets policies, there is a cost associated to offsets. Governments are prepared to take on this additional cost expecting that the money spent on offsets will reap long-term economic, industrial and technological benefit for a nation. It is understood that offsets costs could range from 5 to 20 percent approximately depending on the type of programme, economic viability and sustainability of the project, in-country ease of business, transparency of approval processes and governance and administrative cost[9] (Hoyos, 2013; Gonzales, 2012, p. 35; Balakrishnan, 2007, p. 162). The argument has been the difficulty to quantify offsets cost in every instance though there are empirical evidences to prove that many developing countries have invested in offsets to develop high technology sectors. Often the uneasiness arises when governments believe that they are paying far more for offsets than they should and that the cost of offsets is not transparent. Hence, the onus to prove this cost is upon OEMs to come up with an agreed and tangible offsets cost and the derived benefits as well as outcomes (Hennart and Anderson, 1993, p. 295).

OEMs should also develop their internal 'offsets business code of conduct' as part of their ethical compliance process. The code of conduct should be established in line with other anti-corruption and bribery act as well as international laws that are in place about corruption.[10] Any industry person dealing with offsets should be subject to this code of conduct (Schultz, T. 2016). Corporate governance and business ethics have become an important aspect of international business practice and are now being increasingly taught in universities and business schools (Claessens and Yurtoglu, 2012; Clarke, 2004). It is important that business ethics and governance be extended to offsets in companies. Also, OEMs should conduct due diligence on companies and offsets recipients that they work with and cross check any facts carefully, validate third party contractors and supplier capabilities and conduct audits on technology recipients when needed.

8.5.3 *Role of third party*

Third parties such as agents, intermediaries and offsets consultants often take on an important role in offsets mediation and determination of programme. Appointing an external expert is not always negative as external input is extremely valuable in providing impartial opinions or in highlighting key issues that can be overlooked internally by an organisation. In an offsets environment, a third party is often useful when formulating an offsets policy, developing an offsets proposal, during implementation and when executing a contract. Third parties should be appointed based on their track record, knowledge and expertise in the subject matter. A third party should be someone who is reputable, of high integrity and understands how offsets works. Governments and companies appointing third parties must ensure that they have done an ethical compliance audit on the individual or company to ensure that there has not been any issues with the person being appointed. An appropriately selected third party normally will be able to provide sound advice on the local business environment; industry capability; input into stakeholders and their requirements; do troubleshooting and problem-solving.

Recommendation 12 of the Woolf report explicitly mentioned:

> Advisers engaged to assist in Offsets arrangements in export contracts should be subjected to the same due diligence and approval process as advisers on the principal export contract. Offsets contract should be subject to a due diligence process requiring an explicit assessment of ethical and reputational risks and be capable of being audited for this. The company should also be proactive in encouraging greater scrutiny and transparency by governments of the Offsets elements of defence contracts.
>
> (Woolf Committee Report, 2008, p. 48)

8.5.4 *Role of government of the exporting country*

Governments of defence export nations (sellers) should take a proactive approach in ensuring that there is integrity within offsets practice of their OEMs. Although governments do not have direct control over the activities of businesses but some level of business, ethics can be extended to offsets within international business. Publishing reports of OEMs in a country and their offsets obligations worldwide is a good step to being transparent. To date, the Bureau of Industry and Security, United States Department of Commerce, is the only government organisation that publishes a yearly report on defence offsets. Offsets should also be covered in government briefings for foreign missions including when addressing issues of anti-corruption and bribery practices.

Corruption and non-transparent practice in government procurement is a controversial yet common encounter. Defence had been highlighted as a sector very highly prone to the act of bribery and corruption. As offsets forms part of defence procurement, offsets is not spared from such allegations. There are high chances for similar perceived corrupt practices to happen in other sectors such as construction, transport and oil and gas in areas relating to local content requirement, technology transfer and international joint ventures. These issues are often discussed under ethics in international business. As offsets is less talked about and clouded by secrecy, it seems ethics and governance process in offsets is less matured than in other sectors. The 2010 report produced by TI has certainly been a step in this direction. Hence, both governments and companies must do what is necessary to introduce governance and enforce ethical business practices in offsets management (Richards and Smith, 2002).

Notes

1 Corruption in this context is defined as abuse of power for personal gains, abuse of position of trust for personal benefits, including for friends and family. The *Economist* article defined corruption as rent seeking behaviour.
2 The article on 'Guns and Sugar' in the *Economist* oversimplifies the practice of offsets and focused on some narrow examples that are not reflective of good offsets practice (Economist, 2013).
3 Offsets programmes that are associated to corrupt defence procurement programmes are highlighted. In any case, industries such as mining, construction, oil and gas as well as healthcare and banking are said to be more corrupt than defence. However, the defence sector gets much more visibility due the nature of the business that is clouded by secrecy.
4 Mark Pyman was the Director for TI in London when this report was produced. I recall having a debate with him on the subject of offsets and corruption when he was invited to give a talk about this at Cranfield University, Shrivenham, in 2009. At that time, I was a post-doctoral research fellow at the Centre for Defence Acquisition, Cranfield University.
5 Some of the issues highlighted by TI include excessive secrecy and sensitivity invoked in the name of national security that renders offsets vulnerable to corruption. Further complexity of offsets deals makes commissions hard to detect especially with the widespread use of agents and middlemens.
6 TI had reported the defence sector to be the second most corrupt after the construction industry.
7 The Woolf report identifies high ethical standards, to which a global company should adhere, identifies BAES standards in this regard and provides recommendations on what

the company should do to achieve these standards. The report made 23 recommendations.

J. Murayska, M. Pyman and F. Vilhena da Cunha, *Defence Offsets: Addressing the Risks of Corruption and Raising Transparency* (Transparency International (UK), 2010). Retrieved 6 November 2013.

8 When I was writing the Malaysian offsets policy with an expert team from various departments, there was an issue of overemphasis on governance and eventually the policy was extremely complex, as it had to incorporate so many layers of approval. Rather than creating a pragmatic and less bureaucratic policy, we ended up with one which was overly complex.

9 Other reasons given for offsets cost include cost associated to efficiency of the companies and their ability to effectively absorb offsets investment and industrial and bureaucratic challenges when discharging offsets obligations.

10 International laws on corruption include the United Nations Convention on Corruption (UNCAC), U.S. Foreign Corrupt Practice Act, 1977; U.K. Bribery Act (2010) and the OECD Anti Bribery Convention.

9 Managing offsets risks

9.1 Awareness to risk in offsets

Risk was not given much consideration in offsets management for some time, especially by buyers or offsets authorities. Awareness to risk in offsets management had only gained importance in recent years.[1] Risk was unheard off in offsets practice during the earlier years when I was practising offsets. The onus of undertaking risks and developing risk mitigation was often thought of as the responsibility of sellers. Failure to appreciate risks by both sellers and buyers had often caused confusion, unexpected programme delay, escalation in cost and many other complications in delivering an effective offsets programme. Sellers and buyers are increasingly considering risks and incorporating risks mitigation strategies in their offsets planning and implementation. Risk is now an important component of offsets management and it has become the collective responsibility of both sellers and buyers to anticipate risks and develop risks register as guidance in programme delivery.

My focus in this chapter is not to discuss risks and risks management. There are various books that can provide one with details on risks and risk management (Raczkowski, 2017, pp. 11–210; Hillson, 2016, pp. 7–9; Andersen, Garvey and Roggi, 2014, p. 45; Monahan, 2008; Bernstein, 1998); in this chapter, I focus on risk as part of offsets management from the views of sellers and buyers. I believe it is important for sellers who provide offsets (offsets obligors) and buyers (offsets obligees) who receive offsets to appreciate one another's risks when managing offsets. First, I discuss the risk of offsets obligee and then I focus on the risks of offsets obligor within the offsets management life cycle.

9.2 Evaluating risks in offsets management life cycle: buyer perspective (offsets obligee)

In the initial years of being involved in offsets management, there was lack of emphasis on risk or on developing a risk mitigation strategy. I assume for many governments that was the case, as they were still grappling with offsets and were not sure how to fully implement offsets. In my recent discussions at the 2017 GOCA APAC Government Offsets training session in Kuala Lumpur with offsets authorities, most of them were of the view that they neither have a risk mitigation strategy nor plan (GOCA APAC Government Offsets Training Session, 2017). In many instances, offsets authorities consider possible offsets risk during the contract delivery phase. The decision to consider offsets risks at a later stage of implementation can be disastrous for project delivery (Postula, 2017, pp. 93–113).

It is important that offsets authorities seriously factor in possible risk in offsets, and create a risk register and mitigation strategy. Each offsets authority may have a different plan as to when in the offsets management life cycle they should rationalise risks. However, it is crucial to identify the different types of risks and possible mitigation steps much earlier in the process to ensure minimal project losses if any. What are the possible risks that may generally arise in offsets management? I have highlighted several possible risks that buyers (offsets obligees) may encounter and have suggested mitigation associated to offsets management. The expected offsets risks discussed here include financial risks, organisational or management risks, stakeholder relationship risks, legal or governance risks, technical risks and commercial risks.

9.2.1 *Financial risks*

Financial risk is of major concern to offsets obligees. Table 9.1 summarises the possible financial risks in offsets and suggestions on how to mitigate such risks. First, relates to the cost of offsets. Offsets obligees are often concerned about the cost of an offsets programme and how much they are paying for offsets. The subject of offsets cost is one of the most sensitive and contentious, as offsets cost is often not transparent and is difficult to quantify. I have discussed this topic in my earlier chapters. Offsets obligors and obligees constantly end up arguing about the cost of offsets. It is important to acknowledge that offsets is not free and that offsets practice involves additional costs. The issue to consider is whether offsets obligors and obligees are willing to share this cost or is the cost being borne by just one party? Is the additional cost of investing in offsets justified and expected to bring the intended results. Often, OEMs claim that offsets costs are between 3 percent and 20 percent dependent on the risks of the projects and the country's

Table 9.1 Offsets financial risks matrix

Category	Risks	Mitigation
Financial	Costs of offsets unknown	Consider a margin to work on (5–10%) of contract value Discussion with OEM
	Inadequate budget for offsets project management	Plan, prepare and seek budget approval in advance
	Escalation in cost of project due to project overrun or delay	Foresee the issue and seek advanced budget

Source: Author

offsets implementation governance and overall risks in procurement (Anderson and Terp, 2006, pp. 128–135). Instead of trying to avoid accepting the fact that offsets incurs additional cost, buyers should acknowledge that there is a cost involved for requiring offsets and work on the pretext of how to maximise value for the investment into offsets. The second issue involves inadequate financial budget for offsets project management. Often, offsets authorities fail to factor in project execution costs. In this case, an offsets authority should foresee what is coming and ensure that adequate budget is set aside for offsets project management. Another aspect of financial risks involves financial risk, which could cause cost escalation, is related to project overrun or delay (Damodaran, 2008, p. 119; Anderson, 2011, pp. 42–49). In such instance, offsets authorities should make contingency plans to keep a buffer for unexpected cost escalation due to project delay.

9.2.2 Commercial risks

The second type of offsets risks to offsets obligees involve commercial risks. Table 9.2 summarises the possible commercial risks to offsets obligee and suggested mitigations. Commercial risks involve aspects of IPR, patents and licencing (Pojasek, 2017; Crouchy, Galai and Mark, 2006, pp. 65–72). Other commercial risks may include overseas export control and licencing rules of seller countries for projects that would involve joint design, manufacturing and co-production types of activities (Roggi and Ottanelli, 2012, pp. 11–15). It is important to appreciate these commercial risks for smooth delivery during contract execution phase.

Offsets authorities also undertake risks when approving offsets projects based on proof of additionality and causality. The option to solve this issue is by preparing guidelines and clear instructions on project qualification and approval process for offsets. Offsets authorities may also face risks when executing banking of

Table 9.2 Offsets commercial risks matrix

Category	Risks	Mitigation
Commercial	Negotiating for IPR – patents and licencing with OEM	Understand IPR law and engage experts in IPR and patents
	Export control rules	Discuss in advance with OEM on country export control laws and technology transfer restrictions
	Proof of additionality and causality	Create implementation guidelines or guidance notes and make available to OEMS
	Banking of offsets credits and pre-credits not appropriately registered	

Source: Author

credits and pre-credit offsets. These risks could be overcome through developing clear guidelines on how to bank and claim credits and creating systems or software to record the credits that could be kept up to date (Bulgin, Roger GOCA Offset Training, 2015).

9.2.3   Legal risks

What are the possible legal risks that could arise for offsets obligee? Table 9.3 summarises offsets legal risks and possible mitigation. The possible legal risks include delay in concluding and signing of offsets contract. The delay could be caused by trying to finalise a complex offsets project, difference of opinion between a buyer and seller's legal officers' on clauses and terms and other contractual issues. Contractual delays are hard to predict but developing and following a milestone plan may be useful to keep on track. Other legal issues may include lack of attention to issues of governance in offsets contract (Bettis and Prahalad, 1995; Crouchy, Galai and Mark, 2006, p. 72). I had discussed this issue in detail in Chapter 8 and therefore suffice to mention that governance in the form of lack of transparency and approval processes may be an issue. To overcome issues of governance and increase transparency by spelling out details in the contract, offsets authorities should create a transparent yet not an overly complex governance structure, which spells out clear roles and responsibilities of each stakeholder involved in planning and executing the offsets project. Approval processes may have to be reviewed to reduce unnecessary 'red-tape' and extra layers of approval. Other legal risks may include legal disputes between buyer and seller due to non-performance

Table 9.3 Offsets legal risks matrix

Category	Risks	Mitigation
Legal	Delay in contract signing	Planning and developing a milestone chart, introduce incentive for on-time contract signing and delivery
	Lack of governance	Create a transparent governance structure with clear roles and responsibilities
	Lengthy and complex approval process	Constant review of process and feedback from OEM and stakeholders
	Corruption, or wrong-doing	Anti-corruption act, punishments, whistle blowing
	Legal disputes due to poor performance	Expert negotiation and out of court settlement
	Dispute on release of bank guarantee	Create a clear guidance process on conditions for bank guarantee in guidelines
	Dispute with offsets beneficiaries, or technology recipients	OEM beneficiary conference Pre-audit with professional guidance and OEM assistance

Source: Author

and release of bank guarantee. Non-performance may be settled through expert negotiations or out of court settlement. Precise guidelines should exist on how to release bank guarantees. Finally, other form of legal risks could arise when there is a dispute between offsets authorities and technology recipients on project non-performance. In such instance, offsets authorities could mitigate such risks through pre-industry audits, offsets conferences, professional guidance and being more selective on the selection of technology recipients (Clugston, 2016).

9.2.4 Technical risks

Another type of offsets risks involves technical risks. Table 9.4 summarises the various types of technical risks that could arise in offsets and suggested possible mitigation. I discussed earlier about selection of technology recipient instead of recipient. It is vital that offsets authorities develop a systematic approach to nominate capable companies or technology recipients who will be recipients of offsets projects. At the same time, governments may not have access to better information than firms may; in fact, at the detailed level of products, markets and technologies it is very unlikely to do so. Governments have to ensure that offsets recipients have some level of technical skills, absorptive capability and financial resources to undertake offsets related projects. One other technical risk involves technology valuation. I discussed technology in offsets and technology valuation in my earlier chapters. If offsets authorities do not have a clear guideline to understanding technology and technology valuation this could risk projecting cost escalation and mismatch of partners, which then will not be based on capabilities. Technology risks could be mitigated by developing technology assessment models, working with expert consultants on how to valuate technology and even learning from sellers (offsets obligors) as most of them will be willing to share their method of technology valuation. However, the onus is on offsets obligee to finally valuate and determine the value of technology based on their own understanding and perceived value. Finally, another important technical risk in offsets involves evaluating a winning

Table 9.4 Offsets technical risks matrix

Category	Risks	Mitigation
Technical	Capable beneficiaries	Transparent selection process
	Lack of absorptive capability and capacity	Training, skills development, partnership, pragmatic capacity development in-country and buy-in of expertise
	Technology Evaluation	Developing technology assessment models. Learning from OEM or third party consultants
	Offsets proposal evaluation	Learning from best practices, working with expert consultants/advisors

Source: Author

proposal and the use of multipliers. How do we decide when a multiplier is too high or when is it too low? As the usage of multipliers is often too subjective the best mitigation to risks arising from multipliers is to learn from best practices of other countries that have applied multipliers in offsets, seeking external assistance and experts in offsets to negotiate for best multipliers.

9.3   Evaluating risks in offsets management life cycle: seller perspective (offsets obligor)

What are the possible offsets risks to sellers (offsets obligors)? It is equally important to appreciate and understand possible risks that offsets obligors could face and identify possible mitigations to reduce or negate that risk. I have listed offsets obligors risk into several categories, which includes financial risks, organisational or management risks, reputational risks, relationship risks, supply chain risks, legal risks and IPR risks. Figure 9.1 explains the different levels of offsets management life cycle for an offsets obligor. Where in the offsets management life cycle should an offsets obligor consider risks? It is important to identify and create a risks mitigation plan from the initial stages, but especially at the marketing stage. Neglecting offsets risk until bid preparation phase does not allow adequate time and can create additional risk (Bulgin, 2015). Offsets risks should be considered as part of sales and marketing and incorporated into the main proposal.

An offsets obligor or seller would be expected to consider the risks deriving from offsets including the initial stages of a sales campaign. However, this may not be the case as offsets is often an after-thought in most defence and large

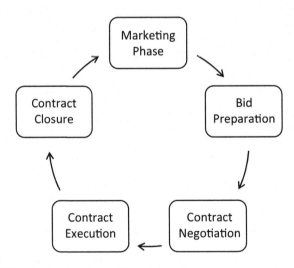

Figure 9.1 Risk reduction in offsets obligor life cycle

Source: Author

procurement contracts. During my discussions and when working with OEMs we agreed that that offsets risks register should be developed from the outset at the marketing phase. Figure 9.1 illustrates the different phases of a sales campaign and the importance of considering offsets risks at the different stages of sales ranging from marketing phase through to bid preparation, contract negotiation and execution and at the contract closure phase. Offsets obligors are advised to develop their risks plan in tandem with their offsets proposal (Bulgin, 2015).

Offsets obligors possible risk mitigation is summarised in Table 9.5. First risk relates to financial risks, which could arise from inadequate budget that is being allocated for offsets. Financial risk could also arise from delayed project approvals and project completion. These delays could expose offsets obligors to budget overruns, expose them to penalties and the terms of bank guarantee being extended (Hillson, 2016, pp. 44–49; Gupta, 2015, pp. 45–60). The offsets obligor may be able to control these risks by ensuring that there is adequate budget or contingency budget and resources to manage the unexpected increase in costs (Glugston, 2016).

Second is the organisational risk that may arise due to lack of control over offsets, as offsets is usually not given the importance or visibility internally within an

Table 9.5 Offsets obligors risks matrix

Type	Cause	Impact	Control
Financial	Late delivery Inadequate budget	Budget overrun Exposure to penalties Terms of bank guarantees extended	Adequate budget and resources Project management
Organisational	Inadequate resources Lack of control Lack of importance	Late delivery Cost overrun Legacy obligations	Develop strategy Provide resources Empower responsible personnel
Reputational	Late delivery	Loss of client trust Market black list Contagion to other customers	Develop strategy Commitment post-contract award
Supply chain	Disruption to existing suppliers Performance risk with new suppliers	Disruption to core business Offsets programme disrupted	Proper audit of new supplies Supply chain strategy
Legal	Lack of governance towards offsets programme	Possible infringement of ITAR and anti-bribery legislation etc.	Governance to include all offsets-related project areas
Intellectual Property	Loss of control	Loss of IP Creating competitors	Supply chain strategy licence agreement

Source: Author

organisation especially by senior management. Those who are not directly involved in offsets may not understand its importance in the sales process. Senior management is also frequently not exposed to offsets, and why it is an important component of sales. The lack of control on offsets within a company could be mitigated by ensuring offsets is made part of a company's corporate strategy. Further, knowledge of offsets must be incorporated into a company's overall training module. The offsets plan should also be translated to internal stakeholders including senior management in a company alongside empowering an offsets department or staff within the organisation to make decisions. Offsets managers themselves should be trained in international business and offsets for them to be able to deliver offsets projects effectively (Bulgin, 2015; Glugston, 2016).

The third aspect involves reputational risks where offsets obligors could jeopardise company reputation for non-performance of offsets projects. Non-performance could result in lack of trust by clients, risks of being blacklisted for future sales, and other customers getting to know of the seller's poor performance. In such instances, reputational risks can lead to catastrophe for future business and jeopardise the seller's opportunity to build long-term partnerships. To mitigate reputational risks, offsets obligors should develop a robust offsets strategy, delivery and monitoring mechanisms. It is important to not dismiss or neglect the post-contract phase but to ensure that a good project team is set up to deliver the offsets project on time according to the schedule with the expected outcome. In addition, offsets obligors should invest in relationship management. It is vital to develop a long-term sustainable relationship, though this may be seen as a cost.

Supply chain risks in offsets cover two aspects: first, disruption to existing suppliers if project or work is taken away or relocated elsewhere and, second, performance risks that could exists due to engaging new suppliers that may lack the experience and capability to deliver according to the specifications and on time (Taylor, 2003b, pp. 338–356; Ianakiev and Mladenov, 2009, pp. 24–26). Supply chain issues could cause disruption to delivery in the main contract as well as offsets contract delivery. Both of these risks should be addressed by ensuring the offsets obligor has a supply chain strategy that considers the risks of introducing new suppliers. Offsets obligors should communicate and plan with company supply chain teams to identify areas for outsourcing and identification of SMEs for subcontracting work. Sellers should also conduct an industry audit prior to appointing a new supplier to ensure that any new supplier has the capability to deliver and if not to make sure appropriate action is taken to equip the supplier with the necessary skills to perform. Supply chain risks could also be mitigated through partnership, where the seller sets up joint ventures and strategic alliances with a local entity, then there is shared responsibility to risk (McCord, 1998, pp. 32–36; Scott, 2008, pp. 153–157). Further, offsets obligors could upskill local workers in the buyer country by transferring of expertise such through education and training.

Legal risks an offsets obligor could face involve lack of governance and transparency in offsets management. These may include issues of corruption and unethical practice. I have discussed the topic of transparency, governance and corrupt practice in detail in Chapter 8. In this chapter, I just wish to point out that such activities may cause infringement of ITAR, anti-bribery and corruption legislation. The legal and governance issues around offsets could be mitigated by developing robust company governance processes and rules that include offsets practice. It is also useful to understand local political practices, culture, norms, procurement and offsets management process and practice of buyer nations and these factors should be factored into an offsets strategy (Magahy, Vilhena da Cunha and Pyman, 2010; Anderson, Forrester, Grevatt and Smith, 2013).

Finally, offsets obligors risk losing IPR ownership. Offsets obligors could end up losing control of IPR and ending in creation of competitors (Anderson, 2012 GICC Conference; Gupta, 2008, pp. 318–325). Thus, as a mitigation option, it is critical to ensure that agreements are in place according to the stipulated rules and regulations, non-disclosure agreements (NDAs) are signed and that buyers and offsets obligees are made aware of IPR rules and regulations via documentation and during briefings, negotiations and conferences. It would also be pertinent to include a consideration of the political risks in offsets which should be considered further.

9.4   Case study

9.4.1   Identification and managing risk in offsets projects

Country Y has a real cyber security threat. Hackers have hit the banking sector several times over a few years crippling the efficiency and reliability of the banking sector in-country. Country Y has been identified as being one of the ten most vulnerable states to cyber threat. In 2014, the banking industry made a loss of $4 billion due to cyberattack. At the same time, country Y's Ministry of Foreign Affairs has also come under attack twice, in 2013 and 2014. Fifty percent of the ministry's computers were hacked and information wiped out. This has called for a major requirement to build-up country Y's cybersecurity capability and the government sanctioned $5.5 billion for that purpose – for procurement of equipment, services and training.

Company W is a leading specialist in cyber technology, has the latest software packages, and provides state-of-the-art training to staff to address cyber threats. Company W submits a bid to the Ministry of Homeland Security for the procurement of cyber equipment. After two months, the procurement authority returns the bid with a comment that the bid has to include an offsets programme, but the Offsets Director of Company W was not aware of this new requirement and claims that he was not told about the offsets requirement at the outset when he was planning and preparing for the bid.

Exercise

1   Identify potential risks to Company W due to the offsets requirement that has been requested after the bid submission.
2   How will Company W manage these risks?

Note

1   It is not the intention of this chapter to provide a basic definition of risk. The concept of risk is traced back to the Italian term *risicare* meaning 'to avoid something current'; in Italian, *risico*, which means principal standing for a venture whose outcome is unknown or uncertain and whose successful outcome is impossible to predict. Various risk management books provide detailed definitions of risk and risk management. A general definition is one where risk and uncertainty are an intrinsic element of human existence covering all aspects of socio-economic life the entirety of determinants that influence human act. For further definitions, see Hillson (2016), Andreson, Garvey and Roggi (2014), and Raczkowski (2017).

10 Conclusion and future of offsets

10.1 Offsets is here to stay

Offsets is complex, challenging and constantly evolving. So why should governments and companies apply offsets? I explained in the earlier chapters that offsets, if used effectively, is able to deliver economic and industrial benefits specifically in knowledge transfer, skills, jobs and exports leading to industrial and technological development. We understand that there is continuous effort to eliminate offsets as it is perceived to be negative and seen as a protective tool by proponents of free market enterprise. However, we know that offsets is becoming increasingly popular for governments that view offsets as providing the advantage of enabling development instead of being pure net purchasers. At the national level, government intervention through policy tools such as offsets is necessary in a world where there is information asymmetry leading to increasing technological divides. For companies, tools like offsets may seem a burden that could incur additional cost and delay for their business activity, but there is an increasing awareness that 'a fly-by-night' strategy is dysfunctional and offsets is necessary to ensure long-term partnerships for sustainable development in countries where they operate. If companies want to operate successfully in the international business space and if they want to establish a long-term presence in their host countries, then it is important to deliver offsets.

Past literature on offsets focused on whether offsets works and the impact of offsets. This book highlights the rationale for offsets, how offsets works and how offsets can work better for effective offsets outcomes and outputs. In this concluding chapter, I address issues that will determine the importance of offsets, but also how offsets should be used to deliver sustainable industrial and technological development for medium- to long-term benefits. Governments and companies should jointly consider the following suggestions when moving forward with offsets.

10.2 Future of offsets

10.2.1 Applying offsets beyond defence

There is a critical need to apply offsets beyond defence. Why? There are great examples of large corporations, such Merck, GlaxoSmithKline, Microsoft, Google, Walt

Disney and BMW, undertaking corporate social responsibilities (CSR) as part of their business presence in host countries. However, these are isolated examples. In this book I discussed offsets mainly in the context of defence, based on my personal experience and involvement in this sector. Of late, I have seen how offsets is being used in the civil sector, though the examples are far and few. For example, when undertaking work in Oman, I realised how offsets was implemented by the Partnership for Development Authority (PfD) within defence, but also in the non-defence sectors, specifically oil and gas. The benefit was that both defence and civil sectors were learning from the best practice and there was effective cross-fertilisation and knowledge transfer in the process. Similarly, in Malaysia, offsets models which started in defence are now applied in civil sectors by the Technology Depositary Agency (TDA), responsible for the transportation sector such as air, rail and MRT projects and in healthcare. I was also made to understand during my recent trip to Thailand that the government of Thailand, specifically through the National Science and Technology Development Agency (NSTA), has been learning from Malaysia on developing their offsets policy, which will be applied to the civil sector instead of defence. Others are studying this model closely in the region, as there is a greater interest to adopt offsets in the civil sector.

However, the adoption and implementation of offsets into the civil sector should consider both the strengths and weaknesses of defence offsets. The defence sector has for long adopted a more structured approach and created a governance process around offsets. Defence offsets however still has inherent issues relating to transparency and oversight. I have discussed some of these weaknesses with defence offsets policy formulation and implementation. These examples should be taken as guidance by the civil sector when developing an offsets policy.

10.2.2　*Offsets for innovative projects*

Offsets projects must demonstrate 'additionality' and 'causality'. Innovation and creativity is vital if a nation wants to avoid the 'middle income trap'. Offsets should be used to facilitate innovation. I discussed in Chapter 2 how offsets as a tool evolves and was used innovatively to create value-added benefits. Innovation is vital for nations to break away from the middle income trap. Governments and companies can learn from various successful offsets models and how offsets had been used to create innovative projects leading to long-term benefits. There are various evidences globally to proof that offsets had been used to leap-frog into specific high technology sectors. For example, Malaysia used offsets to leverage educational programmes for long-term human capital development in specific high technology sectors; the model was quickly emulated by other countries and OEMs. Initially there were suspicions as to whether this will work, but having seen how successful this model has become and the governance structure and transparency in the whole process, it has made many others interested in adopting such a model. Similarly, offsets had also been used for cluster development and creation of centres of excellence in the United Kingdom, France, the USA, Canada, Japan and in the UAE. I talked about clusters in Chapter 6. There are other examples where offsets were used for development of nano-technology, cyber security and biotechnology for example. However, offsets could be used more effectively for innovation. Offsets, having the advantage of governmental support and industrial commitment should be used more effectively to promote innovation. We are now at the age of Fourth Industrial Revolution where development in new technologies such as artificial intelligence, internet of things, robotics and quantum computing are advancing on a global scale. How do we use offsets to develop industrial and technological capabilities in these sectors? How we use offsets to encourage start-ups and entrepreneurship in such areas? What about using offsets to develop skills and knowledge in such areas? As offsets funding is rare and expensive, it should be used for innovative projects that could deliver significant causality and additionality. Governments and companies investing in offsets should consider using offsets for innovative projects that leverage limited resources.

10.2.3 Collaboration in offsets: post development

Traditional offsets models were mostly promoted as 'one-off' where sellers delivered with a view to achieving short-term gains. Sellers were interested in maximising profit and quick ROIs. However, in the long-term this has proven to not be the right model for offsets. Various examples of one-off offsets projects have proven that this view can be detrimental to OEMs and technology recipients. There was one example where the technology was transferred to develop parts for a suspension bridge for the military. The project was approved as the owner of the company was closely related to a senior military official. However, it was clear from the initial stages that the project was not feasible as there would not be any future orders or business. The OEM had made it clear that the cost of equipment and expertise to the government was huge, but there will be minimal ROI. The project still went ahead, but it was a classic case of a one-off project.[1] I strongly believe that offsets projects that promote long-term collaboration are the best way forward to delivering effective offsets projects.

The complex interconnected network of players in collaborative programmes, especially in large government procurement, means there is a high demand to understand how to operate in a collaborative environment. International collaboration in the context of offsets relates to activities undertaken in partnership between sellers and buyers that spans across national boundaries. Offsets particularly requires high levels of collaborative partnerships at various levels involving multiple stakeholders such as foreign contractors, technology recipients or local companies, offsets authorities and various government agencies. Post-development takes a different approach to technology transfer and industrial programmes. In the post-development era, there is no more difference between developed and developing countries. Post development argues that development is a mental structure, which has created the hierarchy of developed and underdeveloped nations. As we are now in the post-development stage, culture is central to development and calls for a broader cultural involvement in development thinking. Post development is about local culture and knowledge and argues for structural change to reach solidarity. Partnership and collaboration are therefore essential in such a post-development era (Rapley, 2004, pp. 350–354). Offsets has moved in the direction of post development in the past decade where national requirements around offsets projects focusing on collaborative programmes relating to international joint ventures, joint research and development, teaching and training where both the foreign and local partners strengths are capitalised, incorporating a diverse and inclusive working environment for maximum results. Future offsets projects will certainly develop along this line, which means it is critical for the offsets community to appreciate and work in a collaborative environment.

10.2.4   *Offsets oversight and governance structure*

I discussed in detail about offsets being closely linked to corruption in Chapter 8 and discussed at length about the need for greater transparency in offsets practice. This is crucial if offsets is to be given its rightful level of recognition and acknowledgement for contribution to development. Despite the sensitivity and secrecy surrounding defence offsets projects, the offsets community must find ways to create oversight and governance in offsets. There are many ways to do this, including through developing codes of conduct, continuous education, incorporating impact assessment exercises and stakeholder forums during project completion. One specific technology to improve transparency will be the adoption of block chain and distributed ledger processes within offsets.

10.2.5   *Offsets strategy*

Having a clear offsets strategy determines success of an offsets programme. I discussed government offsets strategy in Chapter 4 and company offsets strategy in Chapter 6. Buyers and sellers offsets strategies often differ and contradict. A buyer's strategy is to use offsets credits to gain maximum offsets value using minimum offsets multipliers. While a seller's offsets strategy is to deliver minimum offsets value using maximum multipliers for the stipulated offsets credits. The challenge is to create a 'win–win' situation for buyers and sellers to obtain the best value for their offsets credits. In reality, this task is hard to achieve. There is no simple solution to solving this issue, but for buyers and sellers to consider the most pragmatic options for best outcomes. These should include a pragmatic policy that can deliver the intended outcomes, in addition to seller's strategic interest is in maintaining the relationship and making the projects work for both parties in order to efficiently manage the cost of offsets.

10.2.6   *Offsets for transfer of knowledge and skills*

Specific areas where I have seen offsets work most effectively is in knowledge transfer and skill enhancement. As such projects involve local capability, building in the offsets cost can be higher, but the benefits are long-term and much more sustainable. As there is a tendency for offsets projects to focus on technology, the knowledge and skills transferred are most valuable in introducing a nation to a new technology sector and to move up the value chain. This has been the case in aerospace, defence, security and automotive. In Chapter 7, I had addressed the various aspects of technology transfer in offsets. However, as knowledge and skills transfer is very valuable to an OEM and is often seen as the crown jewel of a company, OEMs will either be reluctant to part with the knowledge and skills or will impose high multipliers on buyers. Knowledge is expensive, especially if it leads to future competition. Therefore, buyers and sellers should develop a more matured attitude and create a systematic approach to defining the content, ownership, protection and value attached to the knowledge and skills transfer process (Silva, 2009, pp. 630–634). OEMs and their subcontractors should be more confident that knowledge sharing and skills transfer has inherent benefits to them in the longer term especially as there will be local capability to ensure continuous support to delivery. The issue of knowledge sharing and skills development is still a grey area in offsets; more work should be done to create better understanding to knowledge and skills transfer. OEMs are reluctant to propose such projects due to lack of understanding and importance given to such projects by offsets authorities. If host governments and offsets recipients want to capitalise on offsets for knowledge and skills transfer from OEMs and their technology partners, then offsets policies should provide greater incentives such as high multipliers, joint-funding and infrastructure.

10.2.7 Managing offsets cost

Cost is a sensitive topic in offsets. Companies are not interested in committing to offsets projects due to additional costs incurred in contract delivery. On the other hand, governments argue that they are incurring the offsets cost. When discussing offsets cost, it is crucial to understand who bears the cost, what is being paid for and how is the offsets cost determined. Although some offsets policies mention that offsets should not increase the cost of procurement, in practice, this is not the case. Offsets projects incur additional costs and these costs are paid out of the overall contract. Buyers often justify that the additional cost is the price paid to ensure that they obtain long-term economic and industrial benefits from sellers. The question is whether this cost is justified and whether buyers have obtained the ROIs and multipliers as claimed by sellers. The future should be one where both buyers and sellers acknowledge the existence of offsets cost, discuss how they could share the cost and take on joint responsibility for risks and delivery of the projects.

10.2.8 Offsets management as an academic discipline

Finally, to date, offsets management is yet to be recognised as an academic discipline. Offsets is only sometimes discussed as part of a countertrade activity. The role and importance of offsets is often dismissed mainly because it is associated with defence. In international business, offsets is mainly incorporated using other labels such as local content, international collaboration, international joint ventures and strategic alliances. There are only a few postgraduate level degrees that have incorporated offsets modules as part of a Master's level programme. Offsets was introduced as a module within the MSc in International Defence Marketing that was run by Cranfield University several years ago. That specific MSc programme was discontinued when the European Union was moving towards a solidified and united defence industrial and technological base and a programme of such nature was felt not relevant anymore. ECCO in partnership with the ESSEC Business

School introduced an offsets module as part of an MBA programme. However, the uptake for such a programme is still not popular and companies do not see the importance of offsets education. Further, there is lack of buy-in from government officials to attend such courses.

I argue that the subject of offsets should be introduced in universities at the postgraduate level either as part of an MSc in International Business, International Trade, International Procurement or International Technology Management. It is important that offsets becomes known to the wider business sector and that offsets gains greater visibility as an alternative policy tool that can be used to create development through not only defence but also civil sectors.

In conclusion, it is to be hoped that this text will stimulate far wider interest and debate around the use and application of technology offsets. This is merely the beginning of an open dialogue on an intriguing subject. The author remains active in researching this field and welcomes feedback on proposed concepts.

Note

1 I am unable to provide further details to the identity of the project and parties involved due to commercial sensitivity.

References

Abdalla Alfaki, I.M. and Ahmed, A., 2013. Technological Readiness in the United Arab Emirates Towards Global Competitivness. *World Journal of Entrepreneurship, Management and Sustainable Development*, 9(1), 4–13.

Abramowitz, M., 1993. The Search for the Sources of Growth: Areas of Ignorance, Old and New. *The Journal of Economic History*, 53(2), 217–241. doi:10.1017/S0022050 700012882.

Advanced Electronic Company, 2012. *Defence Industry Offset Association/Global Offset and Countertrade Association (DIOA-GOCA), Conference*. Brewster, MA, USA, Fall.

Agreement on Government Procurement, 15 April 2011 (updated December 2011). *Marrakesh Agreement Establishing the World Trade Organization*, 1994, 1867 U.N.T.S. 154, annex 4(b). Available at: www.wto.org/english/docs_e/legal_e/gpr-94_e.pdf.

Aillianos, Y., 2015. Offset Policy: The Link Between the OEM and Local Industry. In: M.S. Sodhi and R. Bhargava, eds. *Perspectives on India's Defence Offset Policy*. New Delhi and Thousand Oaks, CA: SAGE, pp. 173–179.

Ajaxon, L., 2006. *Offset for Strategic Goals: Swedish IP Practice*. [Online]. The Offset Committee, Association of the Swedish Industries. Available at: www.docstoc.com/docs/86258804/Offset-for-strategic-goals-Swedish-IP-practice [Accessed 4 April 2012].

Akubue, A.I., 2002. Technology Transfer: A Third World Perspective. *The Journal of Technology Studies*, 28(1), 14–21.

Alfredson, T. and Cungu, A., 2008. *Negotiation Theory and Practice: A Review of the Literature*. [Online]. EASYPol Module 179, Food and Agriculture Organization of the United Nations (FAO). Available at: www.fao.org/docs/up/easypol/550/4-5_negotiation_background_paper_179en.pdf.

Al Ghrair, A. and Hooper, N., 1996. Saudi Arabia and Offset. In: S. Martin, ed. *The Economics of Offset: Defence Procurement and Countertrade*. New York, NY: Routledge.

Amara, J. and Pargac, P., 2009. *Offset and Defence Procurement in the Czech Republic: A Case Study*. Working Paper Series 2009/08, Defence Resources Management Institute, School of International Graduate Studies, Naval Postgraduate School. Available at: http://calhoun.nps.edu/bitstream/handle/10945/32568/DRMI_Working_Paper_09-08.pdf?sequence=1 [Accessed 8 June 2015].

Andersen, T.J., Garvey, M. and Roggi, O., 2014. *Managing Risk and Opportunities: The Governance of Strategic Risk-Taking*. Oxford: Oxford University Press.

Anderson, G., ed., 2009. Quid pro Quo: The Changing Role of Offset in the Global Defence Market. *Jane's Industry Quarterly*, 2(4), 1–21, 23 October.

Anderson, G., 2012. China's Approach to Offset in the Global Defence Market: A Competitor Assessment. In: *European Club for Countertrade & Offset Symposium #5*. Frankfurt,

Germany, 14–15 November 2012. Available at: www.ecco-offset.eu/wp-content/uploads/ Agenda-Symposium-5.pdf and www.ecco-offset.eu/wp-content/uploads/SUMMARIES-OF-INTERVENTION.pdf.

Anderson, G., 2012. From Customers to Competitors: How Technology Transfer and Industrial Participation in the Context of Defence and Security Offset Obligations Are Reshaping the Global Market. [Online]. Global Offset and Countertrade Association/ Global Industrial Cooperation (GOCA/GICC) Conference. In: *Spring 2012 Global Industrial Cooperation (GICC) Conference*. Izmir, Turkey, 20–23 May 2012. www. globaloffset.org/conference/2012springizmir/files/AndersonToT_GOCA_May2012.pdf [Accessed 12 July 2012].

Anderson, G., Forrester, C., Grevatt, J. and Smith, M., 2013. Offset and Procurement Compensation Policies: Defence Markets. [Online]. *IHS Jane's*, February. Available at: www. janes.com/products/janes/defence-business/industry-markets-intelligence-centre/ [Accessed 12 July 2012].

Anderson, J.A., 1975. *Public Policy Making*. London: Thomas Nelson & Sons.

Anderson, K. and Terp, A., 2006. Risk Management. In: T.J. Anderson, ed. *Perspectives on Strategic Risk Management*. Copenhagen: CBS Press.

Anderson, R., 2011. *Risk Appetite and Tolerance*. London: The Institute of Risk Management (IRM).

Andolenko, M., 2010. China's Ambitious Energy Program Benefits From AREVA. [Online]. *Energy Business*, Issue 10, Quarter 2. Available at: www.areva.com/global offer/liblocal/docs/EnergyBusiness/EnergyBusiness_Issue10.pdf [Accessed 20 April 2013].

Arcelia, G.L.A., 2014. *Defence Industrial Development and Self-Sufficiency: Offset Effectiveness in Spain*. PhD Thesis, Nanyang Technological University, Singapore.

Archibugi, D. and Coco, A., 2004. A New Indicator of Technological Capabilities for Developed and Developing Countries. *World Development*, 32(4), 629–654.

Ashok, J. and Kharbanda, V.P., 2003. Strengthening Science and Technology Capacities for Indigenisation of Technology: The Indian Experience. *International Journal of Services Technology and Management*, 4(3), 234–254.

Askari, H. and Glover, M., 1977. *Military Expenditures and the Level of Economic Development*. Austin, TX: Bureau of Business Research, University of Texas at Austin.

Athreye, S. and Cantwell, J., 2007. Creating Competition?: Globalisation and the Emergence of New Technology Producers. *Research Policy*, 36(2), 209–226.

Autio, E. and Laamanen, T., 1995. Measurement and Evaluation of Technology Transfer: Review of Technology Transfer Mechanisms and Indicators. *International Journal of Technology Management*, 10(7–8), 634–664. doi:10.5539/ibr.v5n1p61.

Avascent, 2012. *The Half Trillion Dollar Challenge: Building Successful Global Offset Strategies*. [Online]. Available at: www.avascent.com/wp-content/uploads/2013/02/ Avascent-Offsets-2-White-Paper.pdf/ [Accessed 2 November 2013].

Awny, M.M., 2005. Technology Transfer and Implementation Processes in Developing Countries. *International Journal of Technology Management*, 32(1/2), 213–220.

Baesu, C., Bejinaru, R. and Iordache, S., 2015. Contextual Strategies for Conducting Effective Negotiation. *The USV Annals of Economics and Public Administration*, 15(2/22), 148–156.

Balakrishnan, K., 2007. *Evaluating the Effectiveness of Offsets as a Mechanism for Promoting Malaysian Defence Industrial and Technological Development*. PhD Thesis, Cranfield University. Available at: https://dspace.lib.cranfield.ac.uk/bitstream/1826/2504/1/ final%20thesis07ver7.pdf.

Balakrishnan, K., 2011. International Offset Experiences and Policy Prescription. In: L.K. Behera and V. Kaushal, eds. *Defence Acquisition: International Best Practises*. New Delhi: Institute for Defence Studies and Analyses., pp. 321–341.

Balakrishnan, K., 2012. Evaluating the Effectiveness of Policy Implementation for a Successful Industrial Participation and Offsets Outcome. In: *International Seminar on Industrial Cooperation and Offset*. Industrial and Regional Benefit (IRB) Canada, Ottawa, 12–14 September.

Balakrishnan, K., 2013. *Lecture on Offset Management Life Cycle*. MSc in International Defence Marketing, Cranfield University.

Balakrishnan, K., 2015a. Factors that Influence Prime Contractor's Offsets Strategy. In: *European Club for Countertrade and Offsets (ECCO) Conference*. Paris, France, June 27, 2015.

Balakrishnan, K., 2015b. Offsets in International Collaboration. *Lecture Note: International Joint Venture Module*. WMG, University of Warwick.

Balakrishnan, K., 2016a. *The Rationale for Offsets in Defence Acquisition From a Theoretical Perspective*. s.I: University of Warwick.

Balakrishnan, K., 2016b. Understanding Customer Needs. *Lecture Note, ESSEC Business School and European Club for Countertrade and Offsets (ECCO), Offset Training Academy*.

Balakrishnan, K., 2017. 'Managing Industrial project/offsets' Government Offsets training session, Global Offsets and Countertrade Association /Asia Pacific, Royal Chulan Hotel, Kuala Lumpur Malaysia, March 26.

Balakrishnan, K. and Matthews, R., 2009. The Role of Offsets in Malaysian Defence Industrialization. *Defence Peace Economics*, 20(4), 341–358.

Banks, G., 1983. The Economics and Politics of Countertrade. *The World Economy*, 6(2), 159–182.

Baptista, L.O., 2000. *Legal Aspects of Countertrade*. Porto Alegre: Livraria do Advogado.

Baranson, J., 1978. *Technology and the Multinationals: Corporate Strategies in a Changing World Economy*. Lexington, MA: Lexington Books.

Bardach, E., 2006. Policy Dynamics. In: M. Moran, M. Rein and R. Goodin, eds. *The Oxford Handbook of Public Policy*. Oxford: Oxford University Press. Chapter 16.

Barnes, T., Pashby, I. and Gibbons, A., 2002. Effective University Industry Interaction: A Multi-case Evaluation of Collaborative R&D Projects. *European Management Journal*, 20(3), 272–285.

Barrett, S., 2004. Implementation Studies: Time for a Revival? *Public Administration*, 82(2), 249–262.

Bartlett, C.A. and Ghoshal, S., 2002. *Managing Across Borders: The Transnational Solution*. Boston, MA: Harvard Business Press.

Baumgartner, F.R. and Jones, B.D., eds., 2002. *Policy Dynamics*. Chicago, IL: University of Chicago Press.

BBC News, 2013. China in $1.3bn Renault-Dongfeng Auto Joint Venture. [Online]. *BBC*, 5 December. Available at: www.bbc.co.uk/news/business-25227877 [Accessed February 2018].

Beard, J., 2002. Management of Technology: A Three-Dimensional Framework With Propositions for Future Research. *Knowledge, Technology & Policy*, 15(3), 45–57.

Behera, L.K., 2009. India's Defence Offset Policy. *Strategic Analysis*, 32(2), 242–253.

Behera, L.K., 2012a. *A Critique of India's Defence Offset Guideline*. [Online]. New Delhi: The Institute for Defence Studies and Analyses. Available at: www.idsa.in/policybrief/.

Behera, L.K., January 2012b. India's Defense Acquisition System: Need for Further Reforms. *Korean Journal of Defense Analysis*, 24(1), 89–105.

Behera, L.K., 2015. *Defence Offsets: International Best Practises and Lessons for India.* New Delhi: Institute for Defence Studies and Analyses.

Behera, L.K., 2016. *DPP-2016: An Analytical Overview.* [Online]. New Delhi: The Institute for Defence Studies and Analyses. Available at: https://idsa.in/specialfeature/dpp-2016_lkbehera_120416.

Behera, L.K. and Kaushal, V., eds., 2011. *Defence Acquisition: International Best Practises.* New Delhi: Institute for Defence Studies and Analyses.

Bell, M. 1984. 'Learning' and the Accumulation of Industrial Technological Capability in Developing Countries. In: M. Fransman and King, eds. *Technological Capability in the Third World.* St Martin's Press: New York.

Bell, M., 1986. *Technical Change in Infant Industries: A Review of Empirical Evidence.* Washington, DC: The World Bank, p. 92.

Bell, M. and Albu, M., 1999. Knowledge Systems and Technological Dynamism in Industrial Cluster in Developing Countries. *World Development*, 27(9), 1715–1734.

Bell, M., Hobday, M., Abdullah, S., Ariffin, N. and Malik, J., 1995. *Aiming for 2020: A Demand Driven Perspective on Industrial Technology Policy in Malaysia.* Final Report for the World Bank and the Ministry of Science, Technology and the Environment, Malaysia, SPRU, October.

Bell, M. and Pavitt, K., 1993. Technological Accumulation and Industrial Growth: Contrasts Between Developed and Developing Countries. *Industrial and Corporate Change*, 2(2), 157–210.

Bell, M. and Pavitt, K., 1997. Technological accumulation and industrial growth: contrasts between developed and developing countries. *Technology, Globalisation and Economic Performance*, 83137, 83–137.

Bell, M. N., 2002. Technical Change in Infant Industries: A Review of Empirical Evidence, *World Bank Staff Working Paper, Washington.*

Bellais, R. and Guichard, R., 2006, Defense Innovation, Technology Transfers and Public Policy. *Defence and Peace Economics*, 17(3), 273–286.

BenDaniel, D.J., Rosenbloom, A.H. and Hanks, J.J., 2002. *International M & A, Joint Ventures & Beyond: Doing the Deal.* New York, NY: Wiley.

Bennett, D. and Vaidya, K., 2005. Meeting Technology Needs of Enterprises for National Competitiveness. *International Journal of Technology Management*, 32(1), 112–153.

Benoit, E., 1978. Growth and Defense in Developing Countries. *Economic Development and Cultural Change*, 26(2), 271–280.

Benkenstein, M. and Bloch, B., 1993. Models of Technological Evolution: Their Impact on Technology Management. *Marketing Intelligence and Planning*, 11(1), 20–27.

Bernstein, H., 1971. Modernization Theory and the Sociological Study of Development. *Journal of Development Studies*, 7(2), 141–160.

Bernstein, P.L., 1998. *Against the Gods: The Remarkable Story of Risk.* New York, NY: Wiley & Sons, Inc.

Bettis, R.A. and Prahalad, C.K., 1995. The Dominant Logic: Retrospective and Extension. *Strategic Management Journal*, 16(1), 5–14.

Betz, F., 1993. *Strategic Technology Management.* New York, NY: McGraw-Hill.

Beverly, B. and Kevin, S., 1995. Evaluating Technological Collaborative Opportunities: A Cognitive Perspective. *Strategic Management Journal*, 16(Suppl. 1), 43–70.

Biederman, D., 1999. Offsets and Countertrade. *Traffic World*, 259(6), 189.

Bishop, P., 1996. Buyer–Supplier Linkages in the Defence Industry: The Case of Devonport Dockyard Area. *Journal of Defence and Peace Economics*, 28, 171–222.

Biswas, B., 1993. Defense Spending and Economic Growth in Developing Countries. In: J.E. Payne and A.P. Sahu, eds. *Defense Spending and Economic Growth.* Boulder, CO: Westview Press, pp. 223–235.

Bitzinger, R., 1999. Globalization in the Post-Cold War Defense Industry: Challenges and Opportunities. In: A. Markusen and S. Costigan, eds. *Arming the Future: A Defense Industry for the 21st Century*. New York, NY: Council on Foreign Relations Press, pp. 306

Bitzinger, R., 2003. *Towards a Brave New Arms Industry? The Decline of the Second Tier Arms-Producing Countries and the Emerging International Division of Labour in the Defence Industry*, Adelphi Papers 356. London: International Institute of Strategic Studies.

Bitzinger, R., 2009. *The Modern Defense Industry: Political, Economic and Technological Issues*. Santa Barbara, CA: Praeger Security International.

Bitzinger, R., 2015. Defense Industries in Asia and the Technonationalist Impulse. *Contemporary Security Policy*, 36(3), 453–472.

Bitzinger, R., 2017. *Arming Asia Technonationalism and Its Impact on Local Defense Industries*. Abingdon and New York, NY: Routledge.

Blinder, A.S., 2002. *Keynesian Economics*. The Concise Encyclopaedia of Economics, Library of Economics and Liberty. Available at: www.econlib.org/library/Enc1/KeynesianEconomics.html# [Accessed 23 August 2017].

Blunck, F., 2006. *What Is Competitiveness?* [Online]. San Francisco, CA: Scribd Inc. Available at: www.scribd.com/document/51537839/what-is-competitive [Accessed 25 August 2010].

Boer, F.P., 1999. *The Valuation of Technology*. New York, NY: John Wiley & Sons.

Bombardier, 2017. *Bombardier's Chinese Joint Venture Wins Its First Monorail Contract in China*. [Press Release]. December 18, 2017. Available at: www.bombardier.com/en/media/newsList/details.bt-20171218-bombardiers-chinese-joint-venture-wins-its-first-mon.bombardiercom.html [Accessed January 2018].

Bosshart, S., Luedi, T. and Wang, E., 2010. *Past Lessons for China's New Joint Ventures*. [Online]. McKinsey & Company. Available at: www.mckinsey.com/business-functions/strategy-and-corporate-finance/our-insights/past-lessons-for-chinas-new-joint-ventures [Accessed June 2017].

Bower, J.L. and Doz, Y., 1979. Strategy Formulation: A Social and Political Process. In: D.E. Schendel and C.W. Hofer, eds. *Strategic Management*. Boston, MA: Little Brown, pp. 152–166.

Boyce, T., 2000. *Understanding Smart Procurement in the Ministry of Defence*. London: Hawksmere.

Bozeman, B., 2000. Technology Transfer and Public Policy: A Review of Research and Theory. *Research Policy*, 29(4–5), 627–655.

Burgess, K and Antill, P., 2017. *Emerging Strategies in Defence Acquistion and Military Procurement*. Washington: IGI Global, pp. 263–276.

Bush's Press Secretary, 1990. *The WhiteHouse Office of the Press Secretary*, April 16.

Braddon, D., Dowdall, P., Kendry, A. and Reay, S., 1992. *Defence Procurement and the Defence Industry Supply Chain: A Research Report on the Impact of Reduced Military Expenditure on the Defence Market Supply Network*. Research Unit in Defence Economics, University of West of England, Bristol.

Brauer, J. and Dunne, J.P., eds., 2004. *Arms Trade and Economic Development: Theory, Policy and Cases in Arms Trade Offsets*. Abingdon and New York, NY: Routledge.

Briani, V., Marrone, A., Molling, C. and Valasek, T., 2013. *The Development of a European Defence Technological and Industrial Base (EDTIB)*. Brussels: Directorate-General for External Policies of the Union-Directorate B. Available at: www.europarl.europa.eu/RegData/etudes/etudes/join/2013/433838/EXPO-SEDE_ET(2013)433838_EN.pdf.

Bribe Payers Index. 2002. Transparency International [online]. Available at https://www.transparency.org/research/bpi/bpi_2002/0 [Accessed 5 June 2017].

Bribery Act, 2010. [Online]. HMSO. Available at: www.legislation.gov.uk/ukpga/2010/23/contents.

Brzozka, M., 2004. The Economics of Arms Imports After the End of the Cold War. *Defence and Peace Economics*, 15(2), 111–123.

Brzoaka, M. and Ohlson, T., eds., 1986. *Arms Production in the Third World*. London: Taylor & Francis.

Buckley, P.J., 2003. *The Changing Global Context of International Business*. New York, NY: Palgrave Macmillan.

Butt, N., 2015. *Evaluating the Costs and Benefits in Relations to Technology Transfer by Investigating the UAE Offsets Policy: Supplier Perspective*. MSc Dissertation (unpublished), University of Warwick, WMG.

Bulgin, R., 2015. Global Offsets and Countertrade Association GOCA. Training Module. In: *COGA Spring Conference*. Philadelphia, PA, USA, 28 September–1 October.

Cable, V and Persaud, B., 1989. New Trends and Policy Problems in Foreign Investment: The Experience of Commonwealth Developing Countries. In: V. Cabblent, ed. *Developing With Foreign Investment*. London: Croom Helm, pp. 71.

Cairney, P., 2009. Implementation and Governance Problem: A Pressure Participant Perspective. *Public Policy and Administration*, 24(4), 355–377.

Cairney, P., 2012. *Understanding Public Policy: Theories and Issues*. Basingstoke: Palgrave Macmillan.

Canada Department of Business and Industry, 2013. *Canada's Industrial and Regional Benefits: The IRB Policy Within the Government of Canada Procurement Process*. [Online]. Ottawa: Department of Business and Industry. Available at: www.canada.ca/en/services/business.html [Accessed 8 June 2015].

Cardell, S. and Management Consultancies Association, 2002. *Strategic Collaboration: Creating the Extended Organization*. London: Hodder & Stoughton.

Carrincazeane, C. and Frigat, V., 2007. The Internationalization of French Aerospace Industry: To What Extent Were the 1990's a Break With the Past? *Competition and Change*, 11(3), 260–284.

Cavusgil, S., Ghauri, P. and Agarwal, M., 2002. *Doing Business in Emerging Markets: Entry and Negotiation Strategies*. Thousand Oaks, CA: SAGE.

Centre for Exploitation of Science and Technology (CEST), 1991. *The Management of Technological Collaboration*. Report by the Science Policy Research Unit (SPRU), University of Sussex for CEST.

Cetindamar, D., Phaal, R. and Probert, D., 2009. Understanding Technology Management as a Dynamic Capability: A Framework for Technology Management Activities. *Technovation*, 29(1), 45–58.

Chakraborty, S., 2016. *To Evaluate the Barriers to Successful Transfer of Technology to India Through Offsets*. MSc Dissertation (unpublished), WMG, University of Warwick.

Chandra, V. and Kolavalli, S., 2006. Technology, Adaptation, and Exports-How Some Developing Countries Got It Right. In: V. Chandra, ed. *Technology, Adaptation and Exports: How Some Developing Countries Got It Right*. Washington, DC: The World Bank, pp. 19–22.

Chang, H.-J., 2002. *Kicking Away the Ladder: Development Strategy in Historical Perspective*. London: Anthem Press.

Chartered Institute of Purchasing and Supply, n.d. *Countertrade*. [pdf]. Available at: www.cips.org/Documents/Resources/Knowledge%20Summary/Countertrade.pdf [Accessed 3 February 2018].

Chen, H. and Chen, T.-J., 2002. Asymmetric Strategic Alliances: A Network View. *Journal of Business Research*, 55, 1007–1013.

Chenery, H.B., 1960. Pattern of Industrial Growth. *American Economic Review*, 50, 624–665.

Chenery, H.B. and Syrquin, M., 1975. *Patterns of Development, 1950–1970*. Oxford: Oxford University Press.

Cheng, L.K., 1984. International Competition in R & D and Technological Leadership: An Examination of the Posner-Hufbauer Hypothesis. *Journal of International Economics*, 17(1–2), 15–40.

Child, J., Faulkner, D. and Tallman, S., 2005. *Cooperative Strategy: Managing Alliances, Networks, and Joint Ventures*, 2nd ed. Oxford: Oxford University Press.

Chinworth, M., 1992. *Inside Japan's Defence: Technology, Economics and Strategy*. Oxford: Oxford University Press.

Chinworth, M., 2011. Offset Policies and Trends in Japan, South Korea and Taiwan. In: J. Brauer and J. Dunne, eds. *Arms Trade and Economic Development, Theory, Policy and Cases in Arms Trade Offset*. Abingdon and New York, NY: Routledge, pp. 233–245.

Cho, N.H., Han, N.S., Park, J.S., Yang, Y.C., Lee, H.M. and Ahn, J.H., 2006. *A Research on the Offset Technology Valuation*. Korea Institutes of Defence Analysis, Korean.

Choi, H.J., 2009. Technology Transfer Issues and a New Technology Transfer Model. *Journal of Technology Studies*, 35(1), 49–57, Fall.Chowdhury, J., 1992. Performance of International Joint Ventures and Wholly Owned Foreign Subsidiaries: A Comparative Perspective. *MIR: Management International Review*, 32, 115–133.

Chowdhury, A. and Islam, I., 1993. *The Newly Industrialising Economies of East Asia*. London: Routledge.

Chuter, A., 2010. Nations Seek More Offset From Suppliers. *Defense News* (Citing Internet Resources). Available at: www.defensenews.com/story.php?i=4588118 [Accessed 10 May 2011].

Chuter, A., 2013. As Firms Target Exports, Offsets Create Headaches. *Defense News*, 20 May. Available at: www.blenheimcapital.net/downloads/Defense_News_20_May_2013.pdf [Accessed 16 November 2017].

Claessens, S. and Yurtoglu, B.B., 2012. Corporate Governance and Development: An Update (English). In: *IFC Corporate Governance FOCUS Publication; No. 10*. Washington, DC: World Bank Group.

Clark, K., 1986. Company Technology Strategy, R&D Management, V19, N3.

Clarke, T., ed., 2004. *Theories of Corporate Governance: The Philosophical Foundations of Corporate Governance*. London: Routledge.

Clugston, G., 2016. Anti-Corruption in Offsets, Global Offsets and Countertrade Association Advanced Education,Toledo, Spain.

Clulow, V., Gerstman, J. and Barry, C., 2003. The Resource-based View and Sustainable Competitive Advantage: The Case of a Financial Services Firm. *Journal of European Industrial Training*, 220–232.

Cohen, R., 1999. *Negotiating Across Culture: International Communication in an Interdependent World*, 2nd ed. Washington, DC: Institute of Peace.

Cohen, S. and Zysman, J., 1986. Evaluating Offset Agreements: Achieving a Balance of Advantages. *Law and Policy in International Business*, 765.

Cohen, W.M. and Levinthal, D.A., 1990. Absorptive Capacity: A New Perspective on Learning and Innovation. *Administrative Science Quarterly*, 35, 128–152.

Committees on Arms Export Control. 2013. [online]. https://publications.parliament.uk/pa/cm201314/cmselect/cmquad/205/205we05.htm. [Accessed 15 April 2018].

Contractor, F.J. and Lorange, P., 1988. *Cooperative Strategies in International Business: Joint Ventures and Technology Partnerships Between Firms*. Massachusetts/Toronto, Lexington: Emerald Group Publishing.

Countertrade and Offsets, 2017. Quarterly Bulletin [Online]. Available on http://cto-offsets.com.

Crane, G.T. and Amawi, A., eds., 1997. *The Theoretical Evolution of International Political Economy: A Reader*. New York, NY: Oxford University Press.

Crouchy, D., Galai, R. and Mark, S., 2006. *The Essentials of Risk Management*. New York, NY: McGraw-Hill.

CTO Data Services Co., 2011. The EU Directive on Offsets: The Experts View. *Countertrade & Offsets*, 29(4).

Daily Maverick. 2016a. *Fresh Bribery Claims in Swedish Jet Scandal*. [Online]. Avaiable at: https://www.thelocal.se/20150625/saab-payouts-in-jas-gripen-bribery-scandal [Accessed 25 June 2016].

Dahlman, C., 2007. Technology, Globalization and International Competitiveness: Challenges for Developing Countries. In: Department of Economic and Social Affairs (DESA), ed. *Industrial Development for the 21st Century*. New York, NY: United Nations. Part 1.2, p. 29.

Damodaran, A., 2008. *Strategic Risk Taking: A Framework for Risk Management*. Upper Saddle River, NJ: Wharton School Publishing.

Das, G., 2008. Does Trade and Technology Transmission Facilitate Convergence? The Role of Technology Adoption in Reducing the Inequality of Nations. *Journal of Economic Policy Reform*, 11(1), 67–92.

Deger, S., 1986. Economic Development and Defense Expenditure. *Economic Development and Cultural Change*, 35(1), 179–196.

Deger, S. and Sen, S., 1983. Military Expenditure, Spin-off, and Economic Development. *Journal of Development Economics*, 13(1), 67–83.

Deger, S. and Smith, R., 1983. Military Expenditures and Growth in Less Developed Countries. *Journal of Conflict Resolution*, 27(2), 335–353.

Dehoff, K., Dowdy, J. and Kwon, O.S., 2014. *Defense Offsets: From 'Contractual Burden' to Competitive Weapon*. [Online]. McKinsey & Company. Available at: www.mckinsey.com/industries/public-sector/our-insights/defense-offsets-from-contractual-burden-to-competitive-weapon.

DeLeon, P., 1999. The Missing Link Revisited: Contemporary Implementation Research. *Review of Policy Research*, 16(3–4), 311–338.

de Miramon, J., 1985. Countertrade: An illusory solution. OECD Observer, No.134, May, pp. 24–29.

Dhalman, C., 2007. Technology, Globalisation, and International Competitiveness: Challenges for Developing Countries. *ASDF*, 29.

Djeflat, A.K., 1987. The Management of Technology Transfer: Views and Experiences of Developing Countries. *International Journal of Technology Management*, 3(1/2), 149–165.

Dodds, Robert .F., Jr., 1995. Offsets in Chinese Government Procurements: The Partially Open Door. *Law and Policy in International Business*, 26(4), 1119–1145.

Dodgson, M., 1991. The Management of Technological Collaboration. *Engineering Management Journal*, 1(4), 187–192.

Dolowitz, D.P., 2003. A Policy-Maker's Guide to Policy Transfer. *Political Quarterly*, 74(1), 101–108.

Dosi, G., et al (eds), 1990. *The Economics of Technical Change and International Trade*. Wheatsheaf and New York, NY: Harvester.

Dreher, A., Fuchs, A., Parks, B., Strange, A.M. and Tierney, M.J., 2017. *Aid, China, and Growth: Evidence From a New Global Development Finance Dataset*. [Online]. AidData, Working Paper No. 46. Williamsburg, VA: AidData. Available at: http://aiddata.

org/publications/aid-china-and-growth-evidence-from-a-new-global-development-finance-dataset [Accessed 19 April 2017].

Drucker, P.F., 2011. *Technology, Management, and Society*. Boston, MA: Harvard Business Press.

Dunmade, I., 2002. Indicators of Sustainability: Assessing the Suitability of a Foreign Technology for a Developing Economy. *Technology in Society*, 24(4), 461–471.

Dunne, P., 2000. Arms Offset Dubbed a 'Necessary Evil'. *Aviation Week & Space Technology*, 11 December, 49.

Dunne, P. and Freeman-Sam, P., 2003. The Demand for Military Spending in Developing Countries. *International Review of Applied Economics*, 17(1), 23–41.

Dunning, J.H., 1988. *Multinationals, Technology and Competitiveness*. London: Unwin Hyman.

Dymsza, W.A., 1988. Successes and Failures of JVs in Developing Countries: Lessons From Experience. In: F. Contractor and P. Lorange, eds. *Cooperative Strategies in International Business: Joint Ventures and Technology and Partnerships Between Firms*. Boston, MA: Lexington. Chapter 23.

Eaton, J. and Kortum, S., 1999. International Technology Diffusion: Theory and Measurement. *International Economic Review*, 40(3), 537–570.

The Economist, 2013. Guns and Sugar, 25 May, 69–77.

Edwards, J.P., 1977. Strategy Formulation as a Stylistic Process. *International Studies of Management and Organization*, 7(2), 13–27, Summer.

Edwards, J.P., 2011. *The EU Defence and Security Procurement Directive: A Step Towards Affordability?* International Security Programme Paper 2011/05. London: Chatham House. Available at: www.chathamhouse.org/sites/files/chathamhouse/0811pp_edwards.pdf [Accessed 2 February 2015].

Eisenhardt, K.M. and Martin, J.A., 2003. Dynamic Capabilities: What Are They? In: C.E. Helfat, ed. *The SMS Blackwell Handbook of Organizational Capabilities: Emergence, Development, and Change*. Oxford: Blackwell. Chapter 22.

Eisenhardt, K.M. and Sull, D.N., 2001. Strategy as Simple Rules. *Harvard Business Review*, 79(1), 107–116.

Eisenhut, D., 2013. Offset in Defence Procurement: A Strange Animal at the Brink of Extinction? *European Law Review*, 38(3), 393–403.

Elderkin, K. and W. Norquist, 1987. *Creative Countertrade*. Cambridge: Ballinger.

Eliassen, K.A. and Shriver, M., 2002. *European Defence Procurement and Industrial Policy: A Comparative 6 Countries Analysis*. Oslo: Centre for European and Asian Studies at Norwegian School of Management.

Eliasson, G., 2010. *Advanced Public Procurement as Industrial Policy: The Aircraft Industry as a Technical University*. New York, NY: Springer-Verlag.

Eriksson, E.A., et al., 2007. *Study on the Effects of Offsets on the Development of a European Defence Industry and Market*. Final Report for the European Defence Agency 06-DIM-022. Stockholm: FOI and SCS. Available at: www.rijksoverheid.nl/binaries/rijksoverheid/documenten/rapporten/2007/12/12/study-on-the-effects-of-offsets-on-the-development-of-a-european-defence-industry-and-market/7144908-bijlage2.pdf.

Escobar, A., 1995. *Encountering Development: The Making and Unmaking of the Third World*. Princeton, NJ: Princeton University Press.

European Club for Countertrade and Offset (ECCO), 2011. *What Is Offset? Principles*. [Online]. Available at: www.ecco-offset.eu/what-is-offset/principles/ [Accessed 11 January 2018].

European Defence Agency, 2008. *The Code of Conduct on Offsets*. [Online]. Available at: www.infodefensa.com/wp-content/uploads/TheCodeofConductonOffsets%5B1%5D.pdf [Accessed February 2016].

European Defence Agency, The Code of Conduct on Offsets, 2008.[Online]. Available at: http:// www.google.co.uk/url?sa=t&rct=j&q=&esrc=s&source=web&cd=1&cad=rja. [Accessed February 2016].

European Union: Council of the European Union, 1997. *Treaty of Amsterdam Amending the Treaty on European Union, The Treaties Establishing the European Communities and Related Acts.* [Online], 10 November. Available at: www.europarl.europa.eu/topics/ treaty/pdf/amst-en.pdf [Accessed 30 January 2015].

European Defense Industry Group (EDIG), 2011. *Policy Paper on Offsets.* Report EPP / OO/18. Brussels: European Defense Industry Group.

Evans, C., 1986. Reappraising Third World Arms Production. *Survival*, 28(2), 99–118, March/April.

Evans, M. and Davies, J., 1999. Understanding Policy Transfer: A Multi-Level, Multi-Disciplinary Perspective. *Public Administration*, 77(2), 361–385.

Eveland, J.D., 1986. Diffusion, Technology Transfer, and Implementation Thinking and Talking About Change. *Science Communication*, 8(2), 303–322.

Evenson, R.E. and Westphal, L., 1995. Technological Change and Technological Strategy. *Handbook of Development Economics*, 3(1), 2209–2299.

Fasel, D.K., 2000. *Partnering in Action: A Guide for Building Successful Collaboration Across Organizational Boundaries.* Oxford: Pathways.

Felton, P., 2012. Direct Offset in the Nuclear Trade With China. In: *European Club for Countertrade & Offset Symposium #5.* Frankfurt, Germany, 14–15 November 2012. Available at: www.ecco-offset.eu/wp-content/uploads/Agenda-Symposium-5.pdf and www.ecco-offset.eu/wp-content/uploads/SUMMARIES-OF-INTERVENTION. pdf.

Feurer, R. and Chaharbaghi, K., 1994. Defining Competitiveness: A Holistic Approach. *Management Decision*, 32(2), 49–58.

Financial Times, 1995. Longbow Apache Secured 3000 Jobs. *The Financial Times*, 14 July, 14.

Financial Times, 2017. *Ft.com/LEXICON.* [Online]. Available at: http://lexicon.ft.com/ Term?term=strategic-industry [Accessed 31 January 2018].

Fischer, F., 2003. *Reframing Public Policy.* Oxford: Oxford University Press.

Flam, H. and Helpman, E., 1987. Vertical Product Differentiation and North-South Trade. *American Economic Review, American Economic Association*, 77(5), 810–822.

Fluker, L; Muravska, J. and Pyman, M., 2010. *Defence Offsets: Addressing the Risks of Corruption and Raising Transparency.* [Online]. Transparency International (UK). Available at: http://ti-defence.org/publications/20-category-publications-dsp/75-dsp-pubs-offsets-1.html,April 2010 [Accessed 6 November 2013].

Florio, N., Parikh, P. and Hussain, A., 2017. *Aerospace & Defence Global Cross-Border Joint Ventures: Precise, Guided and Complex.* [Online]. Deloitte Center for Industry Insights. [pdf]. Available at: www2.deloitte.com/content/dam/Deloitte/us/Documents/ manufacturing/us-aerospace-and-defense-cross-border-joint-venture.pdf [Accessed May 2017].

Foray, D. and Freeman, C., 1993. *Technology and the Wealth of Nations.* London: Pinter Publishers.

Fozdar, B.I., 2015. Open and Distance Learning (ODL): A Strategy of Development Through Its Potential Role in Improving Science & Technology Knowledge. [Online]. *International Journal of Emerging Technologies in Learning*, 10(2), 9–16. Available at: http://online-journals.org/index.php/i-jet/article/view/4176/3477.

Freeman, R.E., 1984. *Strategic Management: A Stakeholder Approach.* London: Pitman.

Fu, X., Pietrobelli, C. and Soete, L., 2011. The Role of Foreign Technology and Indigenous Innovation in the Emerging Economies: Technological Change and Catching-up. *World Development*, 39(7), 1204–1212.

Furter, L. Denise, 2014. *The Influence of Legislation and Government Policy on Patterns of International Defence Trade and Future Markets: The Case of Offset and Directive 2009/81/ec*. PhD in International Business, Brunel University, West London, UK.

Gale, A. and Luo, J., 2004. Factors Affecting Construction Joint Ventures in China. *International Journal of Project Management*, 22(1), 33–42. doi:10.1016/S0263-7863(03)00012-7.

Garyard, S., Barney, J. and Thompson, G., 2012. The Rising Global Offset Challenge: Addressing the Half Trillion Dollar Question. In: *Global Association for Countertrade and Offset/Defense Industry Offset Association (DIOA/GOCA) Fall Conference*. Brewster, MA, 10 September 2012.

Georgescu, C., Caraiani, G. and Tutor, M., 2013. The Importance and Role of Offsets Within International Economic Exchanges. In: *Knowledge Horizons: Economics*. Bucharest: "Dimitrie Cantemir" Christian University.

Gibson, D.C.R., 1998. *Valuing Technology Transfer in the Context of Defence Offsets*. MDA Dissertation, no. 12. Cranfield University, UK.

Glass, A. and Saggi, K., 1998. International Technology Transfer and the Technology Gap. *Journal of Development Economics*, 55(2), 369–398.

The Global Competitiveness Report 2017–2018, p. 68. *World Economic Forum* [online] at org/reports/the-global-competitiveness-report 2017–2018 (accessed on 15 January 2018).

Globerman, S. and Shapiro, D., 2002. Global Foreign Direct Investment Flows: The Role of Governance Infrastructure. *World Development*, 30(11), 1899–1919.

Glugston, G., 2016. Global Offsets and Countertrade Association (GOCA) Offsets Training Module. In: *Global Offsets and Countertrade Association (COCA), GOCA Conference*. Ottawa, Canada, 24–27 September.

Gonzales, L.A.A., 2012. *Defence Industrial Development and Self Sufficiency: Offsets Effectiveness in Spain*. PhD Thesis (unpublished) , Nanyang Technology University, Singapore.

Goulet, D., 1989. *The Uncertain Promise: Value Conflicts in Technology Transfer*, 2nd ed. New York, NY: New Horizons Press.

Graham, J. and Lam, M.N., 2003. The Chinese Negotiation. *Harvard Business Review*, 81(82–91), 137.

Grant, R.M., 2010. *Contemporary Strategy Analysis: Text and Cases*. Chichester: Wiley.

Grey, B. and Buchan, D., 1992. Bernard Grey and Dan Buchan @ Westland Wins Army Helicopter Order. *Financial Times*

Guardian, 2009. *Secrets of Al-Yamamah*. [Online]. Available at: https://www.the guardian.com/baefiles/page/0,2095831,00.html. [Accessed 14 June 2017].

Gulati, R., 1998. Alliances and Networks. *Strategic Management Journal*, 19(4), 293–317.

Gupta, V.K., 2008. India: IPR and the National Security. [Online]. *Journal of Intellectual Property Rights*, 318–325, July. Available at: http://nopr.niscair.res.in/bitstream/123456789/1780/1/JIPR%2013(4)%20318-325.pdf [Accessed 12 February 2012].

Gupta, V.K., 2015. Offsets: A Finance Perspective. In: M.S. Sodhi and R. Bhargava, eds. *Perspectives on India's Defence Offset Policy*. New Delhi: SAGE, pp. 45–60.

Hall, P., 2011. *Defence Offsets: Causes, Consequences and Questions*, Jakarta International Defence Dialogue. Jakarta, 23–26 March.

Hall, P. and Markowski, S., 1994. On the Normality and Abnormality of Offsets Obligations. *Defence and Peace Economics*, 5(3), 173–188.

Hambleton, K., Weiss, A. and University College, London, 2005. *Conquering Complexity: Lessons for Defence Systems Acquisition*. Norwich: TSO (The Stationery Office).

Hamel, G., 1998. Strategy Innovation and the Quest for Value. *Sloan Management Review*, 39(2), 7–14.

Hamel, G. and Prahalad, C.K., 1989. Strategic Intent. *Harvard Business Review*, 67(3), 63–76.

Hammond, G.T., 1987. Arms, Offsets and Innovation. *The Washington Quarterly*, 10(1), 173–185.

Hammond, G.T., 1990. *Countertrade, Offsets and Barter in International Political Economy*. London: Pinter Publishers.

Harrigan, K.R., 1986. *Managing for Joint Venture Success*. Lexington, MA: Lexington Books.

Harrison, N. and Samson, D., 2002. *Technology Management: Text and International Cases*. New York, NY: McGraw-Hill.

Hay, C., 2006. Globalization and Public Policy. In: M. Moran, M. Rein and R. Goodin, eds. *The Oxford Handbook of Public Policy*. Oxford: Oxford University Press. Chapter 29.

Hayward, K., 2013. *The Chinese Aerospace Industry: A Background Paper*. [pdf]. Royal Aeronautical Society. Available at: www.aerosociety.com/Assets/Docs/Publications/DiscussionPapers/ChineseAerospaceIndustryDiscussionPaper.pdf [Accessed 12 September 2017].

Helfat, C.E., Finkelstein, S., Mitchell, W., Peteraf, M.A., Singh, H., Teece, D.J. and Winter, S.G., 2007. *Dynamic Capabilities: Understanding Strategic Change in Organizations*. Oxford: Wiley-Blackwell Publishing.

Hennart, J.-F., 1989. The Transaction Cost Rationale for Countertrade. *Journal of Law, Economics, and Organisation*, 5(1), 127–153.

Hennart, J.-F. and Anderson, E., 1993. Countertrade and the Minimization of Transaction Costs: An Empirical Examination. *The Journal of Law, Economics, and Organization*, 9(2), 290–313.

Herrnstadt, O.E., 2008. *Offsets and Lack of a Comprehensive U.S. Policy : What do Other countries Know that we don't ?* EPI Briefing Paper. Washington, DC : Economic Policy Institute, April 17.

Henry, A.E., 2011. *Understanding Strategic Management*. Oxford: Oxford University Press.

Herbert, W., 1985. *Arms Production in the Third World*. Stockholm International Peace Research Institute (SIPRI) Yearbook. Oxford: Oxford University Press.

Herrnstadt, O.E., 2008. *Offsets and Lack of a Comprehensive U.S. Policy: What Do Other Countries Know That We Don't?* EPI Briefing Paper, no. 201, 17 April. Washington, DC: Economic Policy Institute.

Hennart, J.F., 1986. *The Causes of Countertrade* . Working paper, Centre for International Management Studies, The Wharton School.

Hennart. J.-F., 1989. The Transaction Costs Rationale for Countertrade. *Journal of Law, Economics and Organization*, 5(1), 127–153.

Hennart, J.-F., and Anderson, E. 1993. Countertrade and the Minimization of Transaction Costs: An Empirical Examination. *Journal of Law, Economics, and Organisation*, 9, 290–313.

Herzog, V.L., 2001. Trust Building on Corporate Collaborative Project Teams. *Project Management Journal*, 32(1), 28–37.

Hill, C.W.L., 2014. *International Business: Competing in the Global Marketplace*, 10th ed. Boston, MA: McGraw-Hill.

Hill, J.S. and Still, R.R., 1980. Cultural Effects of Technology Transfer by Multinational Corporations in Lesser Developed Countries. *Columbia Journal of World Business*, 15(2), 40–51.

Hill J.S. and Still, R.R., 2001. Cultural Effects of Technology Transfer by Multinational Corporations in Lesser Developed Countries. *Columbia Journal of World Business*, 40–51.

Hill, M. and Hupe, P., 2009. *Implementing Public Policy*, 2nd ed. London: SAGE.

Hillson, D., ed., 2016. *The Risk Management Handbook: A Practical Guide to Managing the Multiple Dimensions of Risk*. London: Page Limited.

Hines, C., 2000. *Localisation: A Global Manifesto*. London: Earthscan Publications, p. 27.

Hirschman, A.O., 1958. *The Strategy of Economic Development*. New Haven, CT: Yale University Press.

Hogwood, B. and Gunn, L., 1984. *Policy Analysis for the Real World*. Oxford: Oxford University Press.

Holmes, L., 2015. *Corruption: A Very Short Introduction*. Oxford: Oxford University Press.

Holtom, P., Bromley, M., Wezeman, P.D. and Wezeman, S.T., 2012. *Trends in International Arms Transfers 2011*. SIPRI Fact Sheet, March.

Howarth, C.S., 1994. The Role of Strategic Alliances in the Development of Technology. *Technovation*, 4(4), 243–257.

Howlett, M., Ramesh, M. and Perl, A., 2009. *Studying Public Policy: Policy Cycles and Policy Subsystems*. Oxford: Oxford University Press.

Howse, R., 2010. Beyond the Countertrade Taboo: Why the WTO Should Look at Barter and Countertrade. *University of Toronto Law Journal*, 60(2), 289–314, Spring.

Hoyos, C., 2013. Offsets Side Deals Spark Calls for Transparency. *Financial Times*. [Online]. Available at: www.ft.com/content/4c140b7a-251a-11e3-bcf7-00144feab7de [Accessed 18 May 2017].

Hoyos, C., Tsar, D. and Amann, A., 2013. Q&A: What Are Offsets? *Financial Times*, 9 October. [Online]. Available at: www.ft.com/content/87728d1e-197a-11e3-afc2-00144feab7de [Accessed 16 June 2015].

Hsiung, B., 1998. What Is the Real Value of Offsets and Technology Transfer? *Defence and Foreign Affairs Strategic Policy*, 26(1), 9–12.

Hunt, D., 1989. *Economic Theories of Development: A Competing Paradigm*. London: Harvester Wheatsheaf.

Huq, M., 2004. Building Technological Capability in the Context of Globalisation: Opportunities and Challenges Facing Developing Countries. *International Journal of Technology Management and Sustainable Development*, 3(3), 155–171.

Ianakiev, G. and Mladenov, N., 2009. Offset Policies in Defence Procurement: Lessons for the European Defence Equipment Market. In: *Annual Conference on Economics and Security, 13*. CITY College, Thessaloniki, Greece, 24–26 June.

Independent. 2010. *Independent, BAE Systems Pays $400m to Settle Bribery Charges*. [Online]. Available at: http://www.independent.co.uk/news/business/news/bae-systems-pays-400m-to-settle-bribery-charges-1891027.html [Accessed March 2017].

Jane's Defence Industry, 2013. Offset to Grow by USD50 Billion a Year as Firms Face Problems Clearing Obligations. *Jane's Defence Industry*, 30(3), 1 March.

Jang, W.-J., Chul, H.W., Kim, T.Y. and Joung, T.-Y., 2007. The Defense Offset Valuation Model. *The DISAM Journal*, 29(4), 91–101.

Jang, W.-J. D. and Joung, J.Y.2007. The Defense Offset Valuation Model, *s.I.: Defense Institute of Security Assistance Management*, 29(4), 91–101.

Jarrett, T. and Taylor, C., 2010. *Bribery Allegations and BAE Systems*. Commons Briefing Papers SN05367, House of Commons Library. Available at: http://researchbriefings. parliament.uk/ResearchBriefing/Summary/SN05367#fullreport [Accessed 25 February 2018].

Jegathesan, J., Gunasekaran, A. and Muthaly, S., 1997. Technology Development and Transfer: Experiences From Malaysia. *International Journal of Technology Management*, 13(2), 96–214.

Jenkins, J., Leicht, K. and Jaynes, A., 2006. Do High Technology Policies Work? High Technology Industry Employment Growth in U.S. Metropolitan Areas, 1988–1998. *Social Forces*, 85(1), 267–296, September.

Jenkins, R., 1991. The Political Economy of Industrialisation: A Comparison of Latin American and East Asian Newly Industrialising Countries. *Development and Change*, 22(2), 197–231.

Jenkins-Smith, H. and Sabatier, P., 1993. The Study of Public Policy Process. In: P. Sabatier and H. Jenkin-Smith, eds. *Policy Change and Learning: An Advocacy Coalition Approach*. Boulder, CO: Westview Press.

Jensen, R. and Thursby, M., 1986. A Strategic Approach to the Product Life Cycle. *Journal of International Economics*, 21(3–4), 269–285.

John, P., 2012. *Analysing Public Policy*, 2nd ed. London: Routledge.

Johnson, C., 1984. The Industrial Policy Debate Re-Examined. *California Management Review*, 27(1), 71–89, Fall.

Johnson, G. and Scholes, K., 1999. *Exploring Corporate Strategy*, 5th ed. London: Prentice Hall.

Jomo, K.S., ed., 2001. *Southeast Asia's Industrialization: Industrial Policy, Capabilities and Sustainability*. Houndmills and New York, NY: Palgrave Macmillan.

Jomo, K.S., 2003. *Manufacturing Competitiveness in Asia: How Internationally Competitive National Firm and Industries Developed in East Asia*. London: Routledge.

Jomo, K.S. and Felker, G., 1984. *Technology, Competitiveness and the State: Malaysia's Industrial Technology Policies*. London and New York, NY: Routledge.

Jomo, K.S., Felker, G. and Rasiah, R., eds., 1999. *Industrial Technology Development in Malaysia: Industry and Firm Studies*. London: Routledge.

Jones, E.W., Winter 2001–2002. The Value of Defense Industrial Offsets. *DISAM Journal of International Security Assistance Management*, 24(2), 108–118.

Junni, P. and Sarala, R.M., 2013. The Role of Absorptive Capacity in Acquisition Knowledge Transfer. *Thunderbird International Business Review*, 55(4), 419–438.

Jurgen, B. and Paul, J.D., 2004. *Arms Trade and Economic Development: Theory, Policy and Cases in Arms Trade Offsets*. Abingdon: Routledge.

Karagiannis, N., 2001. Key Economic and Politico-Institutional Elements of Modern Interventionism. *Social and Economic Studies*, 50(3/4), 17–47.

Karass, C.L., 1996. *In Business as in Life: You Don't Get What You Deserve, You Get What You Negotiate*. Stanford University Press.

Kaur, K., 2013. *Defence Acquisitions and Offsets: The Road Ahead*. Manekshaw Paper 42. New Delhi: Centre for Land Warfare Studies, KW Publishers Pvt Ltd.

Keith, B., Vitasek, K., Manrodt, K. and Kling, J., 2016. *Strategic Sourcing in the New Economy: Harnessing the Potential of Sourcing Business Models for Modern Procurement*. New York, NY: Palgrave Macmillan.

Keller, W., 1996. Absorptive Capacity: On the Creation and Acquisition of Technology in Development. *Journal of Development Economics*, 49(1), 199–227.

Kelly, T. and Rishi, M., 2003. An Empirical Study of the Spin-off effect of Military Spending. *Defence and Peace Economics*, 14(1), 1–17.

Kennedy, G., 1974. *The Military in the Third World*. New York, NY: Charles Scribner's Sons.

Kennedy, G., 1975. *The Economics of Defence*. London: Faber and Faber.

Kennedy, G., 1983. *Defence Economics*. London: Gerald Duckworth & Co Ltd.

Keohane, R.O., 2002. *Power & Governance in a Partially Globalized World*. London: Routledge, pp. 632–645.

Keohane, R.O. and Nye, J.S., 2011. *Power and Interdependence Revisited*, 4th ed. Longman Classics in Political Science. Cambridge: Pearson Ltd.

Khan, A.M., 2010. Market Trends and Analysis of Defense Offset. [Online]. *The DISAM Journal of International Security Assistance Management*, 32(1), July. Available at: www.disam.dsca.mil/pubs/Vol%2032_1/Journal%20%2032-1%20Web%20Jul%201. pdf [Accessed 11 April 2012].

Kiely, D.G., 1990. *Defence Procurement: The Equipment Buying Process*. London: Tri-Service Press.

Killing, P., 2012. *Strategies for Joint Venture Success (Routledge Library Editions: International Business)*. Abingdon and New York, NY: Routledge.

Kim, L. and Dahlman, C.J., 1992. Technology Policy for Industrialisation: An Integrative Framework and Korea's Experience. *Research Policy*, 21(5), 437–452.

Kim, L. and Nelson, R.R., 2000. *Technology, Learning and Innovation: Experiences of Newly Industrialising Economies*. Cambridge: Cambridge University Press.

Kim, S.H. and Lee, J., 2015. Absorptive Capacities and Supply Chain Performance: Focus on Korean Firms and Suppliers. *International Information Institute*, 18(3), 825–830.

Kimla, D., 2013. *Military Offsets & In-Country Industrialisation*. [Online]. Frost & Sullivan, Market Insight. Available at: www.frost.com/prod/servlet/cio/275947347 [Accessed 14 May 2013].

Kincaid, B., 2002. *Dinosaur in Permafrost*. Walton-on-Thames: Thesaurus.

Kincaid, B., 2008. *Changing the Dinosaur's Spots: The Battle to Reform UK Defence Acquisition*. London: RUSI.

Kirchwehm, H.A., 2013. Increasing Offset Obligations: How Can Small and Medium Enterprises in India Participate? *International Journal of Applied Research in Business Administration and Economics (IJAR-BAE)*, 48.

Kirchwehm, H.A., 2014a. Why Failed So Often the Offset Part of a Defence Procurement Deal?: A Case Study Based Examination. *Business Management and Strategy*, 5(2), 43–57.

Kirchwehm, H.A., 2014b. Impact of Defence Offsets on the Companies of the Participating Industry: A Case Study Based Examination. *International Journal of Business Research and Management (IJBRM)*, 5(4), 28–40.

Kleinman, M., 2017. GKN Plots Aerospace Tie-Up With State-Owned Chinese Group COMAC. *Sky News*. [Online (Last updated 1:48 P.M., 8 November 2017)]. Available at: https://news.sky.com/story/gkn-plots-aerospace-tie-up-with-state-owned-chinese-group-comac-11118436 [Accessed March 2017].

Klohs, B.M., 2012. Going Global: Best Practices in International Business Development. *Economic Development Journal*, 11(3), 27–34. Available at: http://search.proquest.com/abiglobal/docview/1124470099/11850F79A21D4CBCPQ/60?accountid=14888 [Accessed 28 January 2017].

Kogut, B., 1986. On Designing Contracts to Guarantee Enforceability: Theory and Evidence From East-West Trade. *Journal of International Business Studies*, 17(1), 47–62.

Kogut, B., 1983. Joint Ventures: Theoretical and Empirical Perspectives. *Strategic Management Journal*, 9(4), 319–332.

Korth, C.M., ed., 1987. *International Countertrade*. New York, NY: Quorum Books.

Kostecki, M., 1987. Should One Countertrade? *Journal of World Trade Law*, 21(2), 7–21.

Kottasova, I., 2014. World's Most Corrupt Industries. [Online]. *CNN Money*, 3 December. Available at: http://money.cnn.com/2014/12/02/news/bribery-foreign-corruption/index. html [Accessed 12 July 2017].

Krause, K., 1992. Arms Imports, Arms Production, and the Quest for Security in the Third World. In: B.L. Job, ed. *The Insecurity Dilemma: National Security of Third World States*. Boulder, CO: Lynne Rienner Publishers, pp. 21–142. Chapter 9.

Kremer, D. and Sain, B., 2012. *Offsets in Weapon System Sales: A Case Study of the Korean Fighter Program*. Master's Thesis, US Air Force Institute of Technology, Air University, Wright-Patterson AFB, OH. Available at: www.dtic.mil/dtic/tr/fulltext/u2/a259680.pdf [Accessed 14 December 2017].

Krugman, P., 1979. A Model of Innovation, Technology Transfer, and the World Distribution of Income. *Journal of Political Economy*, 87(2), 253–266.

Krugman, P., 1994. Competitiveness: A Dangerous Obsession. *Foreign Affairs*, 73(2), 28–44.

Lall, S., 1960. Technology Policy and Challenges. In: *Conference on Globalisation and Development: Lessons for the Malaysian Economy*. Faculty of Economics and Administration, University of Malaya, Kuala Lumpur, August 1960.

Lall, S., 1975. Is Dependence a Useful Concept in Analysing Underdevelopment? *World Development*, 3(11), 799–810.

Lall, S., 1978. Transnationals, Domestic Enterprises, and Industrial Structure in Host LDCs: A Survey. *Oxford Economic Papers*, 30(2), 217–248, July.

Lall, S., 1989. *Foreign Investment, Transnationals and Developing Countries*. London: Macmillan.

Lall, S., 1992. Technological Capabilities and Industrialisation. *World Development*, 20(2), 165–186.

Lall, S., 1993. Policies for Building Technological Gap: Lessons From Asian Experience. *Asian Development Review*, 11(2), 72–103.

Lall, S., 1995. Malaysia: Industrial Success and the Role of the Government. *Journal of International Development*, 7(5), 759–773.

Lall, S., 1996. *Learning From the Asian Tigers: Studies in Technology and Industrial Policies*. Houndmills: Macmillan and New York, NY: St. Martin's Press.

Lall, S., 1997. *Transnational Domestic Enterprises & Industrial Structure in Host LDCs: A Survey, the UN Library on TNCs*, 11, p. 111.

Lall, S., 1998. The East Asian Miracle: Does the Bell Toll for Industrial Strategy? *World Development*, 22(4), 645–654.

Lall, S., 1999. *Competing With Labour: Skills and Competitiveness in Developing Countries*. Discussion Paper 31. Geneva, Switzerland: Development Policies Department, International Labor Office.

Lall, S., 2000. The Technological Structure and Performance of Developing Country Manufactured Exports, 1985–1998. *Oxford Development Studies*, 28(3), 337–369.

Lall, S., 2001. Competitiveness Indices and Developing Countries: An Economic Evaluation of the Global Competitiveness Report. *World Development*, 29(9), 1501–1525.

Lall, S. and Morris, T., 1998. 'Market-Stimulating' Technology Policies in Developing Countries: A Framework With Examples From East Asia. [Online]. *World Development*,

26(8), 1369–1385. Available at: http://siteresources.worldbank.org/INTEXPCOMNET/ Resources/Technology_Policies_East_Asia.pdf [Accessed 11 November 2017].

Lall, S. and Najmabadi, F., 1995. *Developing Industrial Technology: Lessons for Policy and Practice*. Washington, DC: The World Bank.

Lall, S. and Teubal, M., 1998. 'Market-Stimulating' Technology Policies in Developing Countries: A Framework with Examples from East Asia. *World Development, 26*(8), 1369–1385.

Landau, D., 1994. The Impact of Military Expenditures on Economic Growth in the Less Developed Countries. *Defence and Peace Economics*, 5(1), 205–220.

Lane, A., 2006. What is technology? The Open University [Online]. Available at http://www.open.edu/openlearn/science-maths-technology/engineering-and-technology/technology/what-technology [Accessed 14 June 2016].

Lawton-Smith, H., 1991. Industry-Academic Links: The Case of Oxford University. *Environment and Planning C: Government and Policy*, 9(4), 403–416.

Learmont, E.M., 2005. *Defence Industrialisation Through Offsets: The Case of South Korea*. MDA Dissertation, Exec 11. Cranfield University, UK.

Lecraw, D., 1988. Countertrade: A Form of Cooperative International Business Arrangement. In: F. Contractor and P. Lorange, eds., *Cooperative Strategies in International Business*. Lexington: Mass Lexington Books.

Lee, T., 2004. Determinants of the Foreign Equity Share of International Joint Ventures. *Journal of Economic Dynamics & Control*, 2004, pp. 96–106.

Leigh, D. and Evans, R., 2009. Secrets of Al-Yamamah. *The Guardian*. [Online]. Available at: www.theguardian.com/baefiles/page/0,2095831,00.html [Accessed 7 March 2017].

Leigh, D. and Evans, R., 2010. BAE Admits Guilt Over Corrupt Arms Deals. *The Guardian*, 6 February. [Online]. Available at: www.theguardian.com/world/2010/feb/05/bae-systems-arms-deal-corruption [Accessed 17 February 2017].

Lim, S.H., 2005. *Analysing the Effectiveness of Korean Defence Offsets*. MDA Dissertation, no. 19. Cranfield University, UK.

Linder, S. and Peters, B.G., 2006. Coming to Terms With Intramural Differences Over Policy Frameworks. *Policy Sciences*, 39(1), 19–40.

Lindquist, E., 2004. Organizing for Policy Implementation: The Emergence and Role of Implementation Units in Policy Design and Oversight. *Journal of Comparative Policy Analysis: Research and Practice*, 8(4), 311–324.

The Local (Sweden), 2015. Fresh Bribery Claims in Swedish Jet Scandal. *The Local*, 25 June. [Online]. Available at: www.thelocal.se/20150625/saab-payouts-in-jas-gripen-bribery-scandal [Accessed 25 June 2018].

Mackun, P. and MacPherson, A.D., 1997. Externally-assisted Product Innovation in the Manufacturing Sector: The Role of Location, In-house R&D and Outside Technical Support. *Regional Studies*, 31(7), 659–668.

Madu, C., 1989. Transferring Technology to Developing Countries: Critical Factors for Success. *Long Range Planning*, 22(4), 115–124.

Magahy, B., Vilhena da Cunha, F. and Pyman, M., 2010. *Defence Offsets: Addressing The Risks of Corruption & Raising Transparency*. [Online]. UK: Transparency International. Available at: www.acrc.org.ua/assets/files/zvity_ta_doslidzhennya/TI_Defence_Offset_Report_20101.pdf.

Mann, P., 2000. Arms Offsets Dubbed a 'Necessary Evil'. *Aviation Week and Space Technology*, 153(24), 11 December, 49.

Mansfield, E., 1975. International Technology Transfer: Forms, Resource Requirements and Policies. *American Economic Review*, 65(2), 372–376.

Manuel, K.M., 2016. *The Buy America Act: Preference for "Domestic Supplies": In Brief*. Congressional Research Services. Available at: https://fas.org/sgp/crs/misc/R43140.pdf.

Markowski, S. and Hall, P., 1998. Challenges of Defence Procurement. *Defence and Peace Economics*, 9(1–2), 3–37. doi:10.1080/10430719808404892.

Markowski, S. and Hall, P., 2014. Mandated Defence Offsets: Can They Ever Deliver? *Defense and Security Analysis*, 30(2), 148–162.

Markowski, S., Hall, P. and Wylie, R., eds., 2010. *Defence Procurement and Industry Policy: A Small Country Perspective*. London: Routledge.

Markwell, D., 2006. *John Maynard Keynes and International Relations: Economic Paths to War and Peace*. Oxford: Oxford University Press.

Marsh, D. and McConnell, A., 2010. Towards a Framework for Establishing Policy Success. *Public Administration*, 88(2), 564–583.

Martin, S., ed., 1996. Countertrade and Offsets: An Overview of the Theory and Evidences. In: S. Martin, ed. *The Econmics of Offsets: Defence Procurement and Countertrade*. Amsterdam: Harwood. Chapter 2.

Martin, S. and Hartley, K., 1995. UK Firms' Experience and Perceptions of Defence Offsets: Survey Results. *Defence and Peace Economics*, 6(2), 123–139.

Marton, K., 1986. *Multinationals, Technology and Industrialization: Implications and Impact in Third World Countries*. Lexington, MA: Lexington Books.

Massey, A., 2001. Policy, Management and Implementation. In: S. Savage and R. Atkinson, eds. *Public Policy Under Blair*. London: Palgrave Macmillan.

Matland, R., 1995. The Implementation Literature: The Ambiguity-Conflict Model of Policy Implementation. *Journal of Public Administration Research and Theory: J-PART*, 5(2), 145–174.

Matthews, C., 2001. *Managing International Joint Ventures: The Route to Globalizing Your Business*. London: Kogan Page.

Matthews, P., 2016. *This Is Why Construction Is So Corrupt*. [Online]. World Economic Forum, 4 February. Available at: www.weforum.org/agenda/2016/02/why-is-the-construction-industry-so-corrupt-and-what-can-we-do-about-it/ [Accessed 24 February 2018].

Matthews, R., 1996. Saudi Arabia's Defence Offset Programmes: Progress, Policy and Performance. *Defence and Peace Economics*, 7(3), 233–251.

Matthews, R., 2002. Saudi Arabia: 'Defence Offsets and Development' in Brauer , J and Dunne, J.P, eds. The Arms Industry in Developing Nations : History and Post-Cold War Assessment, London: Palgrave.

Matthews, R., 2014. *The UK Offset Model: From Participation to Engagement*. [Online]. Royal United Services Institute for Defence and Security Studies (RUSI). Available at: https://rusi.org/sites/default/files/201408_whr_matthews_web_0.pdf [Accessed 15 February 2017].

Matthews, R. and Ansari, I., 2015. Economic Orthodoxy v Market Pragmatism: A Case Study of Europe's Abandonment of Defence Offset. *Public Finance and Management*, 15(4), 378–404.

Maude, B., 2014. *International Business Negotiation*. Palgrave Macmillan.

McConnell, A., 2010. *Understanding Policy Success: Rethinking Public Policy*. Basingstoke: Palgrave Macmillan.

McCord, D., 1998. *An Analysis of the Impact of Military Export Offsets on the United States Industrial Base*. [Online]. MSc, Naval Postgraduate School, Monterey, CA. Available at: https://core.ac.uk/download/pdf/36725468.pdf.

McCorkell, A. and Gillard, M., 2010. Sound Familiar? The BAE Scandal and the Parallels With the Iraq War. *Independent*, 7 February. [Online]. Available at: www.independent. co.uk/news/uk/politics/sound-familiar-the-bae-scandal-and-the-parallels-with-the-iraq-war-1891764.html [Accessed 25 February 2018].

McIntyre, J., 1986. Introduction: Critical Perspective on International Technology Transfer. In: J.R. McIntyre and D.S. Papp, eds. *The Political Economy of International Technology Transfer*. Westport, CT: Quorum Books, pp. 33–39.

McIntyre, J. and Papp, D., eds., 1986. *The Political Economy of International Technology Transfer*. Westport, CT: Quorum Books.

McVey, J., 1980. Countertrade and Barter: Alternative trade financing by third world nations. *International Trade Journal*, 6, 197–220.

Meier, G., 1970. *Leading Issues in Economic Development: Studies in International Poverty*. Oxford: Oxford University Press.

Meissner, F., 1988. *Technology Transfer in the Developing World*. New York, NY: Praeger, pp. 53–58.

Ministry of Defence, 2015. *Common Terms Used in Acquisition*. [Online]. Available at: www.aof.mod.uk/aofcontent/general/commonterms.htm [Accessed 10 May 2016].

Ministry of Defence, India, 2011. *Defence Procurement Procedure: Capital Procurement*. New Delhi: Ministry of Defence. Chapter 1, Appendix D, pp. 44–57. Available at: www. dgqadefence.gov.in/documents/DPP2011.pdf [Accessed 25 April 2013].

Ministry of Defence, UK, 2012. *National Security Through Technology: Technology, Equipment, and Support for UK Defence and Security*. [Online]. (Cm 8278). London: HMSO. Available at: www.gov.uk/government/uploads/system/uploads/attachment_data/file/27390/cm8278.pdf [Accessed 21 August 2012].

Ministry of Economic Affairs Netherlands. *Guidelines to an Industrial Benefits and Offset Program in the Netherlands*. Guidance Brochure Version 1.5. The Hague. Available at: http://stingrayconsulting.nl/PDF/guidelines%20to%20an%20industrial%20benefits%20and%20offsets%20program.pdf [Accessed 8 June 2015].

Mintzerberg, H., Ahlstrand, B. and Lampel, J., 1998. *Strategy Safari: A Guided Tour Through the Wilds of Strategic Management*. London: Prentice Hall.

Miozzo, M. and Walsh, V., 2006. *International Competitiveness and Technological Change*. Oxford: Oxford University Press.

Mirus, R. and Yeung, B., 1986. Economic Incentives for Countertrade. *Journal of International Business Studies*, 17(3), 27–40.

Mirus, R. and Yeung, B., 1993. Why Countertrade? An Economic Perspective. *The International Trade Journal*, 7(4), 411–433.

Mitra, A., 2009. A Survey of Successful Offset Experience Worldwide. [Online]. *Journal of Defence Studies*, 3(1). Available at: https://idsa.in/jds/3_1_2009_ASurveyof SuccessfulOffsetExperiencesWorldwide_AMitra.

Mohamad, A.M., 2005. Technology Transfer and Implementation Processes in Developing Countries. *International Journal of Technology Management*, 32(1/2), 215.

Molas-Gallart, J., 1997. Which Way to Go? Defence Technology and the Diversity of 'Dual-use' Technology Transfer. [Online]. *Research Policy*, 26(3), 367–385. Available at: www.sciencedirect.com/science/article/pii/S0048733397000231 [Accessed 20 April 2006].

Monaghan, A., 2012. Jaguar Land Rover Seals Chinese Joint Venture. *The Telegraph*. [Online (Last updated 8 A.M. 18 November 2012)]. Available at: www.telegraph.co.uk/finance/newsbysector/transport/9684276/Jaguar-Land-Rover-seals-Chinese-joint-venture.html [Accessed 2 January 2018].

Monahan, G., 2008. *Enterprise Risk Management: A Methodology for Achieving Strategic Objectives*. Hoboken, NJ: Wiley.

Moore, M., 1995. *Creating Public Value: Strategic Management in Government*. Cambridge, MA: Harvard University Press.

Moretz, A. Countertrade Opportunities in the People's Republic of China. *Barternews*. [Online]. Available at: http://barternews.com/countertrade_republic_of_china.htm [Accessed 10 February 2010].

Morosini, P., 2004. Industrial Cluster, Knowledge Integration and Performance. *World Development*, 32(2), 305–326.

Mowery, D.C., 2009. National Security and National Innovation Systems. *The Journal of Technology Transfer*, 34, 455–473.

Mowery, D.C. and Oxley, J.E., 1995. Inward Technology Transfer and Competitiveness: The Role of National Innovation Systems. *Cambridge Journal of Economics*, 19(1), 67–93.

Mowery, D.C. and Rosernberg, D., 1989. *Technology and the Pursuit of Economic Growth*. Cambridge: Cambridge University Press.

Mowery, D.G., 1992. International Collaborative Ventures and the Commercialization of New Technologies. In: N. Rosenberg, R. Landau and D.C. Mowery, eds. *Technology and the Wealth of Nations*. Stanford, CA: Stanford University Press. Chapter 11.

Mowery, D.G., 1999. Offset in Commercial and Military Aerospace: An Overview. [Online]. In: C.W. Wessner, ed. *Trends and Challenges in Aerospace Offsets*. Washington, DC: National Academy Press. Available at: https://download.nap.edu/catalog.php?record_id=6315 [Accessed 8 April 2012].

Munusamy, R., 2016. Original Sin: The Arms Deal and South Africa's Sullied Political Story. *Daily Maverick* (South Africa), 22 April. [Online]. Available at: www.dailymaverick.co.za/article/2016-04-22-original-sin-the-arms-deal-and-south-africas-sullied-political-story/#.WrKo2Ux2vIV [Accessed 25 February 2018].

Muravska, J., Pyman, M. and Vilhena da Cunha, F., 2010. *Corruption Risks in Defence Offsets Contracts*. Copenhagen: Transparency International.

Murmann, J.P., 2003. *Knowledge and Competitive Advantage: The Coevolution of Firms, Technology, and National Institutions*. Cambridge: Cambridge University Press.

Murrell, P., 1982. Product quality, market and the development of signaling: East –West trade, Economic Inquiry, pp. 589–603.

Nackman, M.J., 2011. A Critical Examination of Offsets in International Defense Procurements: Policy Options for the United States. [Online]. *Public Contract Law Journal*, 40(2), 511–529. Available at: www.americanbar.org/content/dam/aba/publishing/public_contract_law_journal/pclj_vol40_no2_nackman.authcheckdam.pdf [Accessed 8 August 2012].

Nafzinger, E.W., 2012. *Economic Development*, 5th ed. Cambridge: Cambridge University Press.

Nahar, N., et al., 2006, Success Factors for Information Technology Supported International Technology Transfer: Finding Expert Consensus. *Information and Management*, 43(5), 663–677. doi:10.1016/j.im.2005.02.002.

Nelson, R.R. and Winter, S.G., 1982. *An Evolutionary Theory of Economic Change*. Cambridge, MA: Harvard University Press.

Neuman, S.G., 1985. Co-Production, Barter and Countertrade: Offsets in the International Arms Market. *Orbis*, 29(2), 183–213, Spring.

Niosi, J. and Zhegu, M., 2005. Aerospace Cluster: Local or Global Knowledge Spillover. *Industry and Innovation*, 12(1), 1–25.

Norman, C., 1985. *The Political Economy of Science and Technology*. Oxford: Basil Blackwell Ltd.

O'Donnell, P.K., 2004. *Al-Yamamah Economic Offset Programme: A Measure of Success.* MDA Dissertation, Exec. 10. Cranfield University, UK.

Ogunade, A.O., 2011. *Human Capital Investment in the Developing World: An Analysis of Praxis.* Seminar Research Paper Series 38, University of Rhode Island. Available at: http://digitalcommons.uri.edu/cgi/viewcontent.cgi?article=1029&context=lrc_paper_series [Accessed 12 December 2017].

Oman, C., 1989. *New Forms of Investment in Developing Country Industries: Mining, Petrochemicals, Automobiles, Textile, Food.* Paris: OECD Development Centre.

Organisation for Economic Co-operation and Development (OECD), 2011. *Convention on Combating Bribery of Foreign Public Officials in International Business Transactions and Related Documents.* [Online]. Available at: www.oecd.org/daf/anti-bribery/ConvCombatBribery_ENG.pdf [Accessed 27 October 2017].

Organisation for Joint Armament Cooperation (OCCAR), 1996. *Convention on the Establishment of the Organisation for Joint Armament Cooperation.* Available at: www.occar.int/media/raw/OCCAR Convention.pdf [Accessed 30 January 2015].

Pack, H., 2000. The Cost of Technology Licensing and the Transfer of Technology. *International Journal of Technology Management*, 19(1–2), 78.

Pack, H. and Saggi, K., 1997. Inflows of Foreign Technology and Indigenous Technological Development. *Review of Development Economics*, 1(1), 81–98.

Page, E.C., 2006. The Origins of Policy. In: M. Moran, M. Rein and R. Goodin, eds. *The Oxford Handbook of Public Policy.* Oxford: Oxford University Press. Chapter 10.

Palia, A.P. and Shenkar, P., 1991. Countertrade Practises in China. *Industrial Marketing Management*, 20(1), 57–65.

Parente, S., 2001. The Failure of Endogenous Growth. *Knowledge, Technology & Policy*, 13(4), 49–58.

Parsons, J., 1985. *A Theory of Countertrade Financing in International Business.* Working Paper, pp. 1632–1685. Cambridge, MA: Massachusetts Institute of Technology, Alfred P. Sloan School of Management.

Parsons, W., 1995. *Public Policy.* Aldershot: Edward Elgar.

Patel, P. and Pavitt, K., 1993. *Patterns of Technological Activity: Their Measurement and Interpretation.* University of Sussex. Science Policy Research Unit.

Peng, M.W. and Meyer, K., 2016. *International Business*, 2nd ed. Andover, Hampshire: Cengage Learning EMEA.

Perlo-Freeman, S., 2017a. *Gripen Combat Aircraft Sales to the Czech Republic and Hungary: A Compendium of Arms Trade Corruption.* [Online]. 5 May 2017. Available at: https://sites.tufts.edu/corruptarmsdeals/2017/05/05/gripen-combat-aircraft-sales-to-the-czech-republic-and-hungary/ [Accessed 25 February 2018].

Perlo-Freeman, S., 2017b. *The Al Yamamah Arms Deals: A Compendium of Arms Trade Corruption.* [Online]. Available at: https://sites.tufts.edu/corruptarmsdeals/2017/05/05/the-al-yamamah-arms-deals/ [Accessed 25 February 2018].

Peter, K., 1983. *Strategies for Joint Ventures Successes.* London: Croom Helm.

Peterson, C.D., 2011. Defence & Commercial Trade Offsets: Impacts on the U.S. Industrial Base Raise Economic and National Security Concerns. *Journal of Economic Issue*, 14(2), 485–492.

Petty, F.S., 1999. Defence Offsets: A Strategic Military Perspective. [pdf]. *The DISAM Journal*, 21(4), 65–81. Available at: www.disam.dsca.mil/pubs/v.21_4/petty.pdf [Accessed 15 April 2013].

Platzgummer, P., 2013. Arms Trade Offset and Cases of Corruption: the usage of Anti-Corruption Tools in Special Forms and Arms Acquisition, International Public Management Review, Vol. 14, Fss. 2. pp. 17–38.

Platzgummer, P., 2015. *Performance Management in Arms Trade Offsets: The Rationale and Application of Effective Management Tools.* [Online]. PhD Thesis, University of

St. Gallen, Switzerland. Available at: www1.unisg.ch/www/edis.nsf/SysLkpByIdentifier/4485/$FILE/dis4485.pdf.

Pojasek, R.B., 2017. *Organizational Risk Management and Sustainability: A Practical Step-by-Step Guide*. London: CRC Press.

Porter, M.E., 1985. *The Competitive Advantage: Creating and Sustaining Superior Performance*. New York, NY: The Free Press.

Porter, M.E., 1990. *Competitive Advantage of Nations*. New York, NY: Free Press.

Porter, M.E., 2000. Location, Competition and Economic Development: Local Clusters in a Global Economy. *Economic Development Quarterly*, 14(1), 15–34.

Porter, M.E., 2004. *The Competitive Strategy: Techniques for Analyzing Industries and Competitors*. New York, NY: Free Press.

Posner, M.V., 1961. International Trade and Technical Change. *Oxford Economic Papers*, 13(3), 323–341.

Postula, M., 2017. Risk Analysis as an Instrument of Public Management. In: K. Raczkowski, ed. *Risk Management in Public Administration*. Cham, Switzerland: Palgrave Macmillan. Chapter 4.

Preston, P., 1997. *Development Theory: An Introduction*. Oxford: Blackwell Publishers.

Prime, T., Gale, S. and Scanlan, G.,1997. *The Law and Practice of Joint-Ventures*, 1st ed. Butterworths.

Pyman, M., 2013. Defence and Security Offset Programme. In: *Countertrade and Offset Club (ECCO)*. Juan-les-Pins, France, 21 November 2013.

Raczkowski, K., ed., 2017. *Public Management in Public Administration*. Cham, Switzerland: Palgrave Macmillan.

Ragunathan, P., 1990. India's Move Towards Defence Self-Reliance, and the New Search for Defence Exports. *Defence & Foreign Affairs*, 18(4), April, 29–31.

Ram, R., 1993. Conceptual Linkages Between Defense Spending and Economic Growth and Development: A Selective Review. In: J.E. Payne and A.P. Sahu, eds. *Defense Spending and Economic Growth*. Boulder, CO: Westview Press, pp. 20–39.

Rapaz, S., 2004. *Swiss Defence Offsets*. MDA Dissertation, no. 18. Cranfield University, UK.

Rapley, J., 2004. Development Studies and the Post-development Critique. *Progress in Development Studies*, 4(4), 350–354.

Reissman, A., 2005. Transfer of Technologies: A Cross-Disciplinary Taxonomy. *Omega*, 33(3), 189–202.

Richards, D. and Smith, M., 2002. *Governance and Public Policy in the UK*. Oxford: Oxford University Press.

Roggi, O. and Ottanelli, O., 2012. An Evolutionary Perspective on the Concept of Risk, Uncertainty and Risk Management. In: O. Roggi and E. Altman, eds. *Managing and Measuring of Risk: Emerging Global Standards and Regulations After the Financial Crisis*. World Scientific Series in Finance, 5. Singapore: World Scientific Publishing.

Roman, D.D., 1986. Science Policy, Technology Transfer, Economic Impacts, and Sociological Implications in the West-West Context. In: R.J. McIntyer and D. Papp, eds. *The Political Economy of International Technology Transfer*. Westport, CT: Quorum Books.

Romer, P.M., 1994. The Origins of Endogenous Growth. *Journal of Economic Perspectives, American Economic Association*, 8(1), 3–22. doi:10.1257/jep.8.1.3.

Root, F.R., Contractor, F.J. and Lorange, P., 1988. *Cooperative Strategies in International Business: Joint Ventures and Technology Partnerships Between Firms*. New York, NY: Lexington Books.

Rose, R., 1991. What Is Lesson: Drawing? *Journal of Public Policy*, 11(1:3), 3–30.

Rosenberg, N., 1970. Economic Development and the Transfer of Technology: Some Historical Perspectives. *Technology and Culture*, 11(4), 550–575.

Rosenberg, N., 1982. *Inside the Blackbox: Technology and Economics*. Cambridge: Cambridge University Press.

Rosenberg, N., Landau, R. and Mowery, D., 1992. *Technology and Wealth of Nations*. Stanford, CA: Stanford University Press.

Rostow, W.W., 1971. *The Stages of Economic Growth*, 2nd ed. Cambridge, MA: Harvard University Press.

Rubin, S., 1986. *The Business Managers Guide to Barter: Offset and Countertrade*. London: Economist Intelligence Unit, p. 15.

Russin, R., 1994. Offsets in International Military Procurement. *Public Contract Law Journal*, 24(1), 65–88.

Sabatier, P., 1986. Top-Down and Bottom-Up Approaches to Implementation Research: A Critical Analysis and Suggested Synthesis. *Journal of Public Policy*, 6(1), 21–48.

Sabatier, P., 2007. Fostering the Development of Policy Theory. In: P. Sabatier, ed. *Theories of the Policy Process 2*. Cambridge, MA: Westview Press.

Salamatu, Q.Y, 2014. A study on the relevance of Offsets as a means for developing Nigeria's Defence Industrialization and Technological Base, MSc Dissertation (unpublished), WMG, University of Warwick.

Sachs, W., ed., 1992. *The Development Dictionary: A Guide to Knowledge as Power*. London: Zed Books.

Savitri, C.M., 2016. *Contribution of Offset to Defence Industry in Indonesia, Cranfield Defence and Security*. [Online]. PhD Thesis (unpublished), Cranfield University. Available at: https://dspace.lib.cranfield.ac.uk/bitstream/handle/1826/10263/Savitri%20 PhD%20Thesis.pdf;jsessionid=799B9FA50A142ED4AA5CD4F3ADD7A355?seque nce=1 [Accessed 18 February 2018].

Schmitz, H., 1984. Industrialization Strategies in LDCs: Some Lessons of Historical Experience. *Journal of Development Studies*, 21(1), 1–21.

Schultz, T. 2016. IFBEC Offsets report [Online] in http://www.globaloffset.org/Portals/0/ Conference_PDFs/2016/49.SchultzIFBECOffsetsReport2016GICC.pdf?ver=2016- 05-26-152112-473. [Accessed on 14 May 2018].

Schumpeter, J.A., 1934. *The Theory of Economic Development*. London: Oxford University Press.

Scott, R.E., 2008. The Effect of Offsets, Outsourcing, and Foreign Competition on Output and Employment in the U.S Aerospace Industry. In: C.W. Wessner, ed. *Trends and Challenges in Aerospace Offsets*. Washington, DC: National Academy Press, pp. 153–157.

Serrao, N.T., Ramos, T.P. and Redore, L., 2014. *The Offset Policy Evaluated Through the HX-Br Compensatory Perspective*. [Online]. San Francisco, CA: Academia. Available at: www.academia.edu/15210945/The_Offset_Policy_Evaluated_through_the_HX-Br_ Compensatory_Perspective [Accessed 20 November 2016].

Shrivastava, P., 1995. Environmental Technologies and Competitive Advantage. *Strategic Management Journal*, 16(S1), 183–200.

Silva, E., 2009. Measuring Skills for 21st-century Learning. *Phi Delta Kappan*, 90(9), 630–634.

Singer, H.W., 1984. Industrialisation: Where Do We Stand? Where Are We Going? *Industry and Development*, no. 12, UNIDO, pp. 79–87.

Singh, P.R., 2000. *Arms Procurement Decision Making Volume II: Chile, Greece, Malaysia, Poland, South Africa and Taiwan*. New York, NY: Oxford University Press.

Singh, R.P. and Jain, R.K., 2003. Improving Local Economies Through Technology Transfer: Utilising Incubators to Facilitate Cluster Development. *International Journal of Technology Transfer and Commercialization*, 2(3), 249–262.

Sinha, U.B., 2001. International Joint Venture, Licensing and Buy-Out Under Asymmetric Information. *Journal of Development Economics*, 66(1), 127–151.

Sivard, R.L., 1989. *World Military and Social Expenditures 1989*. Washington, DC: World Priorities.

Skynews, 2017. November 8. GKN plots aerospace tie-up with state-owned Chinese group Comac [Online]. Available at: https://news.sky.com/story/gkn-plots-aerospace-tie-up-with-state-owned-chinese-group-comac-11118436

Smali, A.C., ed., 1985. *Technology Transfer: Geographical, Economic and Technical Dimensions*. Westport, CT: Quorum Books.

Sobolev, S. and Alden, A., 2014. *Top Trends in Defense 2014–2024: Regional Competitions, Economic Development Shape Global Defense Spending*. [Online]. Avascent. Available at: www.avascent.com/2014/07/top-trends-defense-2014-2024-regional-competitions-econ-development-shape-global-defense-spend/.

Soete, L., 1985. International Diffusion of Technology, Industrial Development and Technological Leapfrogging. *World Development*, 13(3), 409–422.

Solow, R.M., 1956. A Contribution to the Theory of Economic Growth. *The Quarterly Journal of Economics*, 70(1), 65–94.

Spear, J., 1997. *The Role of Offsets in the International Trade*. International Studies Association Annual Meeting, Toronto, 19 March. London: Department of War Studies, King's College.

Spear, J., 2013. Defence Offsets: A System-Level View. *Strategic Analysis*, 37(4), 430–445.

Spekman, R.E. et al., 1996. Creating Strategic Allliances which endure. *Long Range Planning*, 29(3), 346–357.

Steinberg, J., 2009. BAE Al-Yamamah Scandal Back in the Headlines. *EIR World News*, 36(15), 56–60. Available at: www.larouchepub.com/eiw/public/2009/eirv36n15-20090417/eirv36n15-20090417_056-bae_al_yamamah_scandal_back_in_t.pdf [Accessed 9 June 2017].

Stiglitz, J., 1987. Learning to Learn, Localized Learning and Technological Progress. In: P. Dasgupta and P. Stoneman, eds. *Economic Policy and Technological Performance*. Cambridge: Cambridge University Press. Chapter 5, pp. 125–153.

Stiglitz, J.E. & Pleskovic, B. (eds).1997. The Annual World Bank Conference on Economic Development, Washington D.C.: World Bank Publication.

Stiglitz, J., 2017. *Globalization and its Discontent: Revisited Anti Globalization in the Era of Trump*. New York: WW. Norton & Company Inc, pp. xii–xli.

Stockholm International Peace Research Institute (SIPRI). 2010. SIPRI Yearbook 2010: Armaments, Disarmaments and International Security. New York: Oxford University Press.

Stockholm International Peace Research Institute, 2016. *Trends in World Military Expenditure, 2015*. [Online]. Available at: http://books.sipri.org/files/FS/SIPRIFS1604.pdf [Accessed 7 June 2016].

Suman, M., 2005. Offsets in International Arms Trade Need for a National Policy. *Security Research Review*, 12, 1–2.

Sunders, S., 2009. Implementation of Offset Policy in Defence Contracts: Indian Army. *Journal of Defence Studies*, 3(1), 71–80.

Sunil, M., 2002. *Government, Innovation and Technology Policy: An International Comparative Analysis*. Cheltenham: Edward Elgar Publishing Limited.

Tatoglu, E. and Glaister, K.W., 1998. Performance of International Joint Ventures in Turkey: Perspectives of Western Firms and Turkish Firms. *International Business Review*, 7, 635–656.

Taylor, D. and Balloch, S., eds., 2005. *The Politics of Evaluation: Participation and Policy Implementation*. Bristol: The Policy Press.

Taylor, T.K., 2002. *Using Offsets in Procurement as an Economic Development Strategy*. New York: College of Business, Alfred University, p. 2.

Taylor, T.K., 2003a. Modeling Offset Policy in Government Procurement. *Journal of Policy Modelling*, 25(9), 985–998.

Taylor, T.K., 2003b. The Proper Use of Offsets in International Procurement. *Journal of Public Procurement*, 3(3), 338–356.

Taylor, T.K., 2004. Using Procurement Offsets as an Economic Development Strategy. In: J. Brauer and J.P. Dunne. *Arms Trade and Economic Development: Theory, Policy, and Cases in Arms Trade Offsets*. Abingdon and New York, NY: Routledge. doi:10.4324/.

Taylor, T.K., 2012. Countertrade Offset in International Procurement: Theory and Evidence. In: M.A. Yulek and T.K. Taylor, eds. *Designing Public Procurement Policy in Developing Countries: How far to Foster Technology Transfer and Industrialisation in the Global Economy*. New York, NY: Springer. Chapter 2.

Thomas, H., ed., 1995. *Globalisation and 3rd World Trade Union: The Challenge of Rapid Economic Change*. London: Zed Books.

Thompson, J., 2010. BAE Systems Pays $400m to Settle Bribery Charges. *Independent*, 6 February. [Online]. Available at: www.independent.co.uk/news/business/news/bae-systems-pays-400m-to-settle-bribery-charges-1891027.html [Accessed 10 February 2016].

Thompson, L.L., 2012. *The Mind and Heart of the Negotiator*, 5th ed. Pearson Ltd.

Tirole, J., 2005. *The Theory of Corporate Governance*. Princeton, NJ: Princeton University Press.

Todaro, M. and Smith, S.C., 2006. *Economic Development*, 9th ed. London: Pearson Ltd.

Toru, Y., 2003. Technology Development and Acquisition Strategy. *International Journal of Technology Management*, 25(6/7), 666–674.

Transparency International, 2010. *Defence Offsets: Addressing the Risks of Corruption and Raising Transparency*. [Online]. London: Transparency International UK. Available at: http://ti-defence.org/wp-content/uploads/2016/03/1004_corruption_risk_offsets.pdf [Accessed 15 January 2018].

Trybus, M., 2014. *Buying Defence and Security in Europe: The EU Defence and Security Procurement Directive in Context*. Cambridge: Cambridge University Press.

Tsang, E.W.K., 1994. Human Resource Management Problems in Sino-foreign Joint Ventures. *International Journal of Manpower*, 15(9/10), 4–21.

Tyler, B. and Steensma, K., 1995. Evaluating Technological Collaborative Opportunities: A Cognitive Perspective. *Strategic Management Journal*, 16(S1), 43–70.

Udis, B. and Maskus, K., 1991. Offsets as Industrial Policy: Lessons From Aerospace. *Defence and Peace Economics*, 2(2), 151–164.

UNCITRAL., 1993. Legal Guide on International Countertrade Transactions, The United Nations Commission on International Trade Law, United Nation. New York.

Ungaro, A., 2013. Trends in the Defence Offsets Market. In: *SIPRI (Stockholm International Peace Research Institute), 17th Annual International Conference on Economics and Security (ICES)*. Stockholm, 14–15 June 2013. Available at: SSRN: https://ssrn.com/abstract=2386528 or http://dx.doi.org/10.2139/ssrn.2386528.

UN General Assembly, 2003. *United Nations Convention Against Corruption*. [Online]. Vienna: United Nations Office on Drugs And Crime. Available at: www.unodc.org/documents/brussels/UN_Convention_Against_Corruption.pdf.

United Nations Conference on Trade and Development (UNCTAD), 1990. *Joint Ventures as a Channel for the Transfer of Technology: Proceedings of a Workshop*. New York, NY: United Nations.

United Nations Conference on Trade and Development (UNCTAD), 2003. *Investment and Technology Policies for Competitiveness: Review of Successful Country Experiences*. Geneva: United Nations, p. 32.

United Nations Development Programme (UNDP). 1999. Fighting Corruption to improve governance. New York: UNDP.

United States. Bureau of Industry and Security (BIS), 2011. *Impact of Offsets in Defence Trade*. [Online]. Fourteenth Report to Congress. Available at: www.bis.doc.gov/index.php/other-areas/strategic-industries-and-economic-security-sies/offsets-in-defense-trade [Accessed 6 April 2011].

United States. Bureau of Industry and Security (BIS), 2015. *Offsets in Defense Trade: Nineteenth Study*. [Online]. Washington, DC: Department of Commerce. Available at: www.bis.doc.gov/index.php/other-areas/strategic-industries-and-economic-security-sies/ [Accessed 16 July 2017].

United States. Bureau of Industry and Security (BIS), 2016a. *Offset Definitions*. [Online]. Washington, DC: Department of Commerce. Available at: www.bis.doc.gov/index.php/other-areas/strategic-industries-and-economic-security-sies/offsets-in-defense-trade [Accessed 10 November 2017].

United States. Bureau of Industry and Security (BIS), 2016b. *Offsets in Defence Trade Sixteenth Study*. [Online]. Washington, DC: Department of Commerce. Available at: www.bis.doc.gov/index.php/forms-documents/other-areas/strategic-industries-and-economic-security/offsets-in-defense-trade/396-offsets-in-defense-trade-sixteenth-study/file.

United States. Bureau of Industry and Security (BIS), 2017. *Offsets in Defence Trade Twenty First Study*. [Online]. Available at: www.bis.doc.gov/index.php/documents/pdfs/1620-twenty-first-report-to-congress-12-16/file [Accessed 12 January 2018].

United States. Congress, Office of Technology Assessment, 1984. *Technology, Innovation, and Regional Economic Development: Encouraging High Technology Development*. Washington, DC: Congress of the United States, Office of Technology Assessment, pp. 8–9.

United States. Department of Commerce Bureau of Industry and Security, 2016. *Offsets in Defense Trade Twenty-First Study*. [pdf]. Washington, DC. Available at: www.bis.doc.gov/index.php/documents/pdfs/1620-twenty-first-report-to-congress-12-16/file [Accessed 11 September 2017].

United States. Government Accountability Office (GOA), 2004. *Defense Trade: Issues Concerning the Use of Offsets in International Defense Sales*. [Online]. GAO-04-954T, 8 July, Washington, DC.

U.S.-China Economic and Security Review Commission, 2005. *2005 Report to Congress of the U.S.–China Economic and Security Review Commission*. One Hundredth Ninth Congress, First Session, Washington, DC, November 2005. Available at: www.uscc.gov/sites/default/files/annual_reports/2005-Report-to-Congress.pdf.

Vaughan Evans, V., 2013. *Key Strategy Tools: The 80+ Tools for Every Manager to Build a Winning Strategy*. Harlow: Pearson Ltd.

Verma, S., 2009. Offset Contracts Under Defense Procurement Regulations in India: Evolution, Challenges, and Prospect. *Journal of Contract Management*, 7(1), 21.

Vernon, R., 1971. *Sovereignty at Bay, the Multinational Spread of US Enterprises*. New York, NY and London: Basic Books Inc, p. 72.

Verzariu, P., 1985. *Countertrade, Barter and Offsets: New Strategies for Profit in International Trade*. New York, NY: McGraw-Hill.

Verzariu, P., 2000. *The Evolution of International Barter, Countertrade, and Offsets Practices: A Survey of the 1970s Through the 1990s*. Washington, DC: Department of Commerce, March.

Vitasek, K., Ledyard, M. and Manrodt, K.B., 2013. *Vested Outsourcing: Five Rules that Will Transform Outsourcing*, 2nd ed. New York, NY: Palgrave Macmillan.

Vitasek, K., Manrodt, K. and Kling, J., 2012. *Vested: How P&G, McDonald's, and Microsoft Are Redefining Winning in Business Relationships*. New York, NY: Palgrave Macmillan.

Von Mises, L., 1881–1973. *Interventionism: An Economic Analysis*, edited by Bettina Bien Greaves, 1998. New York, NY: The Foundation for Economic Education, pp. 10–12.

Wahab, S.A., Rose, R.C. and Osman, S.I.W., 2012. Defining the Concepts of Technology and Technology Transfer: A Literature Analysis. [Online]. *International Business Research*, 5(1).

Webster, A., 1994. UK Government's White Paper: A Critical Commentary on Measures of Exploitation of Scientific Research. *Technology Analysis and Strategic Management*, 6(2), 189–202.

Weigand, R.E., 1977. International Trade Without Money. *Harvard Business Review*, November–December, 30.

Weiss A., 2005. *Conquering Complexity: Lessons for Defence Systems Acquisition.* Norwich: TSO (The Stationery Office).

Welt, L.G.B. and Wilson, D.B., 1998. Offsets in the Middle East. *Middle East Policy*, 6(2), 36–53.

Wheeler, T., 2012. International Strategic Partnership, Boeing Defence, Space and Security. In: *DIOA/GOCA Spring Conference*. Brewster, MA, USA, September 2012.

Willett, S. and Anthony, I., 1998. *Countertrade and Offsets Policies and Practices in the Arms Trade*. Copenhagen: Copenhagen Peace Research Institute Working Paper, 20.

Willett, S. and Anthony, I., 2004. *Countertrade and Offsets Policies and Practices in the Arms Trade*. [Online]. 1–31. Available at: http://www.ciaonet.org/wps/wis01, 2005 [Accessed April 2004].

Williams, R.J.E., 1998. *The UK's Industrial Participation Policy: Strengths and Weaknesses*. MDA Dissertation, no. 12. Cranfield University, UK.

Wills, T., 2012. The Evolution of Technology & Its Impact on the Development of Social Businesses. [Online]. *Forbes*, 1 October 2012. Available at: www.forbes.com/sites/sap/2012/01/10/infographic-the-evolution-of-technology-its-impact-on-the-development-of-social-businesses/#5d5cfc2b66f9.

Woodside, A.G. and Pitts, R.E. (eds), 1996. *Creating and Managing International Joint Ventures*. Westport, CT: Quorum Books.

Woolf Committee Report, 2008. *Business Ethics, Global Companies and the Defence Industry: Ethical Business Conduct in BAE Systems Plc: The Way Forward*. [pdf]. [Online]. London: Column Communications Ltd. Available at: www.giaccentre.org/documents/WOOLFREPORT2008.pdf [Accessed October 2017].

World Industrial Development Report (2002/2003). Vienna: UNIDO, pp. 118–193.

Yang, J. and Lee, H., 2002. Identifying Key Success Factors for Successful Joint Ventures in China. *Industrial Management & Data Systems*, 102(2), 98–109.

Yang, C., Dr. and Wang, T., 2006. Interactive Decision Making for the International Arms Trade: The Offset Life Cycle Model. *The DISAM Journal*, 28(3), 101–109.

Zahra, S. and George, G., 2002. Absorptive Capacity: A Review, Reconceptualization, and Extension. [Online]. *Academy of Management Review*, 27, 185–203. Available at: www.jstor.org/stable/4134351.

Zeng, R., 2012. What Motivates Firms From Emerging Economies to Go Internationalisation? *Technological and Economic Development of Economy*, 18(2), 280–298.

Zhang, N.Y., 2009. *China's Search for Indigenous Industrial Development: A Case Study of the Aviation Industry*. Unpublished PhD Thesis, DCMT, Cranfield University.

Zhouying, J., 2005. Globalisation, Technological Competitiveness and the 'Catch-up' Challenge for Developing Countries: Some Lessons and Experience. *International Journal of Technology Management and Sustainable Development*, 4(1), 34–46.

Ziai, A., ed., 2007. *Exploring Post Development Theory and Practice, Problem and Perspective*. London and New York, NY: Routledge.

Glossary

business strategy   gaining a sustainable competitive advantage in a single strategic business unit

capabilities   how a firm deploys its resources

capability gap   the gap in performance between where a firm is currently positioned against key success factors and where it aims to be

competitive advantage   the strategic advantage processed by one firm over others in a product/market segment or industry which enables it to make superior returns

corporate governance   the way in which organisations are directed and controlled; the process by which corporations are made responsive to the right and wishes of stakeholders

corporate governance   considers the role of the board in its fiduciary role towards the financial owner, the shareholder and their obligors to fend of major disasters while optimising the value-creating potential of the enterprise

dynamic capability   one that is sufficiently dynamic to cope in times of rapid changes namely distinctive processes, knowledge assets and path dependency

enterprise risk management   formal framework that outlines the structure of the risk management process and incorporates various risk, analytical tools and practices and their works; a foundation for identifying, assessing, treating and monitoring all the major risks that could affect corporate performance

government strategy   gaining maximum outcome based on the policy objectives

industry life cycle   suggestions that industries go through four stages: introduction; growth; maturity and decline

innovation   the initial commercialisation of invention by producing and marketing a new good or service or by using a new method of production

international strategy   is based upon an organisation exploiting its core competencies and distinctive capabilities in foreign markets

joint venture   when two organisations for a separate and independent company in which they own shares and equity

offsets obligee   offsets obligee refers to recipients of offsets. These would include buyers which include buyer government, offsets agency, offsets programme recipients and end-users

offsets obligor offsets obligor refers to seller or the company that is responsible for discharging offsets obligations as stipulated in the offset agreement. Offsets obligor is responsible in delivering the offset contract. Offsets obligor could also include subcontractors, seller country or government and other third party engaged by sellers

original equipment manufacturer (OEM) manufacturers of original equipment. In offsets, OEMs are normally referred to as the prime contractors who are responsible for overall offsets planning and delivery of offsets contract

stakeholder person and organisation with stake in the success of the programme; for example, OEMs, local companies, offsets authorities, universities and research agencies, suppliers, national and local government, Armed forces, inter government agencies

strategic alliances when two or more separate organisations share some of their resources and capabilities but stop short forming separate organisation

strategy how a firm or organisation achieves its goal by deploying its scarce resources to gain substantive competitive advantage or intended objectives

transparency is the ease in which a competitor can identify the capabilities which underpins a rival's corrupt practice

value chain the activity in an organisation that go to make up a product or service

vertical integration occurs when an organisation goes upstream, i.e. moves towards its inputs and downstream – moves close to ultimate consumer

Index

Note: Page numbers in *italics* and **bold** denote references to Figures and Tables, respectively.

Printed in the United States
by Baker & Taylor Publisher Services